T0325624

Evolution of Software-Defined Networking Foundations for IoT and 5G Mobile Networks

Sunil Kumar
Amity University, Noida, India

Munesh Chandra Trivedi
National Institute of Technology, Agartala, India

Priya Ranjan
Amity University, Noida, India

Akash Punhani
Amity University, Noida, India

A volume in the Advances in
Wireless Technologies and
Telecommunication (AWTT) Book
Series

Published in the United States of America by
   IGI Global
   Information Science Reference (an imprint of IGI Global)
   701 E. Chocolate Avenue
   Hershey PA, USA 17033
   Tel: 717-533-8845
   Fax: 717-533-8661
   E-mail: cust@igi-global.com
   Web site: http://www.igi-global.com

Library of Congress Cataloging-in-Publication Data

Names: Kumar, Sunil, 1986- editor. I Trivedi, Munesh Chandra, 1981- editor.
   I Ranjan, Priya, editor. I Punhani, Akash, 1985- editor.
Title: Evolution of software-defined networking foundations for IoT and 5G
   mobile networks / Sunil Kumar, Munesh Chandra Trivedi, Priya Ranjan, and
   Akash Punhani, editors.
Description: Hershey, PA : Information Science Reference, an imprint of IGI
   Global, [2021] I Includes bibliographical references and index. I
   Summary: "This book contains research on the security challenges and
   prevention mechanisms in high-speed mobile networks. The book explores
   the threats to 5G and IoT and how to implement effective security
   architecture for them"-- Provided by publisher.
Identifiers: LCCN 2020005540 (print) I LCCN 2020005541 (ebook) I ISBN
   9781799846857 (hardcover) I ISBN 9781799854395 (paperback) I ISBN
   9781799846864 (ebook)
Subjects: LCSH: Internet of things. I 5G mobile communication systems. I
   Software-defined networking (Computer network technology)
Classification: LCC TK5105.8857 .E94 2021 (print) I LCC TK5105.8857
   (ebook) I DDC 004.67/8--dc23
LC record available at https://lccn.loc.gov/2020005540
LC ebook record available at https://lccn.loc.gov/2020005541

This book is published in the IGI Global book series Advances in Wireless Technologies and
Telecommunication (AWTT) (ISSN: 2327-3305; eISSN: 2327-3313)

British Cataloguing in Publication Data
A Cataloguing in Publication record for this book is available from the British Library.

All work contributed to this book is new, previously-unpublished material.
The views expressed in this book are those of the authors, but not necessarily of the publisher.

For electronic access to this publication, please contact: eresources@igi-global.com.

Advances in Wireless Technologies and Telecommunication (AWTT) Book Series

ISSN:2327-3305
EISSN:2327-3313

Editor-in-Chief: Xiaoge Xu University of Nottingham Ningbo China, China

MISSION

The wireless computing industry is constantly evolving, redesigning the ways in which individuals share information. Wireless technology and telecommunication remain one of the most important technologies in business organizations. The utilization of these technologies has enhanced business efficiency by enabling dynamic resources in all aspects of society.

The **Advances in Wireless Technologies and Telecommunication Book Series** aims to provide researchers and academic communities with quality research on the concepts and developments in the wireless technology fields. Developers, engineers, students, research strategists, and IT managers will find this series useful to gain insight into next generation wireless technologies and telecommunication.

COVERAGE

- Digital Communication
- Virtual Network Operations
- Wireless Sensor Networks
- Mobile Communications
- Telecommunications
- Wireless Technologies
- Mobile Technology
- Wireless Broadband
- Network Management
- Cellular Networks

IGI Global is currently accepting manuscripts for publication within this series. To submit a proposal for a volume in this series, please contact our Acquisition Editors at Acquisitions@igi-global.com or visit: http://www.igi-global.com/publish/.

Titles in this Series

For a list of additional titles in this series, please visit:
http://www.igi-global.com/book-series/advances-wireless-technologies-telecommunication/73684

Managing Resources for Futuristic Wireless Networks
Mamata Rath (Birla School of Management, Birla Global University, India)
Information Science Reference • © 2021 • 338pp • H/C (ISBN: 9781522594932) • US $195.00

Principles and Applications of Narrowband Internet of Things (NBIoT)
Sudhir K. Routray (Addis Ababa Science and Technology University, Ethiopia) and Sasmita Mohanty (University of Aveiro, Portugal)
Information Science Reference • © 2021 • 300pp • H/C (ISBN: 9781799847755) • US $195.00

Recent Developments in Individual and Organizational Adoption of ICTs
Orkun Yildiz (Izmir Democracy University, Turkey)
Information Science Reference • © 2021 • 333pp • H/C (ISBN: 9781799830450) • US $195.00

Wireless Sensor Network-Based Approaches to Digital Image Processing in the IoT
Manoj Diwakar (DIT University, India) and Kaushik Ghosh (DIT University, India)
Information Science Reference • © 2020 • 300pp • H/C (ISBN: 9781799832812) • US $195.00

Innovative Perspectives on Interactive Communication Systems and Technologies
Muhammad Sarfraz (Kuwait University, Kuwait)
Information Science Reference • © 2020 • 330pp • H/C (ISBN: 9781799833550) • US $195.00

Handbook of Research on the Political Economy of Communications and Media
Serpil Karlidag (Baskent University, Turkey) and Selda Bulut (Ankara Haci Bayram Veli University, Turkey)

For an entire list of titles in this series, please visit:
http://www.igi-global.com/book-series/advances-wireless-technologies-telecommunication/73684

IGI Global
PUBLISHER of TIMELY KNOWLEDGE

701 East Chocolate Avenue, Hershey, PA 17033, USA
Tel: 717-533-8845 x100 • Fax: 717-533-8661
E-Mail: cust@igi-global.com • www.igi-global.com

Table of Contents

Detailed Table of Contents

Chapter 1

Rashmi Mishra, Delhi Technological University, India & ABES
Engineering College, Ghaziabad, India
R. K. Yadav, Delhi Technological University, India

The evolving area of the upcoming technology in the era of "Mobile Security" is a 5G network. The aim of this technology is to provide security to the mobile nodes for the load balancing, for the voice security, capacity, quality of services, secure end-to-end communication, connectivity of the devices in a highly mobile network with reliable and scalable networks. The enhancement towards technology leads to connect home appliances with IoT devices, industries, business. Therefore, security-related issues will also increase. In wireless communication, devices want to connect all the time, which primes the vulnerabilities, increases network traffic at the device side on the channel, and creates the backdoor for the hacking and cracking mechanisms for the wireless devices.

Chapter 2

Neetu Faujdar, Amity University, Noida, India

Pervasive computing has been greatly supported by the internet of things. The use of internet of things has created the environment that helps in the management of the different modules that are the part of the complete system, which can work effectively without the interference with the other components of the system. The cloud environment with the internet of things can help in getting the greater extend of data sharing. Little attention has been provided to the security of the various stakeholders that are the part of the system. IoT cloud integration involved privacy, security, and personal safety risk of the stakeholders. Not only are these types of security attacks possible, but there is also the possibility of attack on the IoT components like hardware manipulation to disrupt the services. As we are on the network, all the communication attacks of network are also possible. This chapter will cover common aspects of regarding the cloud and internet of things (IOT) with 5G networks.

Chapter 3

Pradeep Kumar Garg, Indian Institute of Technology, Roorkee, India

The internet of things (IoT) is the network of physical objects—devices, vehicles, buildings, and other objects—embedded with software, electronic devices, sensors, and network connectivity that enable these objects to collect and share information or data. Its applications include smart homes, healthcare, industries, transportation systems, logistics, and energy. Building an IoT real-time-based application involves the proper selection of combination of sensors, technology, networks, and communication modules, supported with the concepts of data processing, remote sensing, cloud computing, etc. This chapter highlights advantages and disadvantages IoT and various techniques, such as computer vision, remote sensing, artificial intelligence, cloud computing, big data, ubiquitous computing, which are widely used in various applications. Many new IoT-based applications will evolve, as new devices, sensors, chips, and computational techniques are developed.

Chapter 4

Harsh Khatter, ABES Engineering College, Ghaziabad, India
Prabhat Singh, ABES Engineering College, Ghaziabad, India

Huge-scale highly-dense networks integrate with different application spaces of internet of things for precise occasion discovery and monitoring. Because of the high thickness and colossal scope, the hubs in these systems must play out some basic correspondence jobs, in particular detecting, handing-off, information combination, and information control (collection and replication). Since the vitality utilization and the unwavering correspondence quality is one of the significant difficulties in large-scale highly-dense networks, the correspondence jobs ought to be facilitated so as to efficiently utilize the vitality assets and to meet a palatable degree of correspondence dependability. Right now, the authors propose an on-request and completely dispersed system for job coordination that is intended to distinguish occasions with different levels of basicity, adjusting the information total and information replication as per the desperation level of the recognized event.

Chapter 5

Shakti Kumar, Amity University, Noida, India

Plant disease is a mutilation of the normal state of a plant that changes its essential quality and prevents a plant from performing to its actual potential. Due to drastic environment changes, plant diseases are growing day by day, which results the higher losses in quantity of agricultural yields. To prevent the loss in the crop yield, the timely disease identification is necessary. Monitoring the plant diseases without any digital mean makes it difficult to identify the disease correctly and timely. It requires more amounts of work, time, and great experience in the plant diseases. Automatic approach of image processing and applying the different data science techniques to classify the disease correctly is a good idea for this which includes acquisition, classification, feature extraction, pre-processing, and segmentation all are performed on the leaf images. This chapter will briefly discuss the data science techniques used for the classification of the images like SVM, k-nearest neighbor, decision tree, ANN, and convolutional neural network (CNN).

Chapter 6

The day-to-day advancements have brought the biggest challenge to network providers as it has become difficult to keep up the traditional networks with the ever-advancing technologies for them. It also result as a motivation for vendors to grow by developing, innovating, deploying, and migrating in their services, upgrading to new hardware and infrastructure, as well as hiring newly trained people, which requires a large amount of money and time to implement. It results to a need of a new network architecture who has a capability of supporting future technologies along with solving all sorts of issues known as the network proposal by software. For meeting highly increasing demands, various proposals of load balancing techniques come forward in which highly dedicated balancers of loads are being required for ever service in some of them, or for every new service, manual recognition of device is required. In the conventional network, on the basis of the local information in the network, load balancing is being established.

Chapter 7

Wireless sensor networks have gotten significant attention in recent times due to their applicability in diverse fields. Energy conservation is a major challenge in wireless sensor networks. Apart from energy conservation, monitoring quality of the environmental phenomenon is also considered a major issue. The approaches that addressed both these problems are of great significance. One such approach is node scheduling, which aims to divide the node set into a number of subsets such that each subset can monitor a given set of points known as targets. The chapter proposes a priority coding-based cluster head selection approach as an extension of the energy efficient coverage protocol (EECP). The priority of the nodes is determined on the basis of residual energy (RE), distance (D), noise factor (N), node degree (Nd), and link quality (LQ). The analytical results show that the proposed protocol improves the network performance by reducing the overhead by a factor of 70% and hence reduces the energy consumption by a factor of 70%.

Chapter 8

Manish Bhardwaj, KIET Group of Institutions, India
Neha Shukla, KIET Group of Institutions, India
Arti Sharma, KIET Group of Institutions, India

In MANET, every hub is fit for sending message (information) progressively without prerequisite of any fixed framework. Portable hubs oftentimes move in/out from the system powerfully, making arrange topology unsteady in portable specially appointed system (MANET). Therefore, it turns into an incredibly moving errand to keep up stable system. In this chapter, the authors have proposed an upgraded stable bunching calculation that will give greater soundness to the system by limiting the group head changes furthermore, diminishing grouping overhead. In proposed optimum stable bunching calculation (OSBC), another hub is presented which goes about as a reinforcement hub in the bunch. Such reinforcement hub goes about as group head, when real bunch head moves out (or passed on) from the bunch. Last mentioned, the group head reelect another reinforcement hub. This training keeps arrange accessibility without aggravation. Further, the need of group head and reinforcement hub is determined dependent on the hub degree and the rest of the battery life for portable hubs.

Chapter 9

Kaushal Kumar, A. P. J. Abdul Kalam Technical University, Lucknow, India
Ajit Kumar Singh, R . V. Institute of Technology, Bijnor, India
Sunil Kumar, Amity University, Noida, India
Pankaj Sharma, Sharda University, India
Jaya Sharna, SRM University, Modinagar, India

Energy and speed are very important parts in this fast-growing world. They also play a crucial role in economy and operational considerations of a country, and by environmental concerns, energy efficiency has now become a key pillar in the design of communication networks. With the help of several of base station and millions of networking devices in the fifth generation of wireless communications, the need of energy efficient devices and operation will more effective. This chapter focused on following areas to enhance efficiency, which incorporate EE improvement utilizing radio access techniques like synchronously remote endurance and force move. In this research paper, the authors have searched various methods or techniques that are working with 5G wireless networks and got techniques that can address to increase speed with the help of 5G wireless network. It discusses energy-efficiency techniques that can be useful to boost user experience on 5G wireless network and also discusses the problems that can arrive in and addressed in future.

Chapter 10

The research and development along the 5th generation are moving with extreme speed around the global world. In this paper, the authors are going put light on the concepts of network slicing architecture of the 5G network at multi-level stages. The network slicing concept is another challenge faced by the 5G network. Further, the broad description of 5G architecture and analysis on infrastructure design and applications of network slicing in terms of 5G are done. This technique plays a major part in 5G technology deals with virtualization and software-defined technology. Due to low latency and its explosive growth, it is a technology to look into the deep knowledge it inculcates within. The chapter also focuses on the applications that the industry is looking into, and it has made a large impact on the user's life. With quantitative examples to show, this research will give a proper estimation for network slicing networking.

Preface

OVERVIEW OF SUBJECT MATTER

5G is the upcoming generation of the wireless network that will be the advanced version of 4G LTE+ providing all the features of a 4G LTE network and connectivity for IoT devices with faster speed and lower latency. The 5G network is going to be a service-oriented network, connecting billions of IoT devices and mobile phones through the wireless network, and hence, it needs a special emphasis on security. Security is the necessary enabler for the continuity of the wireless network business, and in 5G, network security for IoT devices is the most important aspect. As IoT is gaining momentum, people can remotely operate or instruct their network devices. Therefore, there is a need for robust security mechanisms to prevent unauthorized access to the devices.

Evolution of Software-Defined Networking Foundations for IoT and 5G Mobile Networks is a collection of innovative research on the security challenges and prevention mechanisms in high-speed mobile networks. The book explores the threats to 5G and IoT and how to implement effective security architecture for them. While highlighting topics including artificial intelligence, mobile technology, and ubiquitous computing, this book is ideally designed for cybersecurity experts, network providers, computer scientists, communication technologies experts, academicians, students, and researchers.

TOPIC FITS IN THE WORLD TODAY

The many academic areas covered in this publication include, but are not limited to:

Artificial Intelligence
Cloud Computing
Energy Conservation
Mobile Technology

Network Security
Network Traffic
Risk Management
Smart Technology
Ubiquitous Computing
Wireless Sensor Network

TARGET AUDIENCE

The volume is mainly intended for professors and academic researchers in the field of networking and communication. However, we consider the book will be of special interest to students at the undergraduate and post-graduate levels who wish to expand their knowledge on topics related to digital communications, IOT, 5G and wireless sensor networks. These topics are introduced in various academic programs. Although the primary potential audience might be academic, there is no reason to exclude a more general public who may be interested in understanding the ways networking may be exercising influence over their daily lives.

CHAPTERS

The book has 10 chapters.

Chapter 1. Security Challenges in Network slicing in 5G

Chapter 2. Security Perspective of Cloud and Internet of Things with 5G Networks: Security Perspective of Cloud and Internet of Things with 5G Networks

Chapter 3. The Internet of Things based Technologies

Chapter 4. Role Coordination in Large-Scale and Highly-Dense Internet-of-Things: Large-Scale and Highly-Dense Internet-of-Things

Chapter 5. Crop Disease Detection Using Data Science Techniques

Chapter 6. Wing of 5G IoT and Other Services: IoT and Other Services

Chapter 7. Priority Encoding based Cluster Head Selection Approach in Wireless Sensor Networks

Chapter 8. Improvement and Reduction of Clustering Overhead in Mobile Ad Hoc Network with Optimum Stable Bunching Algorithm

Chapter 9. The role of dynamic network slicing in 5G: IoT and 5G Mobile Networks

Chapter 10. Network Slicing and the Role of 5G in IOT Applications

CONCLUSION

This book explore the new technologies, future definitions, next generation devices, new protocols and standards for software-defined, software-controlled, programmable networking. The professors and professionals explained you what's required for building next generation networks that use software for communication between applications and the underlying network infrastructure.

This edited book also presents several software defined networking practical aspects including IOT and 5G. Also, explained the some interesting use cases around big data, data center overlays, and network-function virtualization (NFV). This book discovers how different vendors and service providers alike are following SDN as it continues to evolve.

After reading the book, the readers will be able to:

- Explore the current state of the OpenFlow model and centralized network control
- Delve into distributed and central control, including data plane generation
- Examine the structure and capabilities of commercial and open source controllers
- Survey the available technologies for network programmability
- Trace the modern data center from desktop-centric to highly distributed models
- Discover new ways to connect instances of network-function virtualization and service chaining
- Get detailed information on constructing and maintaining an SDN network topology
- Examine an idealized SDN framework for controllers, applications, and ecosystems.

Chapter 1
Security Challenges in Network Slicing in 5G

Rashmi Mishra
ⓘ https://orcid.org/0000-0003-0015-8732
Delhi Technological University, India & ABES Engineering College, Ghaziabad, India

R. K. Yadav
Delhi Technological University, India

ABSTRACT

The evolving area of the upcoming technology in the era of "Mobile Security" is a 5G network. The aim of this technology is to provide security to the mobile nodes for the load balancing, for the voice security, capacity, quality of services, secure end-to-end communication, connectivity of the devices in a highly mobile network with reliable and scalable networks. The enhancement towards technology leads to connect home appliances with IoT devices, industries, business. Therefore, security-related issues will also increase. In wireless communication, devices want to connect all the time, which primes the vulnerabilities, increases network traffic at the device side on the channel, and creates the backdoor for the hacking and cracking mechanisms for the wireless devices.

INTRODUCTION

5G is not individual around "quicker, superior or improved" networks, it is all about distressing approximately every characteristic of our subsists and empowering an assorted innovative customary of amenities. Nevertheless, 5G have their potential, that is, its applications must be distributed very strongly and sanctuary matters

DOI: 10.4018/978-1-7998-4685-7.ch001

essential remain dispensed through the system foundation since from the self-same commencement towards defending equally the systems and clients. Along with 5G, the mobile network takes that security on another close with an extensive diversity of innovative, forward-thinking precautions (McKeown N et.al.,2008). This Chapter pronounces those precautions in deepness, as well as the susceptibilities and bout paths, they are intended towards moderate. Safeguarding mutual equal level of security for all tenders which shape slicing notion, in this case, can also be difficult. There are several features of slicing i.e., isolation and protection might create attack methods such as weak isolation will lead to another resource with better parameters, lower cost. From the industry point of view, following eight major necessities of 5G are recognized (Ericsson,2015):

- *1~10 Gbps data rates in physical networks:* This data rate is almost 10 times faster than the existing LTE networks that are 150 Mbps.
- *Round trip latency is 1 ms:* It is almost 10 times faster than 4G's RTT.
- *High bandwidth in the unit area:* It will increase the connectivity of the devices with very high bandwidth.
- *An enormous number of connected devices:* It will connect thousands of devices in one go.
- *Availability of network:* 99.99% network will be available in 5G.
- *Coverage of network anytime, any ware:* Network should be available anytime as per user location.
- *Energy consumption should be reduced:* Development of technology will lead the usage of 5G network energy consumption is reduced by almost 99%
- *High battery life:* It is very important in the emerging 5G network is that it reduce power consumption.

Many of the wireless industries, university, and research officialdoms have started working in 5G wireless systems such as Ericsson, Qualcomm, Docomo, Huawei, Nokia Solution Networks, METIS, Samsung electronics, 5G training, 5G Forum, 5GNOW. Visions of these companies discussed in the table 1 and reference in table 2 (Ericsson,2015):

Table 1. Company & their vision

Company	Vision
Ericsson	Their vision is to make affordable and sustainable network.
Qualcomm	Empowering innovative amenities
Docomo	Widespread and supplemented contented Each device connected wirelessly
Huawei	Enormous bulk and connectivity
Nokia solutions networks	Accurate communication/channel, Augmented reality and work for Heterogeneous environment.
Samsung Electronics	Evolve IOT, multimedia and enhance cloud computing
5G Forum	Work for Heterogeneous environment.
METIS	Scalable network and Sustainable network
5G Training	PMI (Personal mobile internet) Device to Device communication
5GNOW	Amalgamated mount assembly impression Universal Filtered Multi-Carrier

Table 2. Company, Publisher, Year of Publication

Company	Publisher	Year of Publication
Ericsson	White paper	2015
Qualcomm	White paper	2014
Docomo	White paper	2015
Huawei	White paper	2013
Nokia solutions networks	White paper	2014
Samsung Electronics	White paper	2015
5G Forum	Public-Private Partnership	2013
METIS	A. Osseiranet et al	2014
5G Training	IEEE	2014
5GNOW	G. Wunderet et al	2014

Network Slicing

Is one of most recent technology comes into picture that provides elasticity, scalability, flexibility and provides the security in a way that it creates the logical networks which share the common hardware infrastructure? The primary idea was introduced by (Peterson, L. et.al., 2006) in a paper" A blueprint for introducing disruptive technology into the Internet". Slicing might also use diverse daises, which means slicing mechanisms can be applied in Operating System, kernel level, in the virtualization software systems, firmware or even in regular software. In this wide range of situations, the slicing mechanisms will be provided by diverse sellers. Furthered incorporation concept of software-defined networking and network functions virtualization. But, allowing multiple tenants to share single resources must ensure the security needed for those scenarios (Joseph et al., 2008). The crucks of this research are to describe the overlay network, plant lab in which the environment is created for the sliced network to use the same design and utilize the different services. Having several features of the network slicing in 5G there are various security problems faced by the company and one of the most important area is security such as Denial of Service attack (DoS), attackers may exploit the systems which support the slicing and Slice-initiated attack. Figure 1 (NTT Docomo,2015) shows the network architecture for secure and dynamic network:

Figure 1. Network Architecture for Secure and Dynamic Network

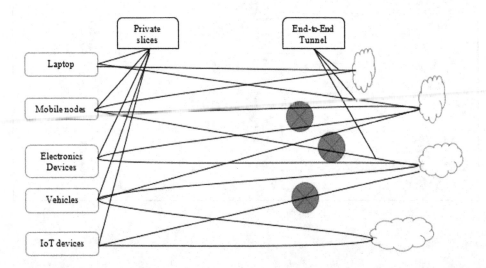

The 5G marketplace is a massive commercial prospect for mobile machinists and their commercial associates (Guermazi A, 2011). Though, the strategies and usage also grow probable cyber threats. Such as a Distributed Denial of Service (DDoS) attacks. Many of the industries provide a layer of security for the operators, vendors, ethics bodies, and connotations procedure an iterative twist of repeated erudition concerning emergent intimidations and retort selections. Some of the actions have to be taken to mitigate an attack for the control aspect. Some of them are proactive while others are applied after the attacks have been taking place. Typically, there are two types of attacks that have been carried out on the 5G network of any business outlook. The first one is a Zero-day attack and the second one is the Day-one attack. A zero-day attack is a threat that does not have predefined signatures or previous history/fingerprints. Classically, the security supervisor recognizes eccentricities in identified upright behavior of the carter cloud, as well as tenders that demand amenity and state. After identification of the abnormal behavior, the action is taken to moderate the attack or to contract supplementary perceptibility to appropriately recognize the challenger. In Day-one attacks, threats that have a predefined signature or fingerprint, a moderation stratagem happens in advance to knob the attack. Controls are carried to formulate the alterations to the carter cloud to smear eminence of amenity fluctuations in per-hop behavior to diminish the impression of an attack (European Commission,2011).

Network Technologies for 5G Security

The new version of the 5G network designed by NGMN is worked on three principles as Flexible security mechanism, Supreme built-in security, Automation. 5G network should provide a highly robust security system for cyber-attack and security assurance. The 5G security mechanism must be supple for authentication and identification, must adjust according to the environment, security control and threats. The two most important concepts in 5G play a vital role such as virtual network function and software-based network control. These features are expected by Network function virtualization enables vendors to implement network function in software called VNFs and deploy them on cloud and Software-Defined Networking separate the core plane from the data plane, SDN deploys on very high-end servers Figure 2 (NTT Docomo,2015) These two mechanisms provide full proof security to the 5G network. The SDN architecture is divided into three layers named Application plane, Control plane, and Infrastructure plane. Application plane consists of QoS management, network management, and security services, Control plane consists of Network Operating Systems which logically centralized the network, it also provides the hardware concept to the Application plane. The infrastructure plane is also known as the Data plane is the instruction of the Control plane which deals with the data traffic flows. OpenFlow is the first worthwhile implementation part of SDN and follows the three-tier architecture named OpenFlow applications, OpenFlow controller and OpenFlow switches.

Figure 2. shows the SDN architecture

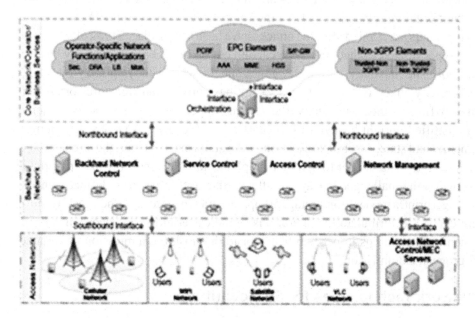

Security Issues Introduced by Network Slicing In 5g

The main feature of the Network slicing is Seclusion. More is Seclusion more is unfailing of network slicing. In a network, if there is a single slice it means a network is un-sliced and it is a well-researched topic. Slicing means the network infrastructure is divided into multiples parts and each part will share the same infrastructures. The minimum requirements are set for each sliced network are coexistence. But for the isolation of each slice Tavakoli et al., defines an abstraction layer for an end to end isolation and the author also introduces the adequate security policies. Other than this author also states that currently no isolation capabilities are defined by any other author. Then is important to design a mechanism for the security of isolation.

In the current mobile network if flooding Distributed Denial of Service attack is attacked by the attacker then only that service will be affected. However, in a 5G network if the DDOS is performed by the attacker then other services will also be affected. This isolation is required for the slicing.

Protuberant forms, such as next-generation mobile networks (NGMN) ETSI's, NFV (for virtual network function life cycle), allotted endorsements aimed at network slicing security in 5G, which assisted the documentation of intimidations in the universal packet essential.

Table 3. shows the threats on SDN layers

	Threats	Description
Application plane	1. Authentication 2. Authorization 3. Access Control 4. Fake rule insertion	In case of roaming, there are no compelling mechanism for authentication and authorization. Management of network resources such as bandwidth and channel capacity. Malicious Node masquerading will generate fake rule.
Control plane	1. DDoS 2. DoS 3. Unauthorized access 4. Availability 5. Scalability	DDoS and DoS attack is possible due to its visibility. No mechanism is there for unauthorized access. Data is not available at the right time, at the right place to the right people due to DoS attack. Centralized mechanism should be there.
Data plane	1. Fake rule flow 2. Flooding attack 3. Jamming 4. Hijacking 5. Compromised of channel	Due to scrapyard nature of Data plane it is more susceptible to this kind of attack. OpenFlow has limited capacity to store the rules. Data plane is totally dependent on the Control plane therefore its security is depending upon controller security.
Ctrl-Data Int	1. Man-in-the-middle attack. 2. TCP-level attack	Due to complex configuration of TLS it is suffers from Man-in-the-middle attack. TLS is susceptible to TCP-level attack.

Security principles on network slicing

Security Principles: Some security principles are followed by any of the substructures for secure communication.

- *Confidentiality:* In (Guermazi and Abid,2011) have proposed a key distribution is used for the secure communication process. In (Yun et al.,2008) says that the communication process in between the sensor nodes should be secure. The idea of confidentiality is used to avert intended or unintended illegal exposé of message contents.
- *Integrity:* In (Diop et al.,2013) use the cryptographic hash function to ensure the integrity of the message. Modifications of data by unauthorized adverts or processes.

- *Availability:* The idea of Availability guarantees that "RIGHT INFORMATION IS AVAILABLE TO THE RIGHT PERSON AT A RIDHT TIME AT A RIGHT PLACE". In (Modirkhazeni et al., 2010) depict that the single point of failure may disturb the entire communication in WSN, therefore the connectivity of the network is well defined for the entire lifetime.
- *Authentication:* In (Misra and Dias,2010) Thomasinous say authentication is essential for the authentication of the civilian applications. In (Shi and Perrig, 2004) depict that authentication is necessary for identifying the malicious packet in the transmission process. The idea of Authentication guarantees that, any renewed node should be authenticated first earlier incoming in the network to guarantee its authenticity.
- *Non-Repudiation:* The idea of Non-Repudiation is to guarantee that the sender can't deny that he was not sent the data or any node cannot refuse to send the data to another node.
- *Access Control:* An Authorized person can access the data to whom he claims to be.

Security Threats and Recommendation

The next-generation mobile network is used in the 5G network and for the security measures that are not implemented as far or not available. The recommendation tourist attractions of the confines in the access network and for the cyber-attacks in the existing infrastructures (Yun Z et al., 2008). Recommendations arc Flash network traffic, security of radio interface keys, User plane integrity, Mandated security in the network, Consistency in subscriber level security policies, DoS attacks on the Infrastructure (A. Osseiranet et al,2014).

- *Flash network traffic:* In today's scenario, mobile nodes are increasing day by day, therefore the in a large number of scales there will be changed in the network traffic pattern that could be either accidental or malicious. Thus, it is recommended that a 5G system must minimize large swipes in traffic tradition and afford elasticity.
- *Security of radio interface keys:* Keys were sent in an insecure manner in the previous generation. But in 5G systems, keys sent in a secure manner such as by using SS7/Diameter.
- *User plane integrity:* In 3G and 4G does not provide a cryptographic veracity shield for the user plan. Therefore, it is recommended that protection will be provided to the transport and application layer. But E2E application-level security will create too much overhead in the transmission.

- *Mandated security in the network:* 3G and the 4G network are having a constraint on service-driven approach and do not provide system layer security. Therefore, it is recommended that it must be instructed in 5G is to investigate the critical security challenges.
- *Consistency in subscriber level security policies:* It is highly in demand that user security parameters will not change if the user is in roaming mode means the operator is changed. In case if the user is in highly roaming mode then it might be possible that security services will not be updated on time. If the user is in roaming mode, the services will be provided by the Mobile Edge Computing and using latency-sensitive services, so will the security services will be updated on the user mobile. This needs security policy, for this recommendation discuss the possibility of using the virtualization technique.
- *DoS attacks on the Infrastructure:* DoS and DDoS attacks might disturb the operation of infrastructures such as energy, health, transportation and telecommunications and many more. So, it is a recommendation that the network should be capable of handling several connections with a different number of operating capabilities and limitations.

Other Security Challenges

Security challenges of the 5G network are divided into 3 categories such as Dos attack, Access of network and the core network (Modirkhazeni A et al., 2010)

Dos attack

DoS attack in 5G network target the bandwidth, memory, processing unit, radios, sensors, operating system, applications, user data, the configuration of the network and the connectivity of the network infrastructure (Diop A et al., 2013). DoS means a large number of connected devices will target the single destination it may be a user and an infrastructure. Attack on user depicts that the user not able to access the services provided by the operator and attack against the infrastructure is to deplete the network resources. Although the operator of the network is not affected the individual subscribers may get affected. Another case of DoS attack is that affected users of the infrastructure may target their infrastructure. Hence for free DoS and DDoS attack, we have to focus on the following areas (Qualcomm,2014):

- The user plane may support two-way communication of the nodes/mobile.
- Authentication of the signaling plane.
- Bandwidth assignment.
- Connectivity checks regularly.
- The management plane should support the network configuration so that the user and signaling plane will be maintained.

Access of the Network

One of the major challenges is data send by the nodes and received by the nodes is not secure and it may increase the jamming of the network. The malicious nodes will send the excessive signaling traffic that leading to a DoS attack. Such type of activity will be identified on time so that the user plane will be protected. Network and services should be accessible by the authenticated nodes/sensors such that vulnerabilities will get protected. 5G network uses higher throughput, lower latencies, extended coverage, etc and various types of access technologies. To keep the network occupied/working, the 5G network will able to recover the network from the jamming attacks of the radio channels. The addition to this node must be secure due to its geographical distribution (Huawei,2013).

Security Challenges in the Core Layer

The enormous dissemination of the IP protocols on the user and core plane makes the 5G network vulnerable to attack. Therefore, the availability of the network must be improved including resilience against signalling-based vulnerability (Misra S et al., 2010). The 5G network should ensure emergency communication if the network is either inaccessible. Other challenges in the 5G network are that there are several infected devices on the network such as IoT devices or M2M devices is ready to attempt the DoS attack or jamming the channel. IoT devices are resource constraint therefore they request the services in two-mode (Shi E et al., 2004). First, these devices will request to perform processing, storing, sharing of information in the cloud. Second, these devices will easily be compromised and the DoS attack will perform by the nodes.

Security Solutions for SDN

The architecture of the SDN provides a high level of security monitoring, traffic analysis and system response for the amenities forensics. By the help of cycle of harvesting intelligence SDN quickly find threat from the network resources, circumstances, and faults. SDN architecture is very useful to find the traffic redirection through flow-tables, update, analyze, reprogram the network without the use of hardware configuration (Rutvij H et al., 2012).

Application Plane Security

Feature of centralized control architecture makes easy to use application by altruistic with network statics and characteristics of the packet. The SDN control plane is worked in between the hardware and applications for hiding the complexities of the existing network. PermOF is predefined system permission is used for access control and access control of SDN applications (G. Wunder et al,2014) . The main working of PermOF is to provide announcements, warning, recite, inscribe and system authorization for certain applications of SDN. Another security measure is NGMN. NGMN is used in the application layer for data integrity, it will defend the data outside the mobile network, end to end security, user plane data integrity, protection form battery consumption in IoT devices.

Control Plane Security

Many of the researchers have been published schemes and security proposals for the control plane such as the Security-Enhanced Flooding Controller, another extended version of the SEFC is also published. Usually, the reactive controller is worked on the flow request when it comes to the controller and proactive controllers are used to installing the flow rules. The control plane is a mediator of the data plane and the application plane. So, by security the control planes the whole network should be secured by adding some secure program northbound API. It will validate the rules which are generated by the application layer and also steadfastness the skirmishes between the applications (Ahmad I et al, 2018). Controller resilience policies have been proposed by the author to mitigate the risk of failure of the controller due to scalability issues by the use of redundancy, distributed controller, storage maximization and maximizing the processing capabilities and resolve the DoS attack. The SDN support wildcard OpenFlow directions will send the aggregated the client data to the server and microflow requests were managed by the controller but this leads to the failure due to the DoS attacks. Therefore, numerous load balancing techniques were proposed and suggested by many researchers with multi-controllers in the network.

Data Plane Security

Data plane sends the packets through the channel also vital for security apparatuses such as authentication/authorization because the application installed were modified, change, update and delete the flow rules in the data plane. Therefore, security mechanisms are needed for authentication and authorization. Multiple controllers have been proposed by the authors if one controller fails and another will provide the flow rules (Jangra1 A., et al). FortNox mechanism is used to permit the controller for checking the illogicality in the flow rules in the application plane. FlowCchecker mechanism is used to find the inconsistencies in the flow rules in the data plane.

CONCLUSION AND FUTURE SCOPE

This chapter is mainly focused on 5G network slicing security for mobile users. 5G network is designed to obtain security beyond the existing limitations. Security in 5G will leads to preserving the load balance, energy constraint of the mobile nodes and size of the clusters/cell which is the main disadvantage of the existing 4G network. Security mechanisms of the 5G network should be designed in such a way that it will be secure from the future threats that were introduced by the attackers and the limitations of the 4G networks should not be propagated in the 5G network. Devices that are connected from the 5G network should also be secure form the malicious program introduced by the adversaries. Load balancing of the network architecture should be developed in such a way that it follows the security policies developed by the SDN and free from saturation attacks. As far as security of controller is concerned, if the security of the controller is not taken into account then it introduces a delay in flow rules and protocols in the switches and if switches will get congested then it leads to the unsought traffic flow. Another constraint is the capacity of the network. If the capacity of the networks is not taken into account then it leads to the DoS attack. So, it is advised to design a mechanism in such a way that it will keep the limitation of mobile nodes or sensor nodes in IoT.

REFERENCES

Ahmad, I., Liyanage, M., Shahabuddin, S., Ylianttila, M., & Gurtov, A. (2018). Design Principles for 5G Security. *A Comprehensive Guide to 5G Security*, 75–98.

Diop, A., Qi, Y., Wang, Q., & Hussain, S, (2013). An advanced survey on secure energy-efficient hierarchical routing protocols in wireless sensor networks. *Int J Computer Sci Issues, 10*, 490–500.

Docomo, N. T. T. (2015). *5G radio access: Requirements, concepts technologies.* White paper.

Ericsson. (2015). *5G radio access*. White paper.

European Commission. (2011). *HORIZON 2020, The EU framework program for Research and Innovation.* Available: http://ec.europa.eu/programmes/horizon2020/

5G Forum. (2015). *Make it Happen: Creating New Values Together.* Available: http://www.5gforum.org/

Guermazi, A., & Abid, M. (2011). An efficient key distribution scheme to secure data-centric routing protocols in hierarchical wireless sensor networks. *Proc ComputSci*, 208–15.

Huawei. (2013). *5G a technology vision.* White paper.

5G Infrastructure Public-Private Partnership. (2013). Available: http://5g-ppp.eu/

Jangra, A., Goel, N., Priyanka, & Bhati, K. (2010). Security Aspects in Mobile Ad Hoc Networks (WSNs): A Big Picture. *International Journal of Electronics Engineering*, 189-196.

Joseph, D. A., Tavakoli, A., & Stoica, I. (2008). A policy-aware switching layer for data centers. *Proceedings of the ACM SIGCOMM*, 51–62. 10.1145/1402958.1402966

McKeown, N., Anderson, T., Balakrishnan, H., Parulkar, G., Peterson, L., Rexford, J., Shenker, S., & Turner, J. (2008). OpenFlow: Enabling innovation in campus networks. *Computer Communication Review*, *38*(2), 69–74. doi:10.1145/1355734.1355746

Misra, S., & Dias Thomasinous, P. (2010). A simple, least-time, and energy-efficient routing protocol with one-level data aggregation for wireless sensor networks. *Journal of Systems and Software*, *83*(5), 852–860. doi:10.1016/j.jss.2009.12.021

Modirkhazeni, A., Ithnin, N., & Ibrahim, O. (2010). Secure multipath routing protocols in wireless sensor networks: a security survey analysis. *Proceedings of the 2nd international conference on network application protocols and services,* 22833. 10.1109/NETAPPS.2010.48

Nokia Networks. (2014). *Looking ahead to 5G: Building a virtual zero latency gigabit experience.* White paper.

Osseiranet, A. (2014). IEEE: Scenarios for 5G mobile and wireless communications: The vision of the METIS project. *IEEE Communications Magazine*, *52*(5), 26–35. doi:10.1109/MCOM.2014.6815890

Peterson, L., & Roscoe, T. (2006). The design Principles of PlanetLab. *Operating Systems Review*, *40*(1), 11–16. doi:10.1145/1113361.1113367

Qualcomm Technologies, Inc. (2014). *Qualcomm's 5G vision.* White paper.

Rutvij, H., & Jhaveri. (2012). *A Novel Approach for GrayHole and BlackHole Attacks in Mobile Ad-hoc Networks*. IEEE.

Samsung Electronics Co. (2015). *5G vision*. white paper.

Shi, E., & Perrig, A. (2004). Designing secure sensor networks. *IEEE Wireless Commun Mag*, *11*(6), 38–43. doi:10.1109/MWC.2004.1368895

5G Training and Certification. (2014). *An Initiative Project in Preparing5G Competence*. Available: http://www.ieee-5g.org/about/

Wunder, G., Jung, P., Kasparick, M., Wild, T., Schaich, F., Chen, Y., Brink, S., Gaspar, I., Michailow, N., Festag, A., Mendes, L., Cassiau, N., Ktenas, D., Dryjanski, M., Pietrzyk, S., Eged, B., Vago, P., & Wiedmann, F. (2014). 5GNOW: Non-orthogonal, asynchronous waveforms for future mobile applications. *IEEE Communications Magazine*, *52*(2), 97–105. doi:10.1109/MCOM.2014.6736749

Yun, Z., Yuguang, F., & Yanchao, Z. (2008). Securing wireless sensor networks: A survey. *IEEE Communications Surveys and Tutorials*, *10*(3), 6–28. doi:10.1109/COMST.2008.4625802

Chapter 2
Security Perspective of Cloud and Internet of Things With 5G Networks

Neetu Faujdar
Amity University, Noida, India

ABSTRACT

Pervasive computing has been greatly supported by the internet of things. The use of internet of things has created the environment that helps in the management of the different modules that are the part of the complete system, which can work effectively without the interference with the other components of the system. The cloud environment with the internet of things can help in getting the greater extend of data sharing. Little attention has been provided to the security of the various stakeholders that are the part of the system. IoT cloud integration involved privacy, security, and personal safety risk of the stakeholders. Not only are these types of security attacks possible, but there is also the possibility of attack on the IoT components like hardware manipulation to disrupt the services. As we are on the network, all the communication attacks of network are also possible. This chapter will cover common aspects of regarding the cloud and internet of things (IOT) with 5G networks.

DOI: 10.4018/978-1-7998-4685-7.ch002

INTRODUCTION

Cloud computing technology, seen as the staggering framework overcome, might convey us to the "cloud society" after the PCs and the Internet conveyed people to the "compose society" (D Singh 2015, Atzori 2010). In the arrangement of Cloud Computing, all the ordinary utilization of PCs will be moved into the fogs (virtualized mass computational servers which organize on the Internet), all we need is a passageway to the Internet and after that we can play out any work on the cloud (R Khan 2012, J Gubbi 2013). Disseminated processing is the latest headway in the movement of figuring power. It cuts down the reason for segment, enabling access to enlisting power effectively only available to the greatest affiliations. It furthermore enables tinier relationship to utilize totally directed enlisting structures, decreasing the essentials for extraordinarily capable IT staff. Dispersed figuring insinuates applications passed on as organizations over the Internet and besides the hardware and structures programming in the server cultivates that give those organizations. At the point when all is said in done, Cloud Computing is internet dealing with, whereby shared resources, programming, and information are given on enthusiasm to PCs, mobile phones, and other practically identical contraptions (M Nia 2015, H Salmani 2016). Disseminated figuring is also another style of preparing in which dynamically adaptable resources are given as virtualized organizations. This licenses pro associations and customers to change their preparing limit dependent upon what sum is required at a given time, or for a given task. Circulated figuring is sifted through on stages like Google, Salesforce, Zoho, Axios Systems, Microsoft, Yahoo, Amazon (M Tehranipoor 2010, G Lafuente 2015).

Cloud Computing Security Issues

Cloud Development Models

Cloud model fix, fixes, stage, amassing, and programming establishment is surrendered as organizations measure or down depend on the web. It has three standards delivery models (J Mineraud 2015, S Abdelwahab 2014):

1. **Private Cloud:** Private cloud is another name utilized by customers nowadays to delineate consumed copies appropriated enlisting in the private structure. These are arranged up in the inward server ranch exercises of an affiliation. In private mists, the data, for example, virtual assets and versatile applications that are given by different customers are gathered together and are made accessible for cloud client for purchasing and selling.

2. **Open Cloud:** Open spread disseminated processing infers that customary standard definition, when the advantages are watchfully given a fine-grained, self relationship towards reason on the web, from an external supplier who is off-website and he gives property and bills on nitty gitty utilize comprehension of the explanation.

3. **Half and half cloud:** Cross breed cloud is a subtype of private cloud which is associated with various cloud affiliations, half regulated given as a specific unit. It changes virtual IT into a blend of both private and open fogs. Cream cloud gives increasingly secure control of data and applications and licenses, a gathering of programming to get the information on the Internet.

Service Delivery Models of Cloud Computing

Imitating cloud shows settlements, however the accompanying security perceives diverse transport circulated processing the board models. The three standards movement cloud the executives models are: Infrastructure-as-a-Service (IaaS), Plateform-as-a-Service (Paas) and Software-as-a-Service (Saas) (W. A. Jansen 2011, S. L. Keoh 2014).

1. IaaS: IaaS is a singular occupant cloud layer in which steady resource cloud comprehension of simply offering to accessible customer based on pay-per-use. This immensely diminishes the requirement for huge beginning enlistment of hardware financing. SaaS: It is a conveyance product that shows which applications are facilitated by a seller or supplier administration and is available for clients within a system, normally the Internet.

2. SAAS: has become a pervasive conveyance inexorably outward as subject innovations that help web administrations and the administration building located design experienced and new techniques formative get to grow dramatically. SaaS is also often connected to a membership model that allows Pay As You Go. Then, the broadband management has the permission to allow the client access from more regions far and wide.

    3 Paas: It is a programming and enhancements found contraptions encouraged servers providers. This can be one layer higher than IaaS. It gives the client a joint scope of natural planners that can inspire the developers to build the applications.

Cloud Computing in Mobile Applications

User module

1. Registration process
2. Login process
3. Service searches
4. Make inquiry process
5. Get information about service-man/woman
6. Send feedback about service
7. Edit profile process
8. Change password process

   Admin Module

1. Login process
2. Register service provider person
3. Manage registered service provider person
4. Manage inquiry from user
5. Assign inquiry to service provider person
6. Send information about person who assign for service
7. Get feedback about service from user
8. Change password process

IOT

IOT is basically components of a device or devices or any other physical article that are linked over an internet network. These devices are linked with each other over a network and can transmit instructions and information with each other. It is a combination of hardware and software components of a device or a machine. Just how a robot works based on the instructions given to it similarly, the functioning of these devices and machines can be controlled and commanded by humans. The decisions taken by these devices depend upon its surrounding environment. These devices are accordingly programmed based upon the actions and the work that are expected from it. In Earlier times internet was associated with laptops and computers only. With advancement in technology internet got linked with smart phones, smart watches and tablets. But now we see that internet is being used everywhere like the concept of smart homes, in automobiles, automatic driving, surveillance and safety, etc. This Figure 1 gives data about number of IOT connected gadgets installed throughout the world from 2015 to 2025 (C. Lesjak 2014, P. N. Mahalle 2013, W. John 2013).

Figure 1. Number of IOT connected gadgets installed throughout the world from 2015 to 2025

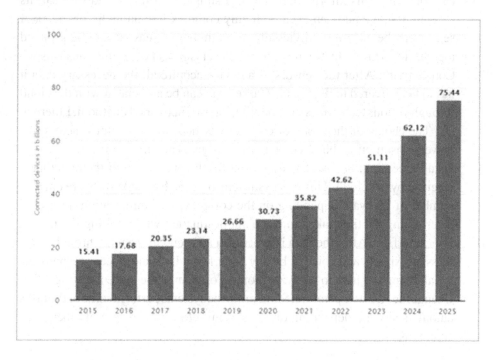

There are assortments of techniques that are used by IOT devices and gadgets to link with each and exchange information with each other. These devices may use wireless network for connectivity. Wi-Fi's and Bluetooth are largely used in workplaces, offices, industries, schools, colleges and even in homes. Some gadgets also use LTE and satellite connection for connection and transfer of data.

It is believed that after few years 5G networks will come under use by the IOT ventures. The main advantage that 5G network provides is that it allows to approximately 1 million 5G devices to connect in a given square kilometer. In this way a large number of sensors can be used together in a little region. After the development of the IOT industry the cloud will gather less information for operation. If operation of information is completed on the device itself and just the important data is received by cloud, then the expenses can be minimized. Various new innovations will be needed for this. IOT comprises of four main sections that is Sensors or gadgets, Connectivity, Data processing and User Interface (Ian F 2015, M.Karakus 2017).

1. Sensors: Sensors. Or gadgets assemble all the information and data from its environment. This information can be a simple data like speed of a car, its acceleration, etc and can even be highly complex like an audio or video. A sensor can be existing individually or a number of seasons can be grouped together to form a gadget or a device. E.g. A car is gadget with numerous sensors.
2. Connectivity: After the sensors of a device acquire all the necessary data it has to be delivered to the cloud. The sensors can be associated with the cloud through various techniques like satellite, internet network, Bluetooth, Ethernet, etc. The choice of the mode of connectivity depends on various factors like power consumption, bandwidth, range of signals and many others.
3. Data Processing: Software is important for the processing of the data that is received by the cloud. This processing can be done by single software or more number of software depending on the complexity of information. E.g. GPS determining the time taken to reach our destination while driving a car.
4. User Interface: After the data is processed it is send to the user through a text message, signal, and voice or by any other form. User interface is responsible for allowing the user to analyze, monitor or change the system settings. E.g. Change the A.C. temperature. Sometimes the systems perform some of the tasks automatically too depending on the system settings or in case of emergency situations.

IOT and automobile industry and its applications

Internet of things is not a extravagant innovation in this era. It's here and quick changing the manner in which we live. The automotive industry is widely benefited by the innovations made through internet of things. It has provided us with significant transportation facility and administration abilities. It is driving us to time where we will have smart, independent and self governing vehicles. Automotive industry is quickest developing marketplace for IOT-based arrangements. It is believed that by the year 2020 greater than 250 million autos are estimated to be associated with internet which features the effects of IOT in the automobile industry. The amount of network units in vehicles is probably going to grow by 67% throughout the following two years, and the purchaser spending on connected systems in automobiles is presumed to double by the end of ten years. Drivers around the world anticipate that their vehicles should become cell phones on wheels, and IOT is demonstrating that vehicle network is by far the best innovation that man has introduced. Applications of IOT in automobile industry are as follows (Brief 2015, P. Demestichas 2013, Van-Giang 2016).

Prescient maintenance technology

Prescient maintenance technology is used to avoid costly repairs in vehicles. This technology depends upon the utilization of IOT network that assemble information of various parts of the automobile. It then conveys that information to the cloud and assesses the dangers of potential breakdown or faults of a vehicle's equipment or in its software. After data is prepared, the driver is informed about any essential or obligatory service or fix to keep away from any potential occurrences. It empowers end clients to get the correct data before time. With IOT network instruments, you can avoid any kind of breakdowns in the course of the ride. Prescient maintenance technology is connected with the algorithms of machine learning. These calculations are astoundingly successful at detecting things such as battery life. Here's the means by which it works (P. Ameigeiras 2015, H. Kim, 2013):

i)   The battery status is examined by a in- vehicle detector system.
ii)   Information is delivered to the cloud.
iii) The battery status is checked by the algorithms of machine learning.
iv)   All sources of information is prepared by the system and accordingly guidance is given to the driver.
     v) Then the system delivers a notification to the driver cautioning them about the low charge in the battery.

Figure 2. How does prescient maintenance technology works

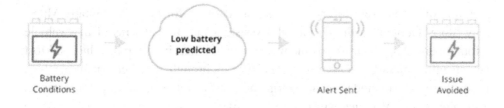

Battery Conditions		Alert Sent	Issue Avoided

The prescient maintenance calculation proceeds in the following way:

i)   Information is gathered from the engine starter, fuel siphon, and the battery.
ii)   Information is transmitted to a cloud server.
     iv)   Any possible system issues in the vehicle are predicted by the cloud.
     v)   Suggestions are conveyed to the driver by means of an associated gadget.

Figure 3. The prescient maintenance calculation method

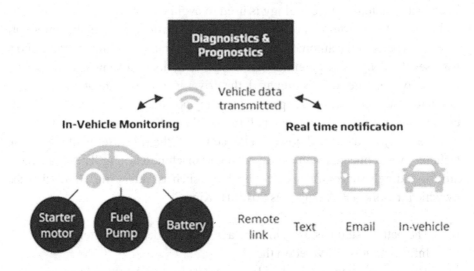

In-car entertainment and information system

The entire vehicle industry is driving towards making innovative and inventive headways to improve accessibility associations and correspondence inside the vehicle, overhaul vehicle assurance and security, and update in-vehicle customer experience. Clever applications are being associated with vehicle infotainment systems to give in-vehicle course, telemetric, and delight. Google has worked together with a couple of automakers to organize its applications, for instance, Google Maps, Play Store, Google Earth and Google Assistant into the systems of in - vehicle infotainment. Apple Car Play is likewise given as a part in different vehicles. Most vehicle infotainment systems utilize the affixed or brought together structure, which needs them to be related with an external device for web accessibility, for instance, a mobile phone. Vehicles will before long have programming and web organize office embedded into their infotainment structures, empowering drivers to move toward maps, on-demand infotainment, and different other web related offices (H. Kim 2013, K. Pentikousis 2013).

Amalgamation of automobile frameworks are used to convey information and entertainment to the vehicle driver and the passengers through sounds and videos, control touch screen components, Voice directions, etc. As per Markets and Markets, the in-car infotainment market is roughly calculated to extend USD 30.47 billion by 2022 which is at a CAGR of 11.79%. Investigation proposes that in-car infotainment market is operated by the expansion in manufacture of automobile, innovative development and expanding interest for opulent automobiles. Fundamental parts of an in-vehicle information and entertainment framework are as follows (W. Li 2016, R. Masoudi 2016):

Coordinated Head-component: It is a touch screen device, a gadget that looks like a tablet or a mini wall TV that is attached on the automobile's dashboard. It has easy to use HMI, the head part goes about as an impeccably associated control panel for the infotainment framework.

Heads-Up Display: It is an indispensable component of exclusive infotainment frameworks, which shows the automobile's ongoing data on the see-through screen coordinated with the automobile's windshield. Heads-up showcase assists in diminishing the driver's diversion while driving and helps him with primary details like speed, route maps, and data from vehicle's OBD port-II, atmosphere, interactive media choices, etc.

Exclusive DSPs and GPUs to help numerous displays: Now day's infotainment frameworks are supported by incredible car processors designed for powerful and smart framework of the automobile. These car processors are effective in showing content on numerous displays (for example Head-up Display, Windshield, Connected cell phones, Head Unit, etc) and conveys an upgraded experience to drivers and travelers in the vehicle.

Operating systems: In vehicle infotainment frameworks need working frameworks that are called "operating systems" fit for handling availability of connections and network and programming applications to coordinate new features in the framework. Operating systems like Android, QNX, Windows, Linux are driving the infotainment fragment.

CAN, LVDS and other network support (according to the prerequisite): The electronic equipment parts in infotainment frameworks are interconnected with specific systematic protocols for communication, example, CAN (Controller Area Network). CAN or some other system enables microcontrollers and gadgets to speak with one another without the host PC.

Connection Modules: Infotainment frameworks incorporate GPS, Wi-Fi, and Bluetooth to provide network with outside systems and gadgets. These functions assist in setting up services like giving route directions, web network and cell phone coordination with the infotainment framework.

Car Sensors Integration: Signal acknowledgment sensors for identifying surrounding light, camera sensors and numerous other sensors in the automobile coordinate with infotainment frameworks to give data related to safety to the driver and if there is any danger around .

Computerized Instrument Cluster: In today's time infotainment frameworks have changed the car cockpit structure from static structure of the in-car instruments to advanced instrument groups and are digitalized. Advanced instrument groups incorporate computerized displays of the old measuring instrument in the vehicle like speedometer, odometer, RPM etc.

Figure 4. System Architecture of IVI

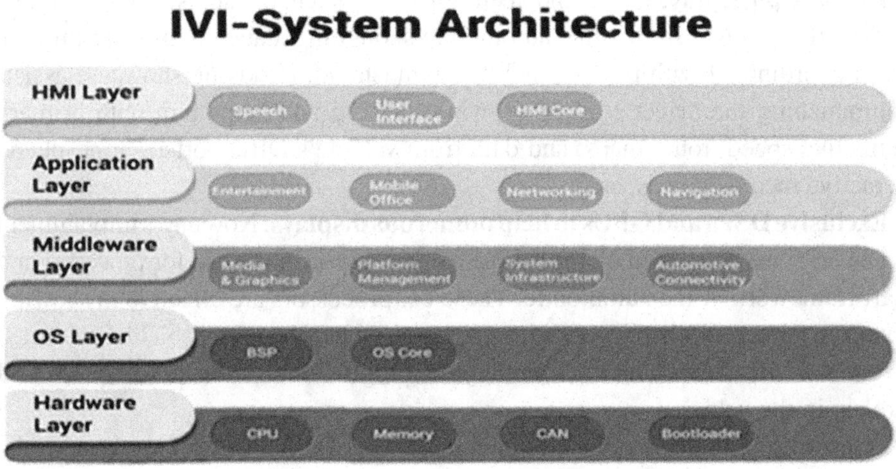

Safety and surveillance

External sensors are additionally utilized as back view cameras and vicinity sensors that guide in blind spot identification and help in accurate parking, and more secure driving. Drivers are secured due to present-day sensors that can detect encompassing traffic on the road and the surrounding environment to guarantee safe driving. Also, with the utilization of mesh arranged vehicles on the road, installed frameworks can anticipate and keep away from crashes and avoid any accidents.

Information examination and dashboard detailing

Connected autos offer driver information crucial for the improvement, prototyping and testing of better self-driving vehicles. As the number of vehicles with IOT empowered frameworks are increasing the nature of information will definitely improve. With information investigation and dashboard detailing devices, associations in the automobile business can keep on improving their contributions and better serve the requirements of their clients.

Real time vehicle scanning system

IOT permits continuous information sharing from vehicles to makers those aides in the improvement and advancement of upkeep, assemblage and production processes throughout the lifecycle of the automobile. By sharing this information with vehicle makers it additionally encourages them to improve prescient experiences to permit quicker reaction times, if there are any difficult or risky issues that might lead to an accident in the future. In this way it becomes simpler for makers to be responsible and proactive in emergency situations.

Connected vehicles enable producers to legitimately and effectively tell the drivers about any issue in the vehicle and automatically operate necessary tasks like booking a vehicle servicing meeting with the closest vehicle dealer or service center. This makes sure that vehicles are consistently serviced without bothering the client. As car IOT advancements keep on developing, they are opening a large amount of chances for automotive market to lift up their businesses. The associated vehicle market includes various sub-sections that include diverse innovation usage. Car makers, media communications suppliers, and software suppliers are taking an interest in every one of these fragments.

5G Network Architecture and its Applications

In the present life 4G arrange is attempting to give solid information and IP network and administrations up to 1 Gbps. 4G systems turns out to improve the advancement of the system execution, cost, effectiveness and give the mass market IP-based administrations. Still the interest is going high because of different example of portable traffic is expanding strain on cell systems. To conquer this issue the future 5G arrange is going to dispatch. 5G system will give the principal foundation to billions of new gadgets with less traffic in the system. Presently a day's 5G innovation is most needed research point for the specialists. So inquires about are as of now in progress investigating distinctive building ways to address their key drivers. SDN (Software Defined Network) innovation has been assuming a vital job to plan the 5G remote system. So in this area will perceive how SDN innovation is developed in the plan of 5G remote system (Tomovic 2014, Van-Giang 2015).

Through consistent effort and confirmation Telecom chairmen are completing an automated change to make a prevalent propelled world. To outfit tries and individuals with a continuous, on demand, all on the web, DIY, social (ROADS) experience requires an end to-end (E2E) encouraged building featuring deft, customized, and keen movement during each stage. The thorough cloud modification of frameworks, movement structures, and organizations is a basic for this enthusiastically anticipated propelled change (SBH Said 2013, J. Costa-Requena 2015).

The "All Cloud" procedure is an enlightened investigation into equipment asset pools, Gives consistently autonomous system cutting on a solitary system foundation to meet differentiated assistance prerequisites and gives DC-based cloud engineering to help different application situations. ° Uses Cloud RAN to recreate radio access systems (RAN) to give enormous associations of numerous models and actualize on-request arrangement of RAN capacities required by 5G. ° Simplifies centre system design to execute on demand setup of system works through control and client plane division, part based capacities, and bound together database the executives. ° Implements programmed arrange cutting assistance age, upkeep, and end for different administrations to diminish working costs through nimble system O&M, circulated programming design, and programmed sending. Administrators change systems utilizing a system engineering dependent on server farm (DC) in which all capacities and administration applications are running on the cloud DC, alluded to as a Cloud Native design (P. Demestichas 2013, Ali-Ahmad H 2013).

The 5G (fifth Generation) is being viewed as client driven idea rather than administrator driven as seen in 3G or administration driven will observed for 4G. Versatile terminals always have the option to join numerous streams approaching from various advances. The 4G cell system uses the multimode versatile system. They expect to give unique client terminal which can participate in various remote systems and beat the structure issue of intensity utilization and cost old versatile terminals (M. Karakus 2017, R Trivisonno 2015).

OWR stands for Open Wireless Architecture which is engaged to enable distinctive extant remote to air coherence similarly as tomorrow remote correspondence standard in an open building stage. Before long, the creating interest and the various instances of flexible traffic place an extending strain on cell frameworks. To consider the tremendous bulk of traffic passed on by the modern organizations and applications, the future fifth period 5G of remote/flexible broadband framework will give the basic establishment to tons of new contraptions with less obvious traffic models will join the framework. The 5G remote frameworks ought to enable the progression and abuse of tremendous utmost and immense accessibility of marvellous and mind boggling heterogeneous structures. In like way, the framework should be fit for dealing with the confusing setting of errands to help the relentlessly contrasting arrangement of new however then sudden organizations, customers and applications (i.e., including astute urban territories, compact mechanical automation, vehicle accessibility, machine-to-machine (M2M) modules, video perception, etc.), all with incredibly isolating essentials, which will push adaptable framework execution and abilities as far as possible. Moreover, it should give versatile and adaptable usage of all available non-circumscribing ranges (e.g., further LTE moves up to support little cells (Non-Orthogonal Multiple Access (NOMA), Future Radio Access (FRA)) for wildly uncommon framework game plan circumstances, in an imperativeness capable and secure way (X. Jin 2013, J. Lee 2014).

The new period of remote correspondence is developing 5G technology. Users can be associated with a few remote access advances at the same time because of acknowledgment of omnipresent processing. Key highlights of 5G incorporate help VPNs stands for Virtual Private Networks and Wireless World Wide Web (WWWW) backing, and utilization of level IP. Utilization of level IP empowers distinguishing proof of gadgets utilizing representative names which permits 5G to be worthy for a wide range of innovations. The quantities of components in the information way are decreased because of the utilization of level IP. This outcomes in low capital cost (CapEx) and operational cost (OpEx). 5Gs significant favourable position is high information paces of up to 10Gbps, which is multiple times quicker than the 4G LTE. Likewise, low system inertness of underneath 1 millisecond which contrasts inactivity of 30-70 ms of 4G, makes 5G, route superior to its more seasoned innovation. Notwithstanding these focal points, high framework limit, vitality sparing enormous gadget backing and cost decrease has proposed 5G as the need of great importance.

For the ultra-thick 5G systems with enormous remote traffic and administration necessities, the foundation must be isolated from the administrations it offers. System usage can be expanded by enabling separated administrations to dwell on the equivalent fundamental foundation. New items and innovations can be bolstered alongside heritage items by WNV by disengaging some portion of the system. The developing heterogeneous remote systems interest for a more grounded system the board instrument. To accomplish this, we require remote system virtualization (K.K. Yap 2010).

Introduction of knowledge against 5G can address the multifaceted idea of Heterogeneous Networks (HetNets) by deciding and offering versatile responses for consider compose heterogeneity. Programming Defined Networking (SDN) has ascended as another astute plan for organize programmability. The fundamental concept towards SDN is to move the control plane outside the switches and engage external control of data through a predictable programming component which is called controller. SDN gives clear considerations to portray the fragments, the limits they give, and the show to conduct the sending plane from a remote controller by methods for an ensured channel. This consideration gets the essential requirements of sending tables for a bigger piece of switches and their stream tables. This united bleeding edge see makes the controller sensible to perform orchestrate the load up limits while allowing basic difference in the framework lead through the brought together control plane (A. Basta 2014).

In heterogeneous systems, multi-connectivity gives an ideal client experience dependent on LTE and 5G capacities, for example, high data transfer capacity and paces of high recurrence, organize inclusion and solid versatility of low recurrence, and open Wi-Fi assets. In situations that require high transfer speed or congruity, a client requires numerous simultaneous associations. For instance, information total from different memberships to 5G, LTE, and Wi-Fi is required to deliver high data transfer capacity. A LTE arrange get to is required to keep up congruity after a client has gotten to a 5G high-recurrence little cell.

The 5G adaptable frameworks should similarly reinforce instruments for traffic detachment. It should achieve from starting Quality of Service (QOS) to end requirements for moving toward applications of 5G. In reality, thus as to ensure a bigger QOS the officials, a few undertakings and task has monitored joining SDN and its introduction in future compact frameworks convincing responses for respecting QOS end-customers. In, maker's inscriptions motivations writing in Open Flow-enabled SDN frameworks, they orchestrate the related functions conforming to stream where QOS can gain by the possibility of SDN. The makers can present the QOS Flow suggestion in order to develop the flexibility of QOS control in SDN frameworks. Delay estimation In SDN frameworks using Queue model delay estimation is analyzed. The designing proposed in a transport the limit of Open Flow in giving execution requirements to different applications (P. Rost 2016).

In the SDN designing, the framework controller keeps up the information in general framework. In the other way, Data plane is appropriated to items switches and switches that offer essential stream sending or guiding subject to stream areas made through the control plane. The per-stream based controller figures guiding approach to give QOS, guarantee and bigger organization assets limits. Moreover, SDN presents an open Application programmability interfaces (API) among the data and control planes Fig.1, shows and offers a programmable framework and offer flexibility to orchestrate movement and rates the association of new headways and organizations, for instance, Open flow, For CES and PCE .This assurance programmability can open intriguing open entryways with respect to 5G adaptable systems. The Open flow is portrayed by the Open Networking Foundation (ONF) as the essential standard show in southbound interface between the data and control plane of SDN designing. It is thoroughly recognized as the predominant SDN show used in interface between the framework controller and framework devices. However, there are various shows that can address an alternative to Open Flow in southbound SDN interface, for instance, the For CES and PCE shows portrayed by IETF. An epic southbound SDN shows are truly a work in progress and testing (B. Naudts 2012).

Single application circumstance for 5G and IOT is the splendid supportable city. Zanella et al. inspects urban IOT developments that are close to regulation, and agree that most by far of splendid city organizations rely upon a brought together structure where data is passed on to a control centre liable for thusly taking care of and taking care of the got traffic. Inside splendid urban territories, sharp transportability is one of the troublesome circumstances where self-administering or helped driving cars demand to constantly screen the direction outside and inside the vehicle and exchange data between the different individuals from the vehicle orchestrate, i.e., vehicle to vehicle (V2V) and vehicle to establishment (V2I) correspondences. Various organizations in a canny city incorporate the leading group of traffic blockage, sullying watching, halting, etc. Consequently, the crucial task of 5G is to facilitate the organization of these different organizations and contraptions in a productive manner, by thinking about the varying thought of the devices (e.g., vehicles moving at different versatility speeds and established traffic road sensors). Adaptability and re-configurability of SDN/NFV is helpful smart urban networks, where fast re-configurations of framework parameters as demonstrated by traffic state would enhance the capacities in supporting and upgrading splendid urban networks organizations. For example emergency organizations could be passed on business orchestrate while re-configurability of SDN/NFV will consider assuring the guarantees required for such emergency organizations. To engage such re-configurability, data from sharp city organizations can be abused, with the ultimate objective that adroit city framework and organizations could stay in amicable manner (P. Sidhu 2015).

In 5G frameworks, C-RAN is gripping from having a central director of modernized work unit, a.k.a. baseband getting ready unit (BBU), to a dynamically expansive thought of limit split. To moreover grow the flexibility, to diminish the capriciousness and to enhance the QOS, 5G frameworks are moving close to an adaptable edge enlisting approach where organizations, (for instance, saving) despite limits are moved closer to the edge. When considering edge-masterminded associations, for instance, C-RAN or adaptable edge, the activity of virtualization and softwarization is as such to re-configure the framework by moving framework limits or organizations and to suitably revive the related traffic ways. If a chop's QOS is separating or the traffic requirement from this cut is over-troubling a given territory of the framework, NFV can trigger a re-region of framework works approaching to the edge and SDN can revive the framework topology to react to the recently referenced changes. In the field of conveying virtualization closer to the edge, the virtualization of BS's low level limits is tended to in. The essential test identified in is the virtualization of procedure heightened baseband limits, for instance, the PHY layer, generally executed on submitted gear or on all around valuable hardware enlivening operators. This use case of physical layer virtualization is analyzed similar to accelerating developments (M. Condoluci 2016).

In organize softwarization engineering the primary 5G arrange sections are Radio Networks, Front take and Backhaul Networks, Aggregation and Core Networks, Network Clouds, Mobile Network and empowering innovations like Mobile Edge

Networks, Service/Software Networks, Software-Defined Cloud Networks, Satellite Networks, IOT Networks. The natures of this proposition are allowed as isolated planes. In independently characterized, the planes are not totally autonomous: primary terms in each plane are identifies with the principle terms of different planes in the design. The structure is isolated in these significant terms which are Application and Business Service Plane, Multi-Service Management Plane, Integrated Network Management and Operations Plane, Infrastructure Softwarization Plane, Control Plane and Forwarding/Data Plane.

Other than and according to ITU-T, SDN displays a couple of level of organizations security provided into 5G mastermind structure, for instance, Data genuineness, Data protection, confirmation. With respect to, SDN will improve security in the accompanying 5G convenient frameworks. Additionally, with the use of Open Flow show in 5G flexible frameworks, the framework will assemble the point of confinement of component parameters will delineate the stream features and choose the critical parameters that impact the QOS of each stream. The Open Flow always uses these parameters in order to develop course of action models and to achieve high QOS. The accompanying 5G focus frameworks is used to astoundingly versatile, flexible and will reinforce more significant level of programmability and robotization. Thus, the 5G focus frameworks will be cloud-based condition. Seen as the accompanying virtualization-based EPC building (vEPC) for the accompanying 5G frameworks. The 5G SDN-based Core Networks will introduce virtualization, and will give innovative courses of action, with to a more prominent degree a consideration on the information unavoidable for 5G compose, moreover SDN will drive the feeds and speeds of data in 5G orchestrates and will intensely give sort out system organizations. The execution of SDN in 5G focus frameworks will give a remote ability to manage the direct of framework contraptions by pushing intensely the distinction in device game plan and the administrators (M. Sama 2014).

Wireless Communication towards the 5G

Evolution of wireless world has been evolved from first generation (1G) and then second generation (2G) and then third generation (3G) to the finally came forth generation (4G). 1G i.e. Advanced Mobile Phone System (AMPS) and 2G (i.e. GSM and GPRS) were designed for circuit switched voice application. In the other hand 3G and 4G were developed for packet switched services. 5G networks will not be based on routing and switching technologies anymore. They will be more flexible, open and able to evolve more easily than previously evolved networks (A. Gudipati 2012).

Software Defined Networks (SDN)

5G network identified the complexity of Heterogeneous Networks (HetNets)by providing the more reliable solution to HetNets. SDN is the new emerging intelligent architecture for the programming of networks. The logic behind the SDN is to move control plane outside the switches and enable the data of external control through a logical software entity called controller. SDN gives the descriptions of components, functions and the protocol to manage the forwarding plane from a remote controller via some secure channel (.

Network Function Virtualization (NFV)

SDN is the most emerging framework for the future 5G networking and how to re-factor the architecture of legacy networks, is virtualization so called Network Function Virtualization. NFV is also called network softwarization i.e. set of network functions by utilizing them in to software packages. The concept of NFV comes from the classical server virtualization that could by installing multiple virtual machines running different operating systems, software and processes.

CONCLUSION

5G technology routes are evolution, convergence and innovation to fulfil the services and applications requirements of the society in near future and beyond. In the near future a network must be designed using a virtualization technology that is why a holistic SDN and NFV strategies are paramount.

5G network will provide the frequency spectrum as well as the physical infrastructure because it is the combination of multi-systems, multi-technologies. The challenging issue towards the 5G network are wireless and mobile network. Even while SDN and NFV will support to overcome these issues. The SDN programming structure presents a complex set of problems facing the increasing weakness, which will change the dynamics around securing the wireless infrastructure.

REFERENCES

Abdelwahab, S., Hamdaoui, B., Guizani, M., & Rayes, A. (2014). Enabling smart cloud services through remote sensing: An Internet of Everything enabler. *IEEE Internet Things Journal, 1*(3), 276–288. doi:10.1109/JIOT.2014.2325071

Akyildiz, I. F., Wang, P., & Lin, S.-C. (2015). *SoftAir: Software de-fined networking architecture for 5G wireless systems. In Computer Netwworkins.* Elsevier.

Ali-Ahmad, H., Cicconetti, C., De la Oliva, A., & Mancuso, V. (2013). SDN-based network architecture for extremely dense wireless networks. IEEE SDN for Future Networks and Services (SDN4FNS).

Ameigeiras, P., Ramos-Muñoz, J., Schumacher, L., Prados-Garzon, J., Navarro-Ortiz, J., & López-Soler, J. M. (2015). Link-level access cloud architecture design based on SDN for 5G networks. *IEEE Network.* Advance online publication. doi:10.1109/MNET.2015.7064899

Atzori, L., Iera, A., & Morabito, G. (2010). The Internet of Things: A survey. *Computer Networks, 54*(15), 2787–2805. doi:10.1016/j.comnet.2010.05.010

Basta, A., Kellerer, W., Hoffmann, M., Morper, H. J., & Hoffmann, K. (2014). Applying NFV and SDN to LTE Mobile Core Gateways, the Functions Placement Problem. *ACM Proceedings of the 4th Workshop on All Things Cellular: Operations, Applications, Challenges, All Things Cellular '14,* 33–38.

Brief, O. N. F. Solution. (2015). *Open Flow enabled SDN and Network Functions Virtualization.* On-line at https://www.opennetworking.org/images/stories/downloads/sdnresources/solution briefs/sb-sdn-nvf-solution.pdf

Condoluci, M., Dohler, M., Araniti, G., Molinaro, A., & Sachs, J. (2016, February). Enhanced Radio Access and Data Transmission Procedures Facilitating Industry-Compliant Machine-Type Communications over LTE-Based 5G Networks. *IEEE Wireless Communications, 23*(1), 56–63. doi:10.1109/MWC.2016.7422406

Costa-Requena, J. (2015). SDN and NFV Integration in Generalized Mobile Network Architecture. *European Conf. Networks and Communications,* 1-6. 10.1109/EuCNC.2015.7194059

Demestichas, P., Georgakopoulos, A., Karvounas, D., Tsagkaris, K., Stavroulaki, V., Lu, J., Xiong, C., & Yao, J. (2013). 5G on the Horizon: Key Challenges for the Radio-Access Network. *Vehicular Technology, 8*(3), 47–53. doi:10.1109/MVT.2013.2269187

Demestichas, P., Georgakopoulos, A., Karvounas, D., Tsagkaris, K., Stavroulaki, V., Lu, J., Xiong, C., & Yao, J. (2013). 5G on the Horizon: Key Challenges for the Radio-Access Network. *Vehicular Technology, 8*(3), 47–53. doi:10.1109/MVT.2013.2269187

Gubbi, J., Buyya, R., Marusic, S., & Palaniswami, M. (2013). Internet of Things (IoT): A vision architectural elements and future directions. *Future Generation Computer Systems, 29*(7), 1645–1660. doi:10.1016/j.future.2013.01.010

Gudipati, A., Perry, D., Li, L. E., & Katti, S. (2013). Soft RAN: Software Defined Radio Access Network. *Proceedings of the Second ACM SIGCOMM Workshop on Hot Topics in Software Defined Networking, HotSDN '13,* 25–30.

Jansen, W. A. (2011). Cloud hooks: Security and privacy issues in cloud computing. *Proc. 44th Hawaii Int. Conf. Syst. Sci. (HICSS),* 1-10. 10.1109/HICSS.2011.103

Jin, X., Li, L. E., Vanbever, L., & Rexford, J. (2013). SoftCell: Scalable and Flexible Cellular Core Network Architecture. *Proceedings of CoNEXT, 2013,* 163–174.

John, W., Pentikousis, K., Agapiou, G., Jacob, E., Kind, M., Manzalini, A., Risso, F., Staessens, D., Steinert, R., & Meirosu, C. (2013). Research Directions in Network Service Chaining. IEEE SDN forFuture Networks and Services (SDN4FNS).

Karakus, M., & Durres, A. (2017). Quality of Service (QoS) in Software De-fined Networking (SDN): A survey. *Journal of Network and Computer Applications, 80,* 200-218.

Karakus, M., & Durres, A. (2017). Quality of Service (QoS) in Software Defined Networking (SDN): A survey. *Journal of Network and Computer Applications, 80,* 200-218.

Keoh, S. L., Kumar, S., & Tschofenig, H. (2014). Securing the Internet of Things: A standardization perspective. *IEEE Internet Things J., 1*(3), 265–275. doi:10.1109/JIOT.2014.2323395

Khan, Khan, Zaheer, & Khan. (2012). Future internet: The Internet of Things architecture possible applications and key challenges. *Proc. IEEE 10th Int. Conf. Frontiers Inf. Technol.,* 257-260.

Kim, H., & Feamster, N. (2013). Improving network management with software defined networking. *IEEE Communications Magazine, 51*(2), 114–119. doi:10.1109/MCOM.2013.6461195

Lafuente, G. (2015). The big data security challenge. *Network Security, 20*(1), 12–14. doi:10.1016/S1353-4858(15)70009-7

Lee, J., Uddin, M., Tourrilhes, J., Sen, S., Banerjee, S., Arndt, M., Kim, K.-H., & Nadeem, T. (2014). Mesdn: Mobile extension of SDN. *ACM Proceedings of the Fifth International Workshop on Mobile Cloud Computing; Services*, 7–14.

Lesjak, C., Ruprechter, T., Haid, J., Bock, H., & Brenner, E. (2014). *A secure hardware module and system concept for local and remote industrial embedded system identification. In Proceeding Emerging Technology Factory Automation.* ETFA.

Li, W., Meng, W., & Kwok, L. F. (2016). A survey on openflow based soft-ware defined networks: Security challenges and countermeasures. *Journal of Network and Computer Applications*, *68*, 126–139. doi:10.1016/j.jnca.2016.04.011

Mahalle, P. N., Anggorojati, B., Prasad, N. R., & Prasad, R. (2013). Identity authentication and capability based access control (IACAC) for the Internet of Things. *Journal Cyber Security Mobility*, *1*(4), 309–348.

Masoudi, R., & Ghaffari, A. (2016). Software defined networks: A survey. *Journal of Network and Computer Applications*, *67*, 1–25. doi:10.1016/j.jnca.2016.03.016

Mineraud, J., Mazhelis, O., Su, X., & Tarkoma, S. (2015). *A gap analysis of Internet-of-Things platforms.* Available: http://arxiv.org/abs/1502.01181

Naudts, B., Kind, M., Westphal, F., Verbrugge, S., Colle, D., & Pickavet, M. (2012). Techno economic Analysis of Software Defined Networking as Architecture for the Virtualization of a Mobile Network. *Workshop on Software Defined Networking (EWSDN), 2012 European*, 67–72. 10.1109/EWSDN.2012.27

Nguyen, Do, & Kim (2016). *SDN and Virtualization-Based LTE Mobile Network Architectures: A Comprehensive Survey.* DOI doi:10.100711277-015-2997-7

Nguyen & Kim. (2015). Proposal and evaluation of SDN-based mobile packet core networks. *Journal on Wireless Communications and Networking*, 172.

Nia, M., Mozaffari-Kermani, M., Sur-Kolay, S., Raghunathan, A., & Jha, N. K. (2015). Energy-efficient long-term continuous personal health monitoring. *IEEE Transaction on Multi-Scale Computing System*, *1*(2), 85–98. doi:10.1109/TMSCS.2015.2494021

Pentikousis, K., Wang, Y., & Hu, W. (2013). MobileFlow: Toward Soft-ware-Defined Mobile Networks. *IEEE Communications Magazine*.

Rost, P., Banchs, A., Berberana, I., Breitbach, M., Doll, M., Droste, H., Mannweiler, C., Puente, M. A., Samdanis, K., & Sayadi, B. (2016, May). Mobile network architecture evolution toward 5G. *IEEE Communications Magazine*, *54*(5), 84–91. doi:10.1109/MCOM.2016.7470940

Said, S. B. H., Sama, M. R., Guillouard, K., Suciu, L., Simon, G., Lagrange, X., & Bonnin, J.-M. (2013), New control plane in 3GPP LTE/EPC architecture for on-demand connectivity service. *Proceedings of second IEEE International Conference on Cloud Networking (CLOUDNET)*, 205–209. 10.1109/CloudNet.2013.6710579

Salmani, H., & Tehranipoor, M. M. (2016). Vulnerability analysis of a circuit layout to hardware Trojan insertion. *IEEE Transactions on Information Forensics and Security, 11*(6), 1214–1225. doi:10.1109/TIFS.2016.2520910

Sama, M., Ben Hadj Said, S., Guillouard, K., & Suciu, L. (2014). Enabling network programmability in LTE/EPC architecture using OpenFlow. *12*th *International Symposium on Modelling and Optimization in Mobile, Ad Hoc, and Wireless Networks (WiOpt)*, 389–396.

Sidhu, P., Woungang, I., Carvalho, G. H. S., Anpalagan, A., & Dhurandher, S. K. (2015). An Analysis of Machine-Type-Communication on Human-Type-Communication over Wireless Communication Networks. *IEEE 29th International Conference in Advanced Information Networking and Applications Workshops (WAINA)*, 332–337.

Singh, D., Tripathi, G., & Jara, A. J. (2014). A survey of Internet-of-Things: Future vision architecture challenges and services. *Proc. IEEE World Forum Internet Things*, 287–292. 10.1109/WF-IoT.2014.6803174

Tehranipoor, M., & Koushanfar, F. (2010). A survey of hardware Trojan taxonomy and detection. *IEEE Design & Test of Computers, 27*(1), 10–25. doi:10.1109/MDT.2010.7

Thakurdesai, P. A., Kole, P. L., & Pareek, R. P. (2004). Evaluation of the quality and contents of diabetes mellitus patient education on Internet. *Patient Education and Counseling, 53*, 309–313.

Tomovic, S., Pejanovic-Djurisic, M., & Radusinovic, I. (2014). SDN based mobile networks: Concepts and benefits. *Wireless Personal Communications, 78*(3), 1629–1644. doi:10.100711277-014-1909-6

Trivisonno, R., Guerzoni, R., Vaishnavi, I., & Soldani, D. (2015). SDN-based 5G mobile networks: Architecture, functions, procedures and backward compatibility, Transmission. *Emerging Telecommunication Technology, 26*(1), 82–92. doi:10.1002/ett.2915

Yap, K. K., Sherwood, R., Kobayashi, M., Huang, T.-Y., Chan, M., Handigol, N., McKeown, N., & Parulkar, G. (2010). Blueprint for introducing innovation into wireless mobile networks. *ACM Proceedings of the Second ACM SIGCOMM Workshop on Virtualized Infrastructure Systems and Architectures, VISA '10*, 25–32.

Chapter 3
The Internet of Things– Based Technologies

Pradeep Kumar Garg
Indian Institute of Technology, Roorkee, India

ABSTRACT

The internet of things (IoT) is the network of physical objects—devices, vehicles, buildings, and other objects—embedded with software, electronic devices, sensors, and network connectivity that enable these objects to collect and share information or data. Its applications include smart homes, healthcare, industries, transportation systems, logistics, and energy. Building an IoT real-time-based application involves the proper selection of combination of sensors, technology, networks, and communication modules, supported with the concepts of data processing, remote sensing, cloud computing, etc. This chapter highlights advantages and disadvantages IoT and various techniques, such as computer vision, remote sensing, artificial intelligence, cloud computing, big data, ubiquitous computing, which are widely used in various applications. Many new IoT-based applications will evolve, as new devices, sensors, chips, and computational techniques are developed.

INTRODUCTION

The network of several interconnected devices is termed as Internet of Things (IoT) (White Paper, 2018). The use of connect devices, and research & development into smart object networking gave birth to IoT. The IoT can be defined as *"smart objects, machines interacting and communicating with other machines using sensors, smart environments and infrastructures"*, resulting in enormous data generated which is processed and converted into useful activities employed to command & control the

DOI: 10.4018/978-1-7998-4685-7.ch003

things, and make living much comfortable. It is a unique system of interconnected computing devices, mechanical & digital devices, sensors, smart objects, smart infrastructures, and human-beings that are interconnected together with unique identifiers. It has the ability to transfer the huge data collected over a network without the need of human-to-computer interaction.

The IoT essentially is the network of connected things, such as sensors and actuators, as well as communication technologies along with the required hardware & software to collect data for a large number of applications, data mining, data analytics, and developing innovations. Figure 1 presents a concept behind the development of IoT. Here, the A's refer to the utilization of technology globally (anytime, anywhere, any device, any network, etc.) and C's indicate the functions of IoT, such as collection, convergence, connectivity and computing. The IoT today has already developed much beyond the A's and C's (Gupta, 2016).

The development in networking technologies also enabled the usage of networking in motion-based objects which resulted in improvement of real-time applications. Using these technologies, object's behavior may be automatically detected, and an alarm may be raised in case of any suspicious, threatening or illegal activities are observed by the intelligent surveillance system. Intelligent surveillance system requires the usage of both control system and IT technologies to reduce the needs of people, which helps users to monitor, control and operate their system from anywhere with the help of IoT-based devices. In essence, the IoT involves sensors that are embedded in all kinds of devices and send data streams *via* Internet connections to one or more central (Cloud) locations.

The IoT is a most promising technology these days. The AI is playing an important role in the connected ecosystem of devices & sensors, and allowing these devices to perform certain defined tasks. It is estimated that by the end of 2020, there will be about 30 million IoT gadgets or devices all over the globe. The market revenues for IoT-based security services are expected to be more than $11 billion by 2021. Gartner predicted that more than 80% of enterprise projects involving the use of IoT will include an Artificial Intelligence (AI) component by year 2022. More than 50% of the enterprises will start using AI and machine learning approach by 2022 to effectively utilize their IoT data (Evans, 2011).

Figure 1. A's and C's concept in IoT (Gupta, 2016)

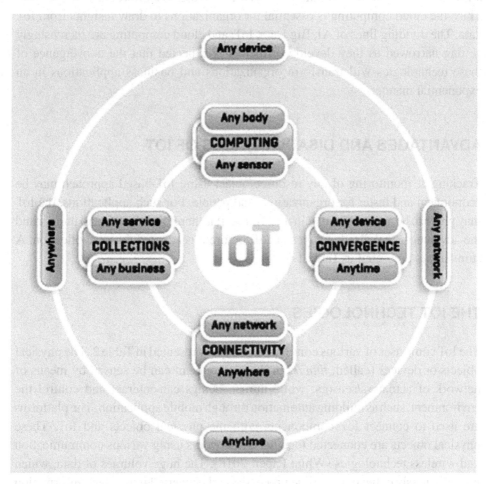

Several technologies, such as IoT, AI, Big Data, and cloud computing have taken lead in transforming the businesses and processes in organizations, world-wide. With digital revolution and transformation, these technologies are gaining popularity in almost all the businesses. Each of these is no longer considered as a sophisticated technology, but in present day context they have become almost a necessity to implement. All IoT devices are expected to follow five basic steps: measuring, sending, storing, analyzing, and acting. The last step 'acting' means an infinite number of things, ranging from a physical action to providing information, which will entirely depend on the 'analysis of data' using appropriate algorithm.

While Big Data deals with the science of storing and analyzing the ever-growing digital data; the number of connected devices and sensors are contributing to this growth of digital data. On the other hand, the cloud computing helps to leverage the big data analytics through anytime-anywhere access to this data through cloud servers. Thus, the cloud computing is essential for organizations to draw insights from IoT data. The dividing lines of AI, Big Data, IoT, and cloud computing are increasingly getting narrowed as they develop further. It is expected that the convergence of these technologies will transform organizations and business applications in an exponential manner.

ADVANTAGES AND DISADVANTAGES OF IOT

Tracking & monitoring of any resource/object using IoT-based approach may be economical and faster for organizations and people. For such applications, the IoT may prove to be a game changer in near future. It is therefore important to understand the advantages and disadvantages of IoT, before it is adopted for an application. A summary is presented in Table 1.

THE IOT TECHNOLOGIES

The IoT comprises of various components that are presented in Table 2. The physical objects or devices (called, *things*) in the environment can be sensed by means of network of actuators/sensors, while human beings can interact and control the environment, such as building automation through mobile application. The platforms are used to connect IoT components with the physical objects and IoT. These physical objects are connected together by networks using various communication and wireless technologies (White Paper, 2018). The huge volumes of data, which is continuously collected is online processed and converted into valued information useful for various applications to run on IoT components. The data generated can be used and analysed in a Geographic Information System (GIS) to yield automatic reports and patterns, which can greatly assist the businesses in making relevant decisions. The GIS software can also convert these data into actionable reports to improve the operational efficiency.

Sensors are commonly used in most places to guide and help the human beings (Jayavardhana et. al., 2013). Through sensor fusion technology, data collected from several sensors is highly accurate than obtained from each individual sensor. Sensor fusion helps in context awareness and higher levels of recognition, having good potential for IoT. Individual sensor which has limitations can be corrected by complementary sensing nodes. For different IoT applications, the sensing nodes may vary widely. For example, the RFID readers sense the existence of a particular object, person, and intruders in the buildings (Want 2004, Said and Tobla, 2016).

These sensors (nodes) have a unique ID, and therefore each one can be controlled individually *via* a remote command. The IoT-based tracking and monitoring of any resource is proving to be economical. The IoT, therefore, will have a significant major impact on our lives.

Table 1. Advantages and disadvantages of using IoT (Machado and Shah, 2017)

S.No.	Advantages	Disadvantages
1	Huge data is produced but this data in raw form may not be useful. It is processed to convert into *information*. More information helps in making better decisions and actions.	The IoT-based large network requires large devices and gadgets; each one is connected with its unique Internet Protocol (IP) addresses. *Compatibility* and tagging of these devices can be a big concern, particularly in absence of any international standards.
2	With IoT, *monitoring* of activities will become easier, so it helps in taking actions well on time.	With large number of devices connected in a cloud-based system, *complexity* to build a secure and large network is a challenging task.
3	It saves lot of *time* in data collection using sophisticated smart devices and gadgets.	System build on large network has big concern over *privacy/ security/safety,* as it may have chances of being hacked.

Table 2. IoT components (Bojanova, 2015)

IoT components	Description
Physical objects	Any entity, also called, Things
Virtual objects	Examples include: Electronic coupons, Books, Wallets, QR code
Sensors	Sense the objects and surrounding physical environment to collect data
Actuators	Affect the physical environment
Human	Human, for example, can control the environment *via* software or mobile applications
Networking components	The components and devices are connected together by networks, using various wireless and wireline technologies, standards, and protocols.
Platforms	The middleware is used to connect components, such as physical objects, people, and services to the IoT, and provides various functionalities, such as: Access to devices, Ensuring proper installation/behaviour of devices, and Interoperable connection to local network, cloud or other devices.
Data storage and processing	Cloud service is the best example of huge data storage and processing technology that can be used for: Processing Big Data and converting it into valuable information, Building and running innovative applications, and Optimizing business processes by integrating the device data.

The IoT practically has wide applications in serveral field, such as infrastructure, traffic & transportation, smart building, smart agriculture, energy, smart environment, smart security, smart wearable, agriculture, healthcare and others, as shown in Figure 2. The development in networking and computing, internet, improved sensors, software and wireless networks has encouraged the use and applications of IoT systems world-wide. The IoT is considered as a universal global neural network in the space that will cover every application of our lives in future.

Figure 2. Application fields of IoT

Several IoT based technologies have been developed which are helping the community and businesses to make more utilization of the data collected from various sources for different applications. Some of the important technologies are listed below:

IOT and Computer Vision

Computer vision is a subset of AI technology that has already played a great role in many applications. Some of the examples where computer vision is improving the quality of life include various social media platforms, law enforcement and industrial productions. Connecting computer vision systems to the IoT creates a powerful network capability. Several algorithms are capable of detecting the edges and movements within the video frames. These algorithms with the advances in silicon technology relating to image sensors, programmable logic, micro-controllers and graphics processing units (GPUs) can be used to develop wide range of embedded applications (Atzori, 2016). Computer vision techniques with advanced data analytics and AI would create ample opportunities for IoT-based innovations and applications.

Computer vision technology is being used now in the banks world-wide to deposit the cheques remotely. The state-of-art technology in computer vision is being used by nearly 300 million visually impaired people to "see" like normal persons. Using computer vision, nearly 2 billion photos are uploaded onto Facebook application every day. One of the important applications computer vision is employed is in the healthcare. It provides information for more precise diagnoses, and may even suggest the possible treatments to doctors, based on diagnoses. The technology offers a variety of visual detection methods in medical science to assist medical professionals in locating the malign organs of the patients.

The computer vision technology, combined with Internet Protocol (IP) connected devices, is useful to both commercial and government. Sensors embedded devices which can easily sense light waves in different spectral ranges are widely used in various real-time applications, such as manufacturing firms for quality assurance, object detection and tracking for security aspect in visual surveillance, acquiring remote sensing images from Drone/UAVs (Unmanned Aerial Vehicles) and satellites for resource monitoring & management. Machine vision is also employed in path design of UAVs for anti-collision purposes so as to avoid the fixed obstacles and objects, including other UAVs flying nearby.

Another key application for computer vision is in the inspection systems. Using sensor-based devices, it becomes easier to monitor safety in real-time i.e., industrial or any restricted place, to take timely action in case any suspicious activity is observed. A safer environment can be created by making use of machine learning techniques with network technologies. By creating different situations, the algorithm or technique can sense the unsafe scenarios and immediately issues alert messages. For example, if the sensors detect leakage of gases, fire, increased temperatures or high humidity, information can be updated to the security authorities and work can be stopped, if required, by raising an alarm. Many industries today use computer vision technology to monitor and report the current status of infrastructure which is important for the smooth operation of industries.

Machine learning is the obvious next stage after computer vision. Machine learning is an AI technology, that has the capability to automatically extract the patterns and detect the outliers from the Big data generated by various sensors and devices. These data/information may include, such as temperature, pressure, humidity, air quality, rainfall, NO_2 concentration, vibration, and sound. It is estimated that machine learning approaches can make predictions up to 20 times faster with greater accuracy as compared to traditional tools and methods. These algorithms make use of other neural network methods to '*train*' the system to identify the specific features from large number of photographs and videos. The accuracy of results is based on training the algorithm. The neural network is shown many different images and videos that are tagged with the features of interest, and these images are usually stored in a large server system or in the cloud. The advanced surveillance cameras use neural network based machine learning algorithms to offer additional video analysis features, such as crowd density monitoring, stereoscopic vision, facial recognition, people count and behavior analysis, as compared to traditional features, such as monitoring & recording the features. The latest version of OpenCV incorporates deep neural networks for machine learning applications. The increased performance of GPUs opens up new opportunities for using machine learning algorithms.

For autonomous materials handling by robots, computer vision can help to follow the locations, and at the same time detect the moving people or obstacles, if any. It would allow industry personnel and robots to work together more efficiently in a safe manner. Many industries are now also employing machine vision for picking product picking automatically, as these products are identified *via* their barcode. Thereafter, a robot with gripper is aligned to pick and hold a particular product and place it into the transport trolley. For making this entire process successful, the cameras and their data processing are essential, as these autonomous robots are required to be continuously monitored as part of entire IoT applications. The advancements in computer vision, Big Data analytics, machine learning, deep learning, neural network and image processing algorithms can be efficiently used to detect the motion-based objects in real-time applications (Rossana et. al., 2017, Sharma, 2018) or fully automatic systems, like robots and drones can be employed for safety applications.

IoT and Remote Sensing

With the advent of new acquisition platforms, smaller and more efficient sensors as well as cloud computing techniques, remote sensing is gaining popularity for significant innovations. Various IoT-based applications for data analysis, visualization & virtualization, environmental condition assessment, precision agriculture and military have evolved with extensive use of remote sensing data (Pallavi and Jayashri, 2017). The UAVs have benefits to go deeply in remote areas, such as mountainous and snow covered regions, oil pipelines and gas installations, forested areas, mining areas for taking high resolution images. The UAVs have the capability to identify a particular target in an area which can be further examined more closely (https://www.iotone.com/term/remote-sensing/t630).

Remote sensing for mapping purposes has undergone significant changes from visual interpretation of aerial images to computer based measurements from the evolution of multispectral imagery to hyperspectral imagery; from low resolution imagery to very high resolution imagery; and from 2D mapping to 3D mapping and visualization (SIITAg, 2018). Remote sensing technology provides data in several forms; Visible images, LiDAR (Light Detection and Ranging) data, Synthetic Aperture Radar (SAR) images, Infrared (IR) images, Thermal Infrared (TIR) images, Sonar, Electric field sensing, and Drone/UAV images (https://arxiv.org/abs/1806.00746). Some applications of remote sensing may require continuous or frequent observations where small changes over time are required to be studied (IoT-UK, 2017).

The IoT is commonly used in applications requiring time series data. The disciplines of remote sensing and IoT are used to basically collect data at a large scale efficiently without requiring human's intervention. Both have evolved to create data and analytics that reduce vast amount of dynamic data into sizeable results. Thus, remote sensing and IoT are essentially complementary methods that contribute different strengths to an application. In fact, under these circumstances, remote sensing methods can essentially be considered '*extrinsic IoT*' to contrast it with the more traditional definition of IoT, which uses embedded or intrinsic sensors, as shown in Figure 3. They bring together external observations possible only from extrinsic sensors and the data stream delivered by embedded IoT sensors. For example, sensors installed in a pipeline may detect a pressure drop across a section, but external hyperspectral sensors can correlate this pressure drop to the presence of oil or water in the ground. The data produced and analysed by these technologies have the potential to offer a wide range of new applications that can reduce costs, and improve the system's performance. The advances using remote sensing and IoT include the emergence of platforms, like robots, drones and spectrographic sensors, which due to their easy mobility and low costs can be mounted on the smaller platforms for frequent uses (Stokes, 2018).

Figure 3. Various applications of remote sensing technology

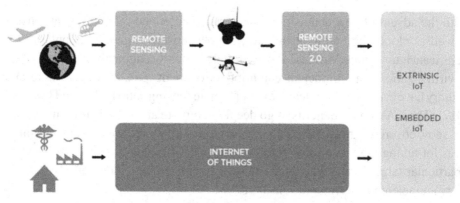

A convergence of IoT and satellite imaging is also very useful in geospatial related studies where information in time & space is required to be correlated. Applications are being developed to integrate mobile technologies, IoT and satellite intelligence to create a picture about the global economy in real-time. This is the new frontier which will drive further growth in the geospatial industry; the ability to fuse that data from multiple platforms, such as video, still imagery, color imagery, and SAR images (https://internetofthingsagenda.techtarget.com/definition/remote-sensing).

The fusion of all geospatial data can be processed using machine and deep learning methods, and used for large number of real-time applications, including exploration and monitoring of several resources, mapping, and tracking in time & space. For example, construction is a dynamic sector where delayed projects with enhanced budgets, and disputes in large-scale construction projects can be easily resolved by using drones/UAVs, remote sensing, computer vision and IoT (https://skymapglobal.com/infrastructure-monitoring-with-satellite-imagery-a-case-study/). The managers and administrators can use cloud platform communications and data analysis tools to monitor the progress in buildings, roads, bridges and highways (Tostes et. al., 2013). The platform combines imaging across successive time periods to automatically detect the progress.

Management of warehouse inventory is a laborious task. Keeping the updated inventory of parts and products in a large warehouse and inspecting these can take several days in some facilities. Drones with layouts of facilities can be used to identify and count the inventory after flying these through such warehouses between various shifts in staff. The drones can also be advantageous to check the condition of stocked material against big data files stored on cloud servers.

IoT and Artificial Intelligence

The AI allows machines to behave and interact just like human-beings by mimicking the human reasoning capability. It tries to mimic human brains; the way human brain thinks, behaves and react to the respective actions. A large volume of data may not be useful to an organization if it cannot lead for any effective decision making. The AI analyses the huge volume of data and coverts them into meaningful information. Connected IoT devices having AI-based algorithms are increasingly used for facilitating streamlined functioning of devices as well as automation (McKinley, 2020). The AI can be categorised into three types; (i) Strong AI- which produces a machine whose intellectual level is comparable with that of a human being, (ii) Applied AI- which aims to produce commercially viable smart systems, and (iii) Cognitive simulation- where computers are used to test the theories about how the human mind works.

The unstructured data can be collected from different sources, such as sensors, gadgets, social media and so on. The AI then uses the perceptions to analyze the logic and incorporates machine learning to utilize the unstructured data and derives from it the useful information. The AI derives accurate predictions from large volume of data for taking up effective & efficient decisions for applications, such as image recognition, language processing, computer vision, and robotics. The AI brings in '*intelligent connectivity*' to the IoT users since AI can select & analyse the data from these connected devices based on its relevance. The AI can also provide results of consumer behaviour, for example, Amazon can suggest the customers some books based on their last purchase, or Pandora can suggest new songs as per existing playlist (McKinley, 2020).

The IoT devices are generating vast amounts of useful data, whereas AI is an essential tool to deal and analyse this huge volume of data for quick analysis. IoT with AI can also directly create new products and services. The IoT encompasses connecting various machines and making use of the large (Big) data generated from these machines, whereas AI involves simulating the intelligent behaviour of all kinds of machines and deriving meaningful results. The AI plays a major role in IoT-based applications. It deals with some sort of intelligence established by machines and also tries to impersonate the natural intelligence of a person. The AI makes the machines learn from the knowledge stored in the knowledge database based on the experiences of experts. In other words, it imitates the cognitive functions that human being performs using their intelligence, such as learning, problem solving and many more, based on supervised or unsupervised learning paradigms (Sharma et. al., 2017).

It is estimated that the IoTs along with the other devices over IP are generating approximately 3.5 quintillion bytes of data every day. Both technologies, the IoT and AI provide power house of collected data that can be used to develop and test the effectiveness of predictive models, experimental analysis, such as smart assistant used in smart homes to manage the homes (Quadri and Sathish, 2017, https://pinaclsolutions.com/blog/2017/cloud-computing-and-iot). The data needs to be supplemented with context and creativity to derive some actionable results. The *Intelligent Connectivity* would help to carry out (i) Predictive analytics (inform what will happen?), (ii) Prescriptive analytics (inform what should we do?), and (iii) Adaptive/continuous analytics (inform what are the appropriate actions or decisions and how should the system adapt to the latest changes?).

Drones and robots controlled by AI can be used to send these devices where human-beings can't reach, creating new opportunities for monitoring and inspection of sites and machineries. Law enforcement agencies use AI for facial recognition to identify the suspected criminals. If the photograph of a suspected criminal in a crime is made available with the police, the AI can search the database with the photos to find the best match having maximum probability, including all the details of the person available in the database. A good example of AI based robot is the use of automated vacuum cleaners.

Other notable applications where AI and IoT are integrated are autonomous cars, augmented intelligence in oil & gas industries, smart homes, aviation & transport, industrial drones, security, and utilities or wearables. The latest example of AI and IoT working in tandem is driverless or autonomous cars. In such applications, the cars can be used as "things" and the power of AI is used to predict the behavior of cars and pedestrians in various circumstances. In addition, all autonomous cars would operate as a network; it means when one car learns something form the surroundings, all the cars would learn it. The AI and IoT are obvious companions to be used in smart city applications to create the components of the city connected and making the city as *'intelligent city'*. With the development in AI technology, fleet management is being revisited in order to monitor the fleet of planes, trains, trucks or automobiles in real-time to find more efficient routing and scheduling to ultimately reduce the travel and delivery time.

IoT and Cloud Computing

Cloud computing technology can be considered as a base technology in using IoT, as it shares a complementary relationship with the IoT. It offers several features, like computing, storage, retrieval, services, and applications using the Internet. It provides an on-demand delivery of computing power, database storage, applications and IT resources, anywhere and anytime. It enables organizations to hire the services of computing resources of some other organizations, such as virtual servers, in place of creating a massive computing infrastructure on their own campus (Christos et. al., 2016). Since IoT generates huge amounts of data, it can be stored on clouds, and then this data is analyzed and shared using cloud computing techniques. The IoT generates an unprecedented amount of Big Data with the help Internet-based infrastructure. According to an estimate, by year 2020 there will be about 5,200 gigabytes of data for everyone on the Earth, and to analyse this there will be a need to deploy around 340 application servers per day (or 120,000 servers per year) in order to support the connected devices.

Cloud efficiently serves as brain in order to improve the decision making power and also to optimize the internet-based interactions. It can be simple, like checking whether the temperature value is within the acceptable range, or complex, such as the use of videos to identify specific objects (i.e., intruders in the building). The collected data can be used smartly for any intelligent monitoring purpose and issuing alarm alerts with other smart gadgets or devices. It offers the advantage is to be able to transform digital data in a cost effective manner. The key features of cloud computing technology along with the characteristics of IoT over the internet are (i) large storage, (ii) efficient service, (iii) high energy efficiency, (iv) high computational capability, and (v) large number of real-time applications (Buyya et. al., 2009). When IoT is integrated with cloud, several new challenging issues are to be addressed, such as quality of service, data security, reliability, efficiency and integrity (https://www.newgenapps.com/blog/top-10-cloud-computing-examples-and-uses).

Cloud is gaining popularity world-wide. While working in the cloud, the data, hardware and software are located at a different place, and the end users do not know on which computer the software runs, or where those computers are exactly located. The users have virtual infrastructure which is scalable. It offers two types of scaling processes: (i) *Vertical Scaling* which increases the capacity of a server by adding resources if required by an application, and (ii) *Horizontal Scaling* that helps businesses to expand hardware resources with increasing processing requirements; thus making it a preferred platform to host Big Data analytics. The emergence of highly scalable cloud computing platforms, such as Amazon Web Service (AWS) or Microsoft Azure is giving rise to new technologies, such as Docker and Kubernetes databases (McKinley, 2020). Cloud offers immensely high bandwidth and processing power to help Big Data for their real-time streaming of for an application. The cloud computing offers three primary services, as given below:

(i) *Infrastructure as a Service (IaaS)*- The service provider offers entire infrastructure along with the maintenance related tasks.

(ii) *Platform as a Service (PaaS)*- The service provider offers resources, such as storage, runtime, queuing, databases, etc. However, the responsibility of configuration and implementation related tasks depend on the users.

(iii) *Software as a Service (SaaS)*- This service is the most facilitated one which offers all the necessary settings and infrastructure provided under *IaaS* for the platform and infrastructure are in place.

Cloud computing provides speed and scalability, while IoT-based applications are mainly built based on the mobility of objects and widespread networking of these objects (Table 3). The combination of cloud computing and IoT facilitates innovative monitoring services and processing of data collected from sensor devices. The files can also be stored in Google Drive instead on personal computers. For example, Google Drive uses Google's cloud services. In addition, many tech-savvy companies, such as Amazon, Alibaba, Google and Oracle offer a wide range of solutions to businesses world-wide, by employing machine learning tools and cloud technology. These IoT-based companies have access to a huge amount of Big Data for many real-time applications as these data are stored in the cloud. Now-a-days, cloud-based services offer a big competition between IT sector and software industries. Billions of customers are taking these services using large number of connected apps, devices and gadgets. It is therefore important to provide flawless services to the customers *via* IoT cloud (Christos et al, 2016).

Table 3. Interconnections between IoT and Cloud computing

Parameter	Internet of Things	Cloud Computing
Big Data	Source for Big Data	Way or means to manage the Big Data
Reachability	Very limited	Far spread and widely
Storage	Limited or almost none	Very large, and virtually endless
Role of Internet	Acts as a point of convergence	Acts as a means for delivering the services
Computing Capabilities	Limited	Virtually unlimited
Components	Requires hardware components	Requires virtual machines which imitate hardware components

Data collected from several sensors, and analysed using huge computational power on each sensor may be extremely expensive, time consuming and energy intensive. Alternative is that this huge data can be stored in the cloud from all the sensors, and processed from there, whenever required. The large amount of data are produced by IoT devices which needs to be collated and analysed together for deriving the best results. These connected devices are not just limited to the devices available in that organization, but can encompass from personal devices of individual users to the large and sophisticated devices available through internet cloud-based services. Cloud computing in combination with IoT also enables better collaboration for developers (Atzori et. al., 2016), as developers can work on several associated projects without any delay, as they all will have access to the remotely collected data.

Table 4. Contributions of cloud computing in IoT

IoT characteristics	Storage over Internet	Service over Internet	Applications over Internet	Energy efficiency	Computationally capable
Smart solution in the bucket of transport	Ö	Ö	Ö		Ö
Smart power grids incorporating more renewable	Ö	Ö		Ö	Ö
Remote monitoring of patients		Ö	Ö		Ö
Sensors in homes and airports	Ö	Ö	Ö	Ö	Ö
Engine monitoring sensors that detect & predict maintenance issues		Ö	Ö	Ö	Ö

Real-time video analytics offers applications, such as surveillance activities, medical operations, crime analysis, etc. Smart cameras are available which can select and analyze the best video frames, and even identify features within specific portion of frames for further processing at cloud-based platform. Computationally efficient analytics is performed by such cameras using cloud platform, whereas a detailed complex algorithm may be used on the cloud for feature analysis from images. For example, smart cameras can be used for traffic analytics during a road incident, allowing these cameras to capture the images of the incident (i.e., what activity), restricting themselves to the areas of interest (i.e., where- geographical location). The smart cameras will stream only the relevant frames to the cloud in real-time for complex analytics of the accident site. The real advantage is that the derived results are fed back to the smart cameras or the control room in near-real time, using parallel architecture setup of the cloud server.

Another latest technology based on the concept of cloud computing, called '*Mobile Cloud Computing*' (MCC), which can also provide access to the available information/data from anywhere-anytime by eliminating or minimizing the need of costly hardware devices (Said and Tolba, 2016). The MCC bridges the cloud computing technology and mobile devices so that the mobile devices become resourceful and efficient to provide more computational power, memory, storage, energy and context awareness. Table 4 lists the main features of MCC when combined with the characteristics of IoT, including the key points of cloud computing technology which improve the features of IoT technology. For example, feature of IoT which has significantly affected by the cloud computing is 'Sensors in homes and airports', whereas in cloud computing, the features which has affected more by IoT technology are 'Service over Internet' and 'Computationally capability'.

The next innovation in the field of cloud computing is Fog computing or Edge computing. It is known that large number of IoT devices don't have their own computational power, therefore Fog computing can play an important role to provide an optimum way not only to collect the data but also process these data from these devices rather than the cloud based platforms (Roy et al., 2015). Fog computing thus provides a better way to gather and process the data at local computing devices, in place of storing the data at the cloud or remote servers. In this approach, sensors and other connected devices keep sending the data to a nearest computing device, such as a switch or a router, and there it is analysed. It is estimated that by 2020, about 5.8 billion IoT-based devices and gadgets available in enterprises and governments will be using Fog computing technology.

IoT and Big Data

The IoT is a promising technology that can streamline the operations between machine to machine and/or machines to humans by producing huge volumes of digital data. The IoT and Big Data are buzzing the technology around the globe. Big data refers to massive, unstructured and complex data sets that may be important to many businesses. The Big Data has almost become like the new currency in the businesses. These data sets are so large and complicated that the traditional data processing software cannot tackle them. The data storage also remains a great concern. Companies are gradually shifting to the cloud due to less complex structure and lower costs involved. The recent developments in technology have exponentially reduced the cost of data storage and computations. Big Data analytics engines with the support of cloud platforms are accessing this data to produce useful insights (McKinley, 2020).

The concept of big data and IoT has been around for many years, but its mainstream application started only recently. Demand for Big Data arise the need for the adoption of both IoT and cloud platforms. With the use of IoT, the quantum of Big Data obviously increases. The adoption of IoT and Big Data necessitates the use of cloud technology. So, any organization willing to transform the IoT data and utilize its full potential will have to adopt the cloud-based systems.

Both IoT and Big Data are very much necessary for any technological innovation. The effective utilization of intelligent data systems based on predictive technologies, such as AI and machine learning is expected to give pave to new and innovative data infrastructure, such as Hadoop, Spark, etc., (Sarkar, 2017). The IoT and Big Data analytics are the fastest growing sectors in IT field. The number of IoT devices is expected to grow to 20 billion by 2020, whereas the Big Data industry is expected to have value US\$ 66.8 billion by 2021. Data analytics with extensive computational power is offering companies to extract maximum value from the data to get the best insights. With more data in hand and a safe storage platform, the businesses will grow very fast. The cost of computation for the businesses is likely to go down as the cost of deploying these technologies significantly decrease with time.

According to last five years statistics, average volume of data generated every day is 2.3 trillion gigabytes (Sarkar, 2017). There are five V's involved in Big Data, as given below:

Value - It represents if the data is relevant or not.
Variability- It may have spatial and temporal variability.
Variety- It can have variety with various types.
Velocity- It deals with the rate at which data is received, and is acted upon.
Volume- Organisations have big volume of unstructured data.

Big Data includes a large set of semi-structured, structured, or unstructured data generated by IoT-based connected sensors and devices, and subsequently analyzing these data efficiently to derive useful information required for improved decision making. The IoT and Big Data have evolved completely independently, but they have become dependent on each other in last few years, due to evolving real-time applications. The Big data is analyzed in the machines on cloud where there is a flexibility of accumulating the computing power on demand, making it quite simpler, easier and feasible to implement several analytics on sorted data units, as shown in Figure 4.

Figure 4. Block diagram of IoT gateway

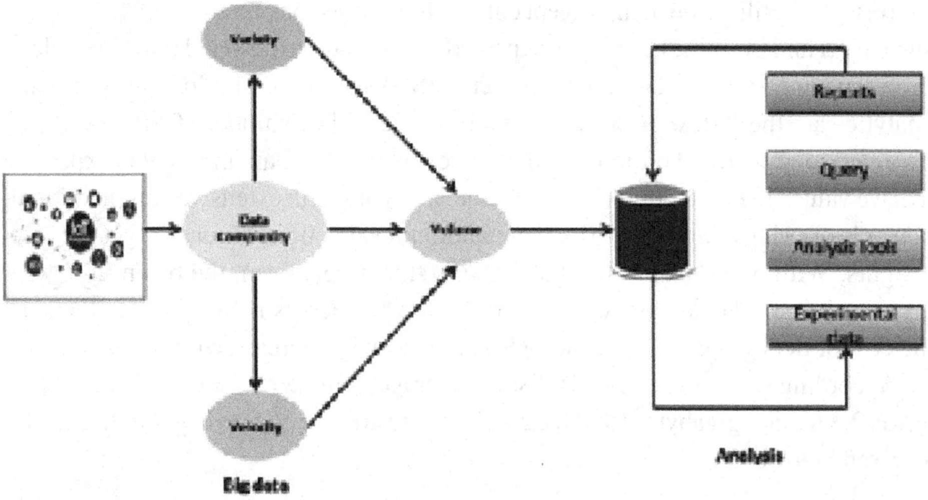

It is estimated that around 4.4 trillion GB data will be generated through the IoT devices and gadgets by the year 2020. The role of Big Data in IoT mainly includes gathering, analyzing, sharing, storing and transmitting that data or results of the analysis in real-time manner. Big Data processing normally follows five main sequential steps, as below;

(i)   The IoT devices and sensors generate a large amount of unstructured Big Data.
(ii)   The Big Data system is a shared distributed database, where the data is stored in Big Data files.
(iii) Since the Big unstructured data are collected *via* the internet, hence, it needs very fast analysis tools with large queries to make quick decisions from the data.
(iv)   The stored IoT Big Data can be analysed using analytic tools, such as Hadoop, MapReduce or Spark,
(v)   Finally the reports of analyzed data are prepared.

Big Data has massive amount of data, but it may not provide any meaningful information to make real-time decisions. In fact, there is normally a time-lag between the collected data and the analyzed data. But as soon as the data are anlaysed, these are used almost in real-time to optimize the operations or take appropriate decisions. The IoT data analytics require managing the streaming of data, and making faster analytics for real-time decisions. Managing the streaming of data would enable to ingest, aggregate (i.e., derive mean, median, mode) and compress real-time data from available sensors and devices at the edge. The edge analytics technique is therefore very useful to automatically analyze the real-time sensor data and provides real-time decisions or actions. These decisions or actions would not only optimize the performance but also identify the unusual performance or behaviors.

The IoT and Big Data analytics can be useful for a number of applications to examine and reveal the trends, find the correlations, and present new information from the Big Data. The organizations can therefore derive the benefits from analyzing large amounts of IoT-based Big Data, and using the information extracted from them to improve their businesses and operations. The Big Data thus can assist the businesses and organizations to improve their understanding of the collected data, and making them useful for decision-making activities.

The combined features of the IoT and Big Data can also bring changes in the e-health care system of any country. This application provides new ways of having remote diagnosis and treatment. It also provides opportunity to have better understanding of the disease which might be useful for the development of innovative healthcare solutions and devices. In transportation-related applications, IoT sensors are installed in the vehicles in order to track them while in movement. This application helps the transport companies to continuously track their vehicles. In addition, it provides information on drivers about utilization of their time as well as routes travelled, which could be used to plan the routes for fuel efficiency. This information is valuable not only for optimizing routes of the vehicles but also planning steps for improvement of productivity of organizations. The IoT and Big Data are also being used frequently in agricultural applications. In agricultural areas, the wireless sensors system is installed which monitors the moisture levels and rainfall, and transmits these data regularly to farmers on their mobiles over internet. This information is useful to farmers to understand the moisture levels of crops in the field, and take decisions to release the amount of water to the crops. It optimizes the water requirements of the crops.

Many organizations dealing with the Big Data are now replacing traditional model to the *PaaS* model in order to have access to a flexible and scalable method to analyze the IoT-based Big Data. The IoT creates a network of smart devices which may be used to pool these various types of data. It is known that the increased data may need increased security, as it will have increased chances for malicious attack or leakage. The IoT data security is a big challenging issue amongst the data security experts world-wide. Any security lapse may keep the entire network of connected devices at greater risk. It is therefore essential to have testing, verification and authentication of the smart devices that are connected to the IoT network. The protocols can be used to have a secured and controlled mechanism of receiving, storing and transmitting the data. For example, the Mosquitto is a very popular protocol and Hadoop may be adopted to store the data generated by IoT networks (Verma, 2018).

The GPU technology would be used in the analytics database of next-generation, allowing even more downsizing of the hardware, i.e., 5 TB may be available on a laptop or a big database in the car in near-future. As the IoT continues its expansion, there is a need to consider safety and cyber security issues. The hackers may enter into the systems or network of systems, containing sensitive data, and can hack the useful data that may be used to shut down power of the entire city or entire IT systems of an organization. Many security platforms are being developed to provide complete safety to IT systems and important data. For example, internet security platforms, such as Zscaler with a cloud-based solution can provide protection and security to IoT devices against unauthorized users to access the data.

IoT and Ubiquitous Computing

Mark David Weiser, widely known as the Father of Ubiquitous Computing (UC), coined the term UC in 1988. The UC can take place using any device, in any location, and in any format, as opposed to desktop computing. Weiser defined ubiquitous computing as *"the method of enhancing computer use by making many computers available throughout the physical environment but making them effectively invisible to the user"* (Rossana et. al., 2017). The UC-based smart devices are completely interconnected and continuously available.

In UC, the processing of data is linked with each activity or object under investigation. This paradigm is also called as *pervasive computing, ambient intelligence*, or, more recently, everywhere, where each term describes slightly different meaning. The term pervasive or ubiquitous computing means *"existing everywhere."* The aim of pervasive computing is to make these devices smart with respect to their surroundings and improve these based on the human experience. The applications of pervasive computing or ubiquitous computing are growing towards the use of micro-processors in everyday objects enabling them to communicate information from each-other. A typical example of use of pervasive computing is the smart electric meters which have replaced the old electric meters.

The UC requires human interaction with computers in virtually everything. It is considered to be the opposite of virtual reality (VR). In the VR, people work inside a computer-generated environment, but the UC virtually forces the computer to live out in the environment with people. The UC effectively enhances the use of computer by making many computers available with internet connectivity throughout the physical environment, while they are invisible to the users due to their remote connectivity (Koshizuka and Sakamura, 2010).

The main aim of UC is the creation of smart sensors and devices that are interconnected, making the communication and exchange of data easier with less complication. Important features of the UC include:

(i)   It must rely on converging Internet, wireless technology and advancement in IT and electronics,

(ii)   It must consider the human factor, rather than completely relying on the computing environment,

(iii)   It must promote the use of low-cost processors with large memory and storage requirements,

(iv)   It must capture the real-time attributes,

(v)   It must have interconnected and continuously available computing devices and sensors, and

(vi)   It must primarily focus on many-to-many relationships, instead of one-to-one, many-to-one or one-to-many in the environment (Want, 2004).

The UC is expected to dramatically reduce the cost of smart devices and gadgets, and therefore reduces the tasks for an average consumer. Collaboration and interoperability between various IoT based applications for real-time enrich the concept of UC, such as LIFX's Wi-Fi lighting, connect sense smart outlet, Eyedro smart home electricity monitor device in order to save electricity in an efficient manner (Dong et. al., 2016, Araújo et. al., 2017).

Relationship Between Big Data and Cloud Computing

With the availability of enormous amount of data, cloud computing plays a significant role in their storage and management. Big data processing on clouds can be carried out globally, whereas operating & maintaining such huge servers at different locations of the world is expensive for an organization. As the data is stored on virtual servers, it significantly reduces the cost of big data processing. Cloud computing uses high-level software and applications, independent on the efficiency of users' devices, but dependent on the network servers and their speed. Cloud computing offers high-speed data flow over the network, which results in faster processing of Big Data. The exponentially growing Big Data requires cloud-based analytics platform for their effective analysis. For example, the Hadoop, and AWS, Google and Microsoft have emerged as the cloud-based analytics platform for Big Data, in a cost-efficient manner which is scalable for all sizes of businesses. The emergence of new model such as *AaaS* model provides a faster and scalable way to integrate different types of structured, semi-structured and unstructured data, analyze them, transform and visualize them in real-time (McKinley, 2020).

A cloud computing environment may generally have several collection terminals and service providers. The users collect the data from the collection terminals using Big Data tools, whereas, they can save, store and process the Big Data from the service providers. Therefore, cloud computing requires a big infrastructure which is able to provide on-demand resources and services to ensure uninterrupted services to the users. Since the cloud environment is scalable, hence it should be able to provide adequate data management solution without considering the volume of data. The cloud computing service providers may also offer security policies as per the requirements of the users. Cloud computing can provide two important services; efficient management and security of data when dealing with the confidential data (Verma, 2018).

Relationship Between Big Data and IoT

The IoT streamlines operations in many sectors allowing interaction between machines to machines and machines to humans. Big Data and IoT are inter-related to each-other, as connected sensors and devices provide data to the Big Data system for their analysis and generation of final reports. The intersection of IoT and Big Data has created new IT applications and challenges regarding data storage, integration, and analytics. It has created ample opportunities than the challenges. It is projected that the IoT will bring a market of US$ 19 trillion in next ten years for internet industry, and this provides more opportunities & scope for research & development in both IoT and Big Data (McKinley, 2020).

Relationship Between IoT and Cloud Computing

The IoT has evolved with the new concept of the Internet network, enabling communication between several objects which include smart devices, mobile devices, and sensors & gadgets. The IoT and cloud computing has a complementary relationship, as IoT generates large amounts of data, cloud service providers allow data transfer *via* the internet. The IoT provides effective communication between all elements of architecture, which include objects, gates, network infrastructure and cloud infrastructure.

In a cloud infrastructure, data can be processed and analyzed quickly for an application to make early decisions. Cloud computing helps collaborate in IoT development. Using cloud platform, IoT developers can store the data remotely and access it easily. Cloud computing also helps advance analytics and monitoring of IoT devices. The IoT devices which utilize common APIs, and back-end infrastructure can receive instant security updates through cloud as soon as any security breach takes place in the infrastructure. It is estimated that almost 4.4 trillion GB data will be generated by the year 2020, putting up pressure on its infrastructure which can be easily resolved through cloud computing. It is expected that more than 90 percent of IoT data will be hosted on the cloud platform within the next five years (Verma, 2018).

Figure 5. Relationship between IoT, Big Data and cloud computing

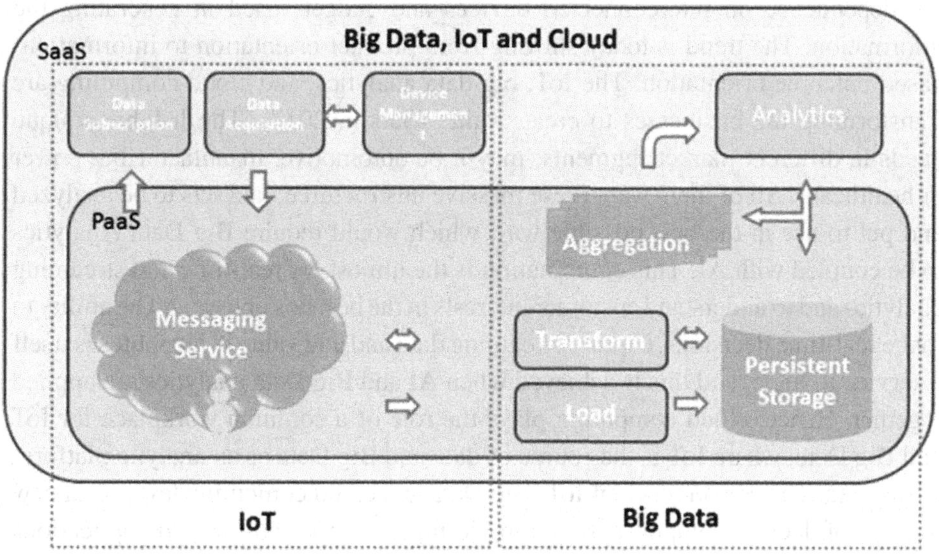

Relationship Between IoT, Big Data and Cloud Computing

The IoT, AI, Big Data, and cloud computing are different technologies, and each one of them has emerged and evolved in independent ways. Recently, these are being developed as interdependence, and therefore provide new opportunities of innovations, and enhanced efficiency & productivity. For most industries and organizations, as these technologies seem to work in cohesion to drive innovations and automation in business processes, there is a need to understand the relationship between them (Figure 5). The convergence of these technologies is playing most important role in many industries where faster processing and productivity are required for both business and revenue growth. Big Data and cloud storage are helping the organizations to merge the processed data and ensure more efficiency and productivity. From material usage data to the sharing of real-time inventory data, big data analytics and cloud computing are providing useful platform for the data to deliver insights for augmenting the industrial processes. The use of robotics, connected machines, and equipment and data analytics together are providing opportunities to create automation in industrial processes. Together these technologies help in modern industrial environments to enhance the productivity and business in a significant manner. The Amazon Web Services (AWS), Microsoft Azure, and Google Cloud Platform (GCP) have emerged as consolidated platforms leveraging all these technologies (McKinley, 2020). In future, the convergence of these technologies will further open new grounds for technological innovations.

The convergence of the three technologies is creating a massive shift towards the dependence on interconnected devices and gadgets used in generating the information. The trend is today shifting from product-orientation to information-based outcome orientation. The IoT, big data analytics, and cloud computing are transforming the businesses to create value (Sarkar, 2017). The IoT has unique needs in different market segments; may it be automotive, manufacturing, power or healthcare. All of them want these massive unstructured data sets to be analyzed and put to use in the best possible way, which would require Big Data Analytics to be coupled with AI. This combination is the utmost for real-time and streaming analytics and to understand customer interests in the best possible way. The ability to make real-time decisions, capture streaming data and add value to attributes is itself a service to logic, and this is achieved when AI and Big Data analytics are applied together. Hence, cloud computing plays the role of a common workplace for IoT and Big Data, where IoT is the source of data and Big Data as an analytic platform of the data. The convergence of IoT, Big Data and cloud computing leverage a new horizon of decision support system, providing new opportunities and applications in all the sectors (Verma, 2018).

FUTURE RESEARCH DIRECTIONS

The integration of Big Data, IoT and AI is further driving next generation applications for organizations and real-world. Applications in visualization technology, brain computing interfaces, security in IoT & semantic interoperability, augmented knowledge, machine intelligence, and automation capabilities will be an integral part of future IoT networks to support new business opportunities. It will also encourage innovations from network operation within the IoT (Culler, 20013).

The amalgamation of IoT and Big Data is providing new opportunities and applications in many sectors. They are providing useful information to transform the businesses and get better insights. The IoT devices are ready to collect enormous data for their analysis by organizations dealing with the Big Data. These organizations are further equipping themselves of handling vast amount of data with highest security. The future research expected on Big Data includes the adoption of flexible & scalable solutions to enhance the data security, data storage, and data analysis methods. There is an increased demand for organizations dealing with efficient data storage in safe manner on cloud platform storage; which may lower down the implementation cost.

The cloud computing and IoT together is opening several new applications for businesses and researchers. The development in cloud-enabled devices will enhance the usage of cloud-based systems in future. With the growth in devices working on cloud-based services, a considerable growth is expected in computers and storage services. Integration of Spark-based Hadoop, deep learning, Big Data and cloud-based analytics would be beneficial to introduce the computer vision methods as well as address these challenges (Al-Fuqaha et. al., 2015). As the technology grows further, the IoT-based applications will develop significantly; few examples include: (i) Real-time public safety, (ii) Security and access devices, (iii) Emotional analysis, and (iv) Facial recognition (Stergiou and Psannis, 2017).

New areas for IoT applications may also include sensor networks on land, underwater and in space to monitor the objects and surrounding environment, monitoring large-scale agricultural farms remotely, precision agriculture, perform remote surgery, remote use of laboratories, and developing autonomous devices, including drones/UAVs, taxis and cars (Culler, 2003). The other future applications could include, robotics, advanced forms of AI such as deep learning, machine vision, cloud, fog and edge-based architectures, new chips allowing higher performance, new data management approaches, and some newer forms of connectivity where fog computing ecosystem utilizes 5G etc., (Dong et. al., 2016)

CONCLUSION

In last few years, development of computation tools and technology produced more powerful storage capacity, processors, and memory at very low cost (Tan and Wang, 2010). There are numerous fields where the IoT has already impacted positively, including asset monitoring, security, fleet tracking and management, energy management, smart mobile devices, automotive systems, healthcare, industrial control system, disasters management and weather monitoring.

The computer vision and data analytics industries are developing a generic framework that is expected to solve almost all computer vision-related problems in future. These problems have a wider range from context-based search, multi-threaded real-time video analytics, event recognition & prediction, and many more. The machine learning algorithms would be able to predict the possibilities of failure of a device which can be repaired remotely in order to prevent the complete shutdown, for example, within a smart city from street smart furniture to intelligent services to the area. The technology of IoT and AI will be beneficial for autonomous vehicles (UAVs) and cars to ensure safety, reliability, and efficiency for driver-less movement (Bahga and Vijay, 2015).

A number of applications combining IoT with AI are benefitting the organizations to better understand the processes adopted by them. It is also helping them to predict all the risks involved as well as automate the processes for faster response. Moreover, it allows them to better manage the safety of workers and safety of processes from possible cyber-attacks. The UC allows for data collection on an unprecedented scale with digital devices & gadgets distributed around us with high computing power. The UC is expected to significantly reduce the cost of digital devices & gadgets, and tasks for an average consumer. It is expected that with pooled resources giving individual consumers the benefits of economies of scale, monthly fees similar to a TV cable bill for services will replace the purchases of expensive electronics and smart devices.

REFERENCES

Al-Fuqaha, A., Guizani, M., Mohammadi, M., Aledhari, M., & Ayyash, M. (2015). Internet of things: A survey on enabling technologies protocols and applications. *IEEE Communications Surveys and Tutorials, 17*(4), 2347–2376.

Araújo, I. L., Santos, I. S., Filho, J. B. F., Andrade, R. M. C., & Neto, P. S. (2017). Generating test cases and procedures from use cases in dynamic software product lines. *Proceedings of the 32nd ACM SIGApp Symposium on Applied Computing.*

Atzori, L., Iera, A., & Morabito, G. (2016). The internet of things: A survey. *Computer Networks, 54*(15), 2787–2805.

Bahga, A., & Vijay, M. (2015). *Internet of Things - A Hands-on Approach.* Universities Press.

Bojanova, I. (2015). *What Makes Up the Internet of Things? Computing Now.* https://www.computer.org/web/sensing-iot/content?g=53926943&type=article&urlTitle=what-are-the-components-of-iot-

Buyya, R., Yeo, C. S., Venugopal, S., Broberg, J., & Brandic, I. (2009). Cloud computing and emerging IT platforms: Vision, hype, and reality for delivering computing as the 5th utility. *Future Generation Computer Systems. Elsevier, 25*(6), 599–616.

Christos, S., Psannis, K., Kim, B., & Gupta, B. (2016). Secure integration of IoT and cloud computing. In *Future Generation Computer Systems.* Elsevier.

Culler, D. (2003). 10 emerging technologies that will change the world. *Technology Review,* 33–49.

Dong, T., Churchill, E. F., & Nichols, J. (2016). Understanding the challenges of designing and developing multi-device experiences. *Proceedings of the 2016 ACM Conference on Designing Interactive Systems,* 62–72.

Evans, D. (2011). *The internet of things: How the next evolution of the internet is changing everything*. CISCO White Paper. https://www.cisco.com/web/about/ ac79/ docs/innov/IoT_IBSG_0411FINAL.pdf

Gubbi, J., Buyya, R., Marusic, S., & Palaniswami, M. (2013). Internet of Things (IoT): A vision, architectural elements, and future directions. *Future Generation Computer Systems, 29*(7), 1645–1660.

Gubbi, J., Buyya, R., Marusic, S., & Palaniswami, M. (2013). Internet of Things (IoT): A vision, architectural elements, and future directions. *Future Generation Computer Systems, 29*, 1645–1660.

Gupta, R. (2016). ABC of Internet of Things: Advancements, Benefits, Challenges, Enablers and Facilities of IoT. *IEEE Symposium on Colossal Data Analysis and Networking (CDAN)*.

IOT-UK. (2017). *Satellite technologies for IoT applications*. Report produced by IoT UK.

Koshizuka, N., & Sakamura, K. (2010). Ubiquitous ID: Standards for ubiquitous computing and the internet of things. *IEEE Pervasive Computing, 9*(4), 98–101.

Machado, H., & Shah, K. (2017). *Internet of Things (IoT) impacts on supply chain*. APICS Houston Student Chapter. http://apicsterragrande.org/images/articles/ Machado _Internet_of_Things_impacts_on_Supply_Chain_Shah_Machado_ Second_Place_Grad.pdf

McKinley. (2020). *Big Data, AI, IoT & Cloud Computing: Futuristic Approach?* https://www.techbooky.com/big-data-ai-iot-cloud-computing/

Pallavi, S., & Jayashree, D. (2017). Remote sensing of greenhouse parameters based on IoT. *International Journal of Advanced Computational Engineering and Networking, 5*(10).

Paper, W. (2018) *Internet of Things (IoT), Technology, economic view and technical standardization*. Version 1.0, July 2018, Agence pour la Normalisation etl'Economie de la Connaissance (ANEC).

Quadri, I. S. A., & Sathish, P. (2017). IoT based home automation and surveillance system, *International Conference on Intelligent Computing and Control Systems (ICICCS)*.

Rossana, M. C., Andrade, R. M., Carvalho, I. L. de A., Oliveira, K. M., & Maia, M. E. F. (2017). What changes from ubiquitous computing to internet of things in interaction evaluation? *International Conference on Distributed, Ambient, and Pervasive Interactions, DAPI 2017* (*vol. 10*, 291, pp 3-21). Academic Press.

Roy, S., Bose, R., & Sarddar, D. (2015). A fog-based DSS model for driving rule violation monitoring framework on the internet of things. *International Journal of Advanced Science and Technology*, 23-32.

Said, O., & Tolba A. (2016). Performance evaluation of a dual coverage system for internet of things environments. *Mobile Information Systems*. doi:10.1155/2016/3464392

Sarkar, S. (2017). *Convergence of Big Data, IoT and Cloud Computing for Better Future, Big Data Cloud Computing Internet of Things*. https://www.analyticsinsight. net/convergence-of-big-data-iot-and-cloud-computing-for-better-future/

Sharma, L. (2018). *Object detection with background subtraction. LAP LAMBERT Academic Publishing, SIA OmniScriptum Publishing Brivibas gatve 197*. European Union.

Sharma, L., Lohan, N., & Yadav, D. K. (2017). A study of challenging issues on video surveillance system for object detection. *International Conference on Electrical, Electronic Communication, Industrial Engineering and Technology Management Collaboration: Breaking the Barriers*.

SIITAg. (2018). *Satellite-enabled Intelligent internet of things for agriculture*. https:// business.esa.int/projects/siitag

Stergiou, C., Psannis, K. E., & Andreas, P. (2017). Architecture for security monitoring in IoT environments. *IEEE 26th International Symposium on Industrial Electronics (ISIE)*.

Stokes, P. (2018). *IoT applications in agriculture. the potential of smart farming on the current stage*. https://medium.com/datadriveninvestor/iot-applications-in-agriculture-the-potential-of-smart-farming-on-the-current-stage-275066f946d8

Tan, L., & Wang, N. (2010). Future internet: The internet of things. In *IEEE 2010 3rd International Conference on Advanced Computer Theory and Engineering*, (vol. 5, pp. 376-380). IEEE.

Tostes, A., Izabel, J., Fátima, de L. P., Assuncao, R., Salles, J., & Loureiroet, A. A. F. (2013). From data to knowledge: City-wide traffic flows analysis and prediction using bing maps. *Proceedings of the 2nd ACM SIGKDD International Workshop on Urban Computing*, 12.

Verma, A. (2018). *The Relationship between IoT, Big Data, and Cloud Computing.* https://www.whizlabs.com/blog/relationship-between-iot-big-data-cloud-computing/

Want, R. (2004). Enabling ubiquitous sensing with RFID. *Computer*, *37*(4), 84–86.

Chapter 4
Role Coordination in Large–Scale and Highly– Dense Internet of Things

Harsh Khatter
ABES Engineering College, Ghaziabad, India

Prabhat Singh
ABES Engineering College, Ghaziabad, India

ABSTRACT

Huge-scale highly-dense networks integrate with different application spaces of internet of things for precise occasion discovery and monitoring. Because of the high thickness and colossal scope, the hubs in these systems must play out some basic correspondence jobs, in particular detecting, handing-off, information combination, and information control (collection and replication). Since the vitality utilization and the unwavering correspondence quality is one of the significant difficulties in large-scale highly-dense networks, the correspondence jobs ought to be facilitated so as to efficiently utilize the vitality assets and to meet a palatable degree of correspondence dependability. Right now, the authors propose an on-request and completely dispersed system for job coordination that is intended to distinguish occasions with different levels of basicity, adjusting the information total and information replication as per the desperation level of the recognized event.

DOI: 10.4018/978-1-7998-4685-7.ch004

INTRODUCTION

Remote systems are getting incredibly thick and are being utilized to associate a wide range of gadgets (Asadi et al., 2015). In this way, it is visualized that Large-Scale Highly-Dense Networks (LSHDN) will rise to help Internet-of-Things (IoT) and Machine-to-Machine (M2M) correspondence, and countless low force gadgets will detect and incite on various focuses over the system. Because of the exceptional elements of these systems regarding occasion events and the different jobs that a hub can play, the system ought to depend on efficient organize coordination capacities to stay away from the quick fatigue of the hub's assets and to keep up a palatable degree of correspondence unwavering quality.

Existing arrangements intended to organize the method of jobs over the system are not entirely circulated since they are halfway disseminated approaches that depend on group heads or facilitator hubs. It implies that a large portion of the current solutions may spend, in LSHDN, a lot of system assets imparting control messages.

Related Work

This section shows the main works that address aspects related to the role of sensing, relaying, data-control, and data-fusion. Sections 2.1, 2.2, and 2.3 describe solutions that focus on specific aspects of sensing and relay, data-control, and data-fusion, respectively. Section 2.4 shows the current frameworks that solve whole issues of role assignment and coordination. At the end of this section, there is a summary that discusses the presented solutions.

Sensing and Relaying

A specific hub with the Sensing job performs two principle errands: (I) it screens a marvel, target, or occasion by methods for an electronic circuit, and (ii) it communicates the detected information utilizing a system interface. In arrangements that just think about the Sensing job, it is typically expected that each hub can set up an immediate association with the information gatherer (for example, base-station, sink, door, or information combination focus). In any case, Draves et al. (Draves et al., 2004) show that the immediate association between the sens-ing hubs and the information authority powers the correspondence between far off centers with poor connection quality.

The methodologies that dole out transferring jobs over the system can be separated into Reactive and Proactive. The Reactive Relaying Assignment Role (RRAR) arrangements forward the detected information from the source to the information gatherer without determining in every correspondence jump which is the following hub to get the communicated mes-sages containing the exposed information. Because of the sharing property of the remote chan-nel, in every correspondence bounce, any neighbor hub can catch the related messages. Rather than characterizing before the transmission which center ought to get the information, RRAR arrangements manage the following issue of erasing numerous duplicates of a similar message got on neighbor hubs.

Another transfer task approach is the Proactive Relaying Assignment Role (PRAR). These arrangements decide, in view of different data, before the information transmission, the hub or set of hubs that must assume the handing-off job.

By and large, both Proactive and Reactive Relaying Assignment Role arrangements fluctuate the info data that helps their inner choices, just as the layer where the arrangement is actualized.

The principle bit of leeway of the RRAR approach is that solitary the hubs that get cor-rectly the information take part as hand-off hubs, which increment the unwavering quality and through-put without requiring control messages to choose the transfers. In any case, the principle step back is identified with vitality use brought about by the additional time wherein the hub needs to keep the radio turned on so as to catch the neighbor transmissions.

Data-Control (Aggregation and Replication)

Information Aggregation (DA) is a notable system in remote correspondence, particularly in vitality obliged systems. DA comprises in applying collection capacities to condense the system traffic that streams over the ways. By decreasing the measure of system traffic, the hubs lessen the vitality devouring exercises (for example transmission, gathering, impact, and catching). Be that as it may, Data-Aggregation brings a correspondence side effect, since it diminishes the degree of Data-Accuracy and expands the correspondence weakness in information misfortune event. Ssome occasions require high correspondence unwavering quality and high Data-Accuracy. In this manner, in occasions with high criticality level, rather than diminishing the system traffic, the system must imitate the messages so as to expand the unwavering quality and guarantee improved Data-Accuracy.

With respect to Replication, it is critical to differentiate among storing and the importance of information replication. Storing is a notable methodology that has been adjusted for the impromptu correspondence. By and large, reserving has been applied to build the efficiency of the question based applications, which isn't the situation of occasion based applications.

Information Replication is a methodology generally utilized in postponement and interruption tolerant net-works. In these systems, availability isn't ensured, so the information replication can build the dependability of message conveyance.

One of the most well known information replication arrangement is proposed by Spyropoulos.

Data-Fusion for Event-Detection

The field of system information combination for occasion recognition is immense. It is a between disciplinary subject that includes data and choice hypothesis, signal preparing, and remote correspondence. Genuine situations force a few snags for occasion location in Large-Scale Highly-Dense Networks, for example: limited assets of sensors, time requirements, and the blunder presented in the gathered information. The circulated approaches are desirable over handle these difficulties, since they can adjust the asset utilization, and bring the dynamic procedure closer to the occasion event area. In spite of the fact that the unified methodology is clearly not reasonable for LSHDN, it is by a wide margin the most utilized methodology because of the simpler usage.

Role Coordination Frameworks

In the writing, there are far reaching works that address the coordination of certain jobs, relegating powerfully which hubs ought to perform detecting, handing-off, and information collection.

One of the most crucial job coordination arrangements is named Information-Fusion-based Role Assignment (InFRA) (Nakamura et al., 2009). This work proposes a circulated reac-tive job task approach coordinated with a steering convention. It doesn't address the information combination job, since it accept the presence of information combination calculations ready to distinguish occasions in the sensor field. At the point when an event is identified, InFRA can organize the task of detecting, handing-off, and information accumulation jobs over the system.

Planning to improve InFRA and DRINA, the arrangement, called dYnamic and scal-ablE tree Aware of Spatial correlaTion (YEAST) (Villas et al., 2014) doles out progressively the sens-ing, handing-off, and total jobs. YEAST considers the degree of spa-tial connection of the system and the degree of information precision to be met, which is educated by the application. Considering this data, YEAST characterizes which hubs should play the detecting, transfer, and information total jobs. To accomplish this, YEAST partitions the system into non-covering cells, where every phone con-tains a lot of hubs. Inside every cell, just a single hub plays out the detecting job at once. YEAST adjusts the vitality utilization by changing intermittently the hub playing out the detecting job on every cell. Be that as it may, YEAST doesn't take the deci-sion dependent on the information assembled from the occasion, since it adjusts the task of the jobs dependent on the application prerequisite (for example level of information exactness) and the spatial connection of the system. Furthermore, this arrangement can't utilize different information control calculations, for example, information conglomeration and replication.

Related Work Summary

Table 1 abridges the related works, featuring their fundamental highlights and disadvantages. Among the works that address only detecting and handing-off jobs, Blestas et al. (Bletsas et al., 2006) and Chou et al. (Chou et al., 2007) don't assess the overhead effect of their answer as far as vitality utilization. In addition, Jakllari et al. (Jakllari et al., 2007) and Chen et al. accept situations with low hub thickness and with low elements (for example no versatility and connection disappointment), individually.

Framework for Role Coordination in Large-Scale and Highly-Dense IoT Scenarios

This area introduces a system for job coordination in Large-Scale and Highly-Dense systems. Area 3.1 shows a lot of plan rules, which is utilized to characterize the design of the proposed arrangement. Segment 3.2 presents the outline of the proposed arrangement, indicating the segments in subtleties. At that point, the remainder of this area shows the undertakings executed by the proposed structure.

Applications, Requirements and Objectives

A portion of the run of the mill occasion based applications in Large-Scale and Highly-Dense IoT situations are identified with urban applications where a hub is associated with a huge num-ber of hubs, and every hub may have the option to recognize more than one sort of occasion. For example, in a urban Large-Scale and Highly-Dense IoT situation, the hubs work together and might trade information identified with fire identification, vehicle mishap alert, and crisis and salvage tasks. These necessities are pre-sented as follows:

- **Diversity of Hardware Capabilities:** The Large-Scale and Highly-Dense scenarios of Internet-of-Things depend on hubs with different equipment capacities.
- **Diversity of Event:** Besides the equipment decent variety, the Large-Scale and Highly-Dense IoT situations additionally include assorted variety regarding occasions. It implies the possi-bility of concurrent event of occasions with different criticality levels.

Table 1. Related work summary

Roles	Approach	Main features	Main disadvantage
Sensing and relaying	Blestas et al. (Bletsas et al., 2006)	Reactive timer-based	Spends energy on overhearing
	Chou et al. (Chou et al., 2007)	Reactive threshold-based	Resource expenditure on signaling
	Jakllari et al. (Jakllari et al., 2007)	Proactive distance-based	Low performance in dense scenarios
	Chen et al. (n.d)	Proactive distance-based	Low performance in dynamic scenarios
Data-control (Aggregation)	Tan et al. (n.d.)	Periodic tree refresh MST-based	Centralized solution
	Lin et al. (n.d)	Dynamic tree refresh SPT-based	Centralized solution
	Hussain et al. (n.d)	Dynamic tree refresh MST-based	Centralized solution
	Tan et al. (n.d)	Periodic tree refresh LMST-based	Does not measuare overhead cost
	Luo et al. (n.d)	– SPT-based	Designed for equally deployed networks
Data-control (Replication)	SnW	Distance-based	Constant number of replicas
	Takahashi et al. (n.d.)	Distance-based	Does not measure energy consumption
	Nishiyama et al. (n.d)	Distance and Density-based	Perfect wireless channel
	Thompson et al. (n.d)	Congestion-based	Does not measure energy consumption
Data-fusion for event-detection	Luo et al. (n.d)	Fusion-center-based 1-bit decision	Low accuracy in link failure
	Chaudhariet et al. (n.d)	Fusion-center-based log-likelihood	High energy consumption
	Sheltami et al. (n.d)	Fusion-center-based hybrid decision	Requires full network connectivity
	Cattivelli et al. (n.d)	Fully distributed	Constant channel quality

continued on following page

Table 1. Continued

Roles	Approach	Main features	Main disadvantage
Coordination	Nakamura et al. (Nakamura et al., 2009)	Reactive-based	Always minimizes the energy consumption
	Villas et al. (Villas et al., 2013)	Reactive-based with auxiliary data collection	Same criticality level for every event
	Villas et al. (Villas et al., 2014)	Reactive-based with auxiliary data collection	Roles are addressed Partly

- **Decentralization:** The enormous size of these situations requests appropriated solu-tions ready to adjust the traffic and the preparing functionalities over the system.
- **On request:** The vitality imperative requires the ability of setting off the center functionalities when an occasion is identified. Albeit some proactive functionalities are reasonable for diminishing the location delay and a full proactive arrangement presents restrictive expenses.

Figure 1. Overview of the framework

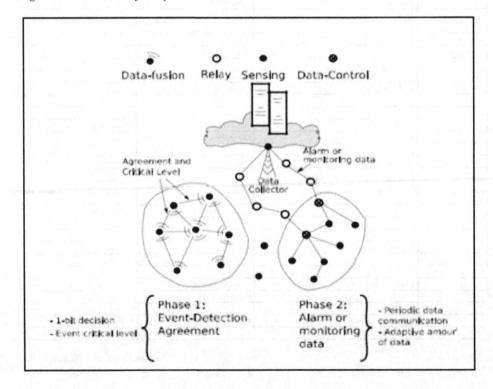

- **Adaptive:** The correspondence in Large-Scale and Highly-Dense IoT situations needs to manage dynamic situations, for example, versatility and connection disappointments.

Figure 2. Phases and tasks of the framework

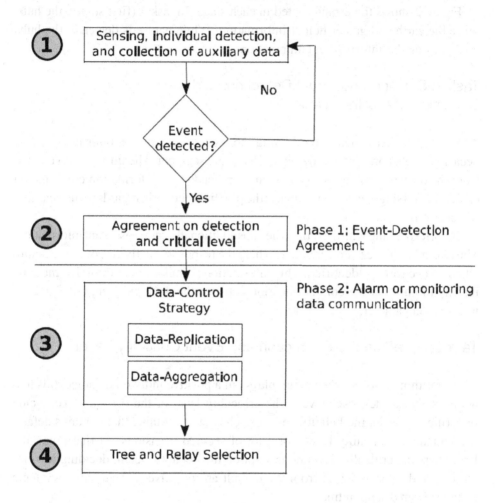

Architecture Overview

As delineated in Fig. 1, the proposed structure performs job coordination of sensing, transferring, information combination, and information control in two stages. The principal stage includes the detecting and identification, while the subsequent stage is identified with the information communication between the hubs and the information gatherer. The primary stage just includes detecting and information combination jobs. On the off chance that the hubs concur that an occasion is happening, at that point the sec-ond stage happens. During the subsequent stage, the hubs impart information to the information authority, and as can be watched, the hubs running the information control job can recreate alert or observing messages.

Figure 2 shows the errands acted in each stage. In task 1 (first stage), the hubs sense the earth and gather helper information. While nature is detected, the hubs perform singular information combination.

Task 1: Sensing, Individual Detection, and Collection of Auxiliary Data

As previously mentioned, the detecting job includes examining information of an occasion or phenom-enon utilizing an electronic segment. The information created from the detecting job goes to an essential procedure of information combination choice, called singular choice, which is the principal choice in regards to the nearness of occasions.

In corresponding with detecting, the hubs additionally gather assistant information. The reason for helper information is to help the responsive activities of the structure when an occasion is identified. This information is important to diminish the time interim to build up the commu-nication between the distinguishing hubs and the information gatherer.

Task 2: Agreement on Detection and Event Criticality Level

As Algorithm 1 shows, when a hub plays out a positive individual choice, this hub additionally decides, exclusively, the criticality level of the occasion. To decide the criticality level, the hub utilizes a pre-characterized table that contains default estimations of criticality levels for a lot of secured occasions. At that point, the hub, alters the criticality level dependent on the default esteem, deciding how far the detected information is from the default an incentive to maintain a strategic distance from disappointments.

Algorithm 1 Phase 1: Event detection and criticality level agreement

```
Initialize:
1: newCriticLevel ¬ 0;
2: Start
3: while (isDecisionInterval()==true) do
```

```
 4: sensing[ ] ¬ aquisition.data();
 5: dataType ¬ aquisition.type();
 6: newCriticLevel ¬ individualDecision(sensing[ ], dataType);
 7: end while
 8: while (isAgreementInterval()==true) do
 9: auxiliaryData ¬listenNeighbors();
10: nghCriticLevel ¬ auxiliaryData.getCriticLevel();
11: broadcastData(newCriticLevel, itsOwnAuxData);
12: if (newCriticLevel > 0) then
13: criticLevelAgreement(newCriticLevel, nghCriticLevel);
14: end if
15: end while
16: End
17: function INDVIDUALDECISION(sensing[ ], dataType)
18: eventDetected ¬ occurrenceTest(sensing[ ], dataType)
19: if (eventDetected == True) then
20: defaultCriticLevel ¬ defaultCriticalityLevel(dataType)
21: newCriticLevel ¬ computeCriticalityLevel(sensing[ ]);
22: newCriticLevel ¬adjust(newCriticLevel, defaultCriticLevel)
23: end if
24: return (newCriticLevel)
25: end function
```

Task 3: Data-Control Strategies Decision

Information total and information replication are the two information control procedures that the hubs can perform on the system traffic. Right now, recognizing hub chooses which methodology it should utilize. To choose the information control system, the hub utilizes the concurred criticality level (Task 2). This choice guarantees that the total and repli-cation job are facilitated in a completely circulated way, which implies that these jobs don't depend on a nearby or focal element (for example group head or organizer hub).

Task 4: Tree and Relay Selection

This errand is combined with the systems that tune the information control technique. Each distinguishing hub must choose a solitary or numerous guardians, contingent upon which information control technique was characterized on task 3. Hence, the

Tree and Relay choice has two instances of execution (see Algorithm 2), which are displayed as follows:

- If the characterized information control procedure is replication, the hub locate various repli-cas and chooses the arrangement of parent hubs that will get the message copies.
- In instance of information total, the hub processes the conglomeration level and chooses a solitary parent hub to send the accumulated information.

Algorithm 2 Phase 2: Data-control decision and tree selection

```
Initialize:
1: Start
2: criticLevel ¬ getCriticLevel();
3: dataControl ¬ decideStrategy(criticLevel);
4: if (isAggregation(dataControl)) then
5: aggLevel ¬ computeAggL(auxiliaryData);
6: selectSingleParent(auxiliaryData);
7: end if
8: else if (isReplication(dataControl)) then
9: numReplicas ¬ computeNumReplicas(auxiliaryData);
10: selectMultipleParents(numReplicas, auxiliaryData);
11: end else if
12: End
```

Discussion

This segment portrays an utilization case situation, representing the execution of the proposed structure, and furthermore shows a subjective correlation between the primary related works.

Illustration

To show the activity of the proposed arrangement, a urban situation is considered. Right now, Large-Scale Highly-Dense Network is utilized to identify and screen occasions identified with crisis circumstances (for example fire, vehicle mishap, and common debacle) and furthermore distinguish vehicle traffic sticks, and climate data (for example downpour and snow event). The sorts of sensors utilized by the system to distinguish these occasions are: smoke, temperature, dampness, area, and vibration. Henceforth, the system hubs are outfitted with the appropriated equipment, and execute consistently Tasks 1 and 2.

Table 2. Qualitative comparison

Requirements	InFRA Nakamura	DRINA Villas	YEAST Villas	Proposed
	et al. (Nakamura et al., 2009)	et al. (Villas et al., 2013)	et al. (Villas et al., 2014)	Framework
Diversity of hardware capabilities	No	No	No	Yes
Diversity of event	No	No	No	Yes
Decentralization	Partly	Partly	Partly	Yes
On demand	Yes	Yes	Yes	Yes
Dynamic adaptive	No	Yes	No	Yes

Qualitative Comparison

Table 2 shows a subjective examination between the principle related works and the proposed system. Concerning of Hardware Capabilities, none of the related works consider, for example, hubs with different vitality assets (for example battery-powered and non-battery-powered batteries). The proposed system considers the vitality asset during the information control choice. For example, in event of exceptionally pundit occasions, the proposed arrangement recreates the messages, and the quantity of imitations considers the vitality accessibility.

CONCLUSION

Coordination of detecting, handing-off, information combination, and information control (conglomeration and replication) is a significant test in Large-Scale Highly-Dense Networks. Right now address this test, showing an on-request and completely distrib-uted job coordination system intended to efficiently utilize vitality assets and to adaptively give a reasonable degree of information conveyance proportion.

The proposed system extends the related works by being a completely circulated approach, and considering gadgets with different equipment abilities (recharge capable vitality saves, non-chargeable batteries, and memory buffer sizes), and occasions with different levels of direness. In addition, the proposed structure is intended to run in powerful situations having connection and hub disappointment, and versatility.

REFERENCES

Asadi, A., Sciancalepore, V., & Mancuso, V. (2015). On the efficient utilization of radio resources in extremely dense wireless networks. *IEEE Communications Magazine, 53*(1), 126–132. doi:10.1109/MCOM.2015.7010525

Bletsas, A., Khisti, A., Reed, D. P., & Lippman, A. (2006). A simple cooperative diversity method based on network path selection. *IEEE Journal on Selected Areas in Communications, 24*(3), 659–672. doi:10.1109/JSAC.2005.862417

Chou, C. T., Yang, J., & Wang, D. (2007). Cooperative mac protocol with automatic relay selection in distributed wireless networks. In *Fifth Annual IEEE International Conference on Pervasive Computing and Communications Workshops, PerCom Workshops' 07*, (pp. 526–531). IEEE. 10.1109/PERCOMW.2007.33

Draves, R., Padhye, J., & Zill, B. (2004). Comparison of routing metrics for static multi-hop wireless networks. *ACM SIGCOMM Comput. Commun. Rev., 34*(4), 133–144. doi:10.1145/1030194.1015483

Jakllari, G., Krishnamurthy, S. V., Faloutsos, M., Krishnamurthy, P. V., & Ercetin, O. (2007). A cross-layer framework for exploiting virtual miso links in mobile ad hoc networks. *IEEE Transactions on Mobile Computing, 6*(6), 579–594. doi:10.1109/TMC.2007.1068

Lu, R., Li, X., Liang, X., Shen, X., & Lin, X. (2011). Grs: The green, reliability, and security of emerging machine to machine communications. *IEEE Communications Magazine, 49*(4), 28–35. doi:10.1109/MCOM.2011.5741143

Nakamura, E. F., Ramos, H. S., Villas, L. A., de Oliveira, H. A., de Aquino, A. L., & Loureiro, A. A. (2009). A reactive role assignment for data routing in event-based wireless sensor networks. *Computer Networks*, *53*(12), 1980–1996. doi:10.1016/j.comnet.2009.03.009

Villas, L. A., Boukerche, A., De Oliveira, H. A., De Araujo, R. B., & Loureiro, A. A. (2014). A spatial correlation aware algorithm to perform efficient data collection in wireless sensor networks. *Ad Hoc Networks*, *12*, 69–85. doi:10.1016/j.adhoc.2011.08.005

Villas, L. A., Boukerche, A., Ramos, H. S., de Oliveira, H. A., de Araujo, R. B., & Loureiro, A. A. F. (2013). Drina: A lightweight and reliable routing approach for in-network aggregation in wireless sen-sor networks. *IEEE Transactions on Computers*, *62*(4), 676–689. doi:10.1109/TC.2012.31

Xu, X., Luo, J., & Zhang, Q. (2010). Delay tolerant event collection in sensor networks with mobile sink. In *INFOCOM, 2010 Proceedings IEEE*, (pp. 1–9). IEEE. 10.1109/INFCOM.2010.5462075

Chapter 5
Crop Disease Detection Using Data Science Techniques

Shakti Kumar
Amity University, Noida, India

ABSTRACT

Plant disease is a mutilation of the normal state of a plant that changes its essential quality and prevents a plant from performing to its actual potential. Due to drastic environment changes, plant diseases are growing day by day, which results the higher losses in quantity of agricultural yields. To prevent the loss in the crop yield, the timely disease identification is necessary. Monitoring the plant diseases without any digital mean makes it difficult to identify the disease correctly and timely. It requires more amounts of work, time, and great experience in the plant diseases. Automatic approach of image processing and applying the different data science techniques to classify the disease correctly is a good idea for this which includes acquisition, classification, feature extraction, pre-processing, and segmentation all are performed on the leaf images. This chapter will briefly discuss the data science techniques used for the classification of the images like SVM, k-nearest neighbor, decision tree, ANN, and convolutional neural network (CNN).

DOI: 10.4018/978-1-7998-4685-7.ch005

INTRODUCTION

Title of the Study

Review of Crop Diseases and Disease detection techniques of Data Science.

Field of the study

India comes in the world largest producer of many vegetables and fresh fruits like papaya, chickpea, banana, mango, guava, okra, lemon and the second largest producer of wheat and rice as per the 2014 FAO world agricultural statistics. Fifty percent population of India depends on the agriculture. Every year farmers faces a very high production loss due to plan diseases and it also affects the economy of the country.

The cause of many Plant diseases is pathogens. These pathogens are infectious organisms those spread from one plant to another plant or non-infectious. Diseases can also be non-infectious generally these are disorders. Plants disorders are like deficient nutrients, soil is polluted, too much or little water. Other reasons are like very hot or very cold weather and very heavy wind or rain and the air pollution from automobiles and industry, and wrong methods of farming.

Diseases and Disorders Found in Plants

Infectious plant diseases are caused by living *(biotic)* agents, or pathogens. These pathogens can be spread from an infected plant or plant debris to a healthy plant. *Microorganisms* that cause plant diseases include *nematodes, fungi, bacteria*, and *mycoplasmas* (Lucas, 1992).

Following are some common symptoms and types of plant leaf diseases.

- Fungal

The disease caused by fungus is like Late blight early blight and downy mildew these diseases are spread by different types of fungus like Phytophthora infesters and Alternaria solani etc. Late blight, early blight and downy mildew shows different type of symptoms like water soaked grey green spots, small brown spots, and the white patches on upper side of leaves shown in Figure 1.

Figure 1. Late Blight

- Bacterial

All type of bacteria is not harmful some of the bacteria are cause disease in plant and this type of bacteria represents leaf spot like brown or black .

- Viral

Diseases caused by the virus are very difficult to identify because they do not show any early symptoms and if any present that is very confusing to identify sometimes confuse with nutrient deficiencies.E.g. Mosaic Virus. Shown in Figure 2

Figure 2. Bacterial leaf spot

   It's a very critical task to detect the disease. Manual detection from naked eyes of crop plant disease is a difficult task as it takes serious observation and consumes much time and it is very difficult to follow different type of guidelines on disease day by day. Automated recognition of plant leaves diseases can be achieved by Image processing. Image Processing with different data science techniques helps better to identify the plant disease and provides a detailed investigation about the disease.

   Image processing and segmentation includes the basic steps as in Figure 3.

Figure 3. Basic steps of image processing

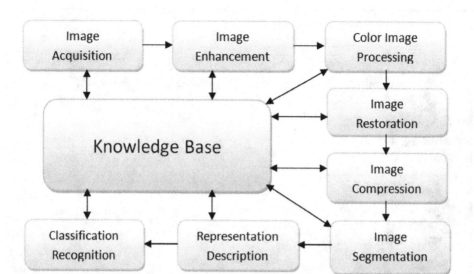

This is the basic flow of steps to process an Image. This is just an overview of steps involving in the process every step in the process applies many techniques to improve the performance of that particular step. Like if we talk about the image pre-processing which comes immediate after the Image acquisition step involves multiple techniques to improve the Image processing and enhance its efficiency to produce better and accurate results. The steps involved are as Image cropping, filtering Of Image, scaling of the Image, Colour transformation, Intensity Adjustment, Brightness thresholding, Histogram equalization, detection of Edges of the Image, smoothing of Images etc.

Image Processing steps are discussed in more details in coming course.

Image Processing

Image Acquisition

Image acquisition is the process to get an image from some source the image can be retrieved directly from digital cameras or any saved image from any physical storage media. Image Acquisition comes first in picture for any type of image processing done because image is necessary to do image processing work on it. At this phase of processing the will be in unprocessed state.

Image Pre-Processing

The dataset which is required by any machine learning model should be noise free because the distorted dataset can decrease the efficiency of the machine learning algorithm applied on that dataset so to avoid this to happen before feeding any data to the ML model the noise and the distortions are removed from the data by cleaning it. Like this in the Image pre-processing the noise is removed from the images and some of the features of the image enhances for efficient working of the machine learning algorithm. Robert(1992) and Sonka(1998) mentioned that the pre-processing of an image makes the picture pure or we can say it removes noise and distortions from the image and makes it relevant to go for further processing step. In pre-processing some of the other steps are also included like cropping of the image to specified dimensions, colour transformation of the image in some cases, scaling of the image, filtering and thresholding of the image etc.

Image segmentation

The need of the automation of the image analysis and interpretation gives birth to segmentation algorithms for many industry applications. Image segmentation technique involves breaking up an image into a set of similar and effective groups called segments. Pixel in each segment will have its own identical attribute. These attributes are like contrast, grey levels, spectral values and textural properties. Example Figure 4.

Figure 4. Image segmentation

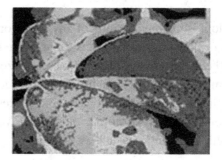

Image R segmentation can identify multiple of regions $\left(R_1, R_2 \ldots \ldots R_N\right)$ such that

$$R = R_1 \cup R_2 \cup R_3 \ldots \ldots \ldots R_N$$

We will adopt the computer vision techniques for Image segmentation which will give us a more granular detail of the leaf object and the symptoms presented on that leaf. Segmentation works tremendously when we think about in-depth details of an image.

Several Techniques and algorithms have been developed some of them are like semantic segmentation, Instance segmentation, region-based segmentation. Graph theoretic approach and the Threshold Segmentation techniques are utilized more. Applications using the image segmentation Include locating object in satellite images, automated driving, medical imaging, Traffic control systems, video surveillance etc.

Feature Extraction

Feature Extraction is the Technique of extracting the key characteristics of an image or object. The key features can be multiple and each feature has its own specific irrefutable property about an object, and is computed such that it quantifies some significant characteristics of the object (Choras,2007).

Such features are as follows:

- Common features: The common features include colour of the image, Texture and the shape of the image other are the sublevels of these common features like pixel level features (working on each Pixel and its location), segmented image features, specific features such as face and fingerprints etc.

Colour Features

Colour is the main feature of any image or an object to distinguish a unique object out of the number of objects same as the human eyes do. Colour feature provides us the important information to categorize the objects and to distinguish the object from background. Colour histogram is widely used technique Colours are commonly defined in three-dimensional colour spaces. The general models are used like RGB colour model, HSV colour model, HMMD colour model etc. Colour feature has multiple advantages such as:

1) Robustness
2) Effectiveness
3) Implementation simplicity
4) Computational simplicity

5)   Low storage requirements

Texture Features

Texture description provides us the important measurement about the image to classify its texture. As we know an image is made up of number of pixels and the matrix of these pixels forms a texture and this overall texture is perceived by human eyes as an image. Texture is very important characteristic for image segmentation and classification. For this we required some invariance like position, scale and rotation. The most basic approach to texture description is to generate the Fourier transform of the image and then to group the transform data in some way so as to obtain a set of measurements.

Textural features are Like Entropy, Wavelets, Statistical measures, Homogeneity and Fractals.

Shape Features

Shape is another important measurement of an image feature. Shape is the collection of all the geometrical information of an object which does not change even when the location, scale and orientation of the object are changed. Shape is invariant to Euclidean similarity transformations.

To do the Shape analysis there are various techniques like

1)   Contour based shape analysis
2)   Region based shape analysis.

Image Classification

Image classification is a technique which classify the image according to the contents available in that image. For this system takes an image as input and produces the output as a class of that image like the input given is a picture of cat and classification algorithm gives output as cat. Classification of an is the part of computer vision technology which is very much in use now a days like Face book image tagging, in self driving cars defence surveillance etc. In this the models are trained on the basis of pre-defined set of patterns. Now a day's different classification techniques are in use some of them are described below.

Image Classification Techniques

Support Vector Machine (SVM)

A support vector machine comes under the tab of supervised machine learning. Support Vector Machine is very useful for small datasets because it works tremendously and produces higher efficiency result. As a Linear model it works well for both type of problems like linear or non-linear. The idea behind Support Vector Machines to create a line or hyper plane which classifies the given input (Kamavisdar, 2013). It separates only when there is the possibility of classification.

In the Figure 5 it is clearly shown that how data is separated by a line or a plane under the data classification mechanism.

Figure 5. Data separated by a Plane

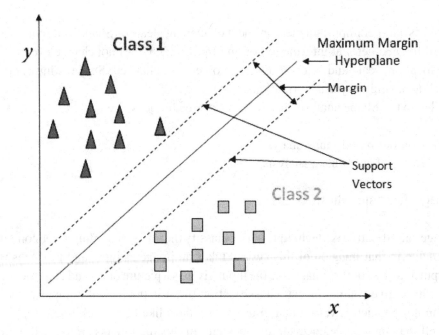

We can define a vector and a plane as "A vector is an object that has both a magnitude and a direction" What do we use to separate the data when there are more than three dimensions? We use what is called a Hyper plane. "A Hyper plane is a subspace of one dimension less than its ambient space" (Kowalczyk, 2017).

For more than one dimensional aspect we use Hyper plane as in the real-life examples we could have to tackle thousands of dimensions of the dataset. If two dimensional vectors are defined as

$$x = \left(x_1, x_2\right)$$

And

$$w = \left(a, -1\right)$$

Then we will get an equation of a line

$$w.x + b = 0$$

Where $w.x$ is the dot product of the w and x

Actually, this equation uses vectors and represents a hyper plane and can be used for any dimensional set of the data. The Perceptron algorithm is invented by Frank Rosenblatt in early 60's. It is the building block of a simple neural network: the multilayer perceptron. The goal of the Perceptron is to find a hyper plane that can separate a linearly separable data set. Once the hyper plane is found, it is used to perform binary classification.

If the augmented vectors

$$x = \left(x_0, x_1 \ldots x_n\right)$$

$$w = \left(w_0, w_1 \ldots w_n\right)$$

As per perceptron the classification of data point x_i:

$$h\left(x_i\right) = sign\left(w.x_i\right)$$

The Perceptron has several advantages: it is a simple model, the algorithm is very easy to implement, and we have a theoretical proof that it will find a hyperplane that separates the data. However, its biggest weakness is that it will not find the same hyper plane every time.

The perceptron is very simple model of algorithm to implement and it definitely separates the data to classify it. But one problem or we can say the weakness of the perceptron algorithm is it was unable to find same hyper plane every time. And this problem is total eliminated by the Support Vector Machine (SVM).

The main Motive of the Support Vector Machine (SVM) is to identify the right Hyper plane. First is the Thumb rule which says that select that hyper plane which separate two classes better. Second is the margin which is the distance between hyper planes and by maximising this distance we can easily identify the best one. Third Support Vector Machine (SVM) classifies the classes efficiently before to maximizing the margin. Fourth if the hyper planes are non-linear then SVM applies additional feature which is

$$z = x^2 + y^2$$

Now it will make it easy to identify the right hyper plane.

K-Nearest Neighbors (KNN)

K-nearest neighbor is very simple and basic classification algorithm but it is very effective machine learning algorithm. It is also the part of supervised learning and it can be utilized to solve both classification and regression problems. It calculates the Euclidean distances k and results the minimum distance between given points which determine the class of the point. The applications of the K-nearest neighbor are like pattern recognition, intrusion detection and data mining etc. It is very basic algorithm but it is very essential algorithm. It is one of the non-parametric type algorithms we can understand it with the help of the following Figure 6.

Plotting these points on a graph we can identify some clusters as blue squares and red triangles and now observe the cluster for a classified point as green circle is nearest neighbour in this process, we can figure out one cluster that near one. In above example it is the blue square group.

Now if we see this n Figure 7 here we are having three classes or we can say three clusters and one is the circle which is covering three classes but there is one unclassified star like point which shows the group in red one is its nearest neighbor and that is more relevant classification. To get these points clear K should be kept as odd number for clear understanding.

Decision tree (DT)

Decision Tree is a machine learning algorithm which is utilized for the classification and regression problems. As the name implies of the algorithm it keeps dividing the input dataset into smaller part until the single instance is left which is then classified.

Figure 6. A Set of Data Points

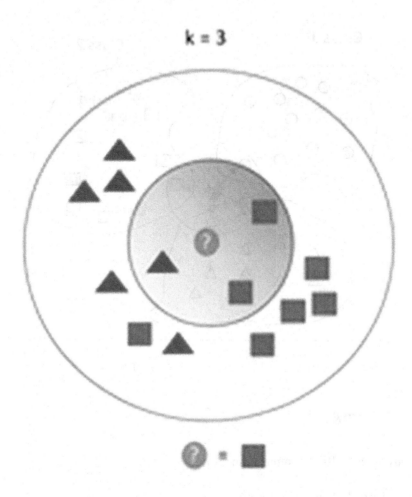

The partitioning is done uniformly at last hierarchical structure is developed which look like a tree thus decision tree the name is given to this algorithm. Figure 8.

Basically, if we split the given data set to a point where only single instance left at the end so we can easily classify the data set given and this split will be based on the homogeneity of the data. And this process makes the data set highly pure. Deshpandey discussed that Entropy and the information gain are used to quantify the homogeneity in classification.

And the Entropy can be defined as follows:

Figure 7. K-Nearest Neighbor (KNN)

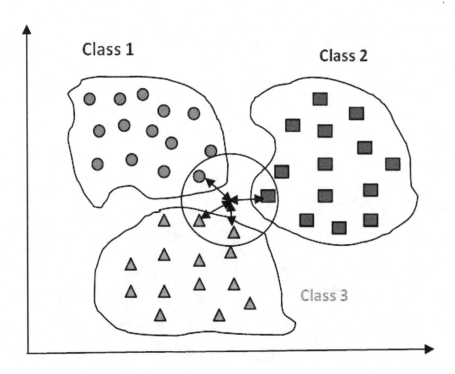

$$H = -\sum p(x)\,logp(x)$$

Entropy is basically the impurity measure.

Artificial Neural Network (ANN)

Artificial Neural Network is one type of model that is used for information processing. The basic concept behind Artificial Neural Network is human mind because it works like human mind as neurons in the human mind processes the information. The ANN is inspired by the biological nerve system of human mind. ANN is widely used for the classification process. The dataset of the images is collected and a model is trained on that image dataset then this model is utilized to identify the same type of object in other images. We can understand the key concept of Artificial Neural Network with the help of following Figure 9.

Figure 8. Decision tree

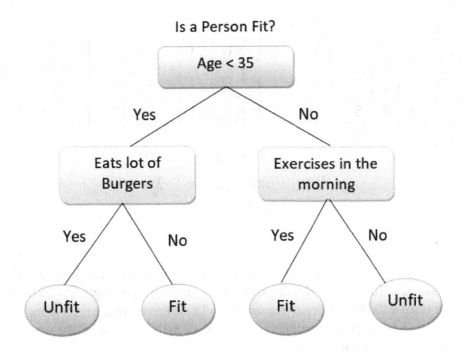

Figure 9. Node in the Neural Network (ANN)

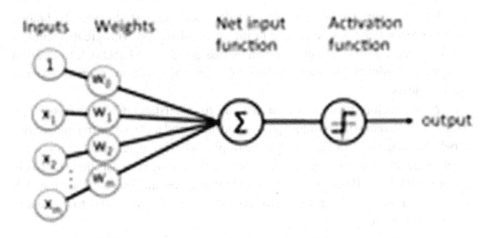

Figure 10. CNN Matrix

8	2	3	3	8
4	5	3	5	1
3	3	2	7	5
1	2	4	5	4
3	2	5	3	5

*

1	0	-1
1	0	-1
1	0	-1

=

7		

8x1+4x1+3x1+2x0+
5x0+3x0+3x-1+3x-
1+2x-1=7

In Artificial Neural Network (ANN) one layer is as Input layer and one is the Output layer and between the Input and Output layers there are multiple Hidden layers which make it the human brain like structure. These layers are the combination of the nodes and all the computational activity is done in the nodes only. The structure of the node will look like as in Figure 9.

Here x are the inputs and w are the weights one activation function works just like the activator of the human brain neurons.

Convolutional Neural Network (CNN)

Convolutional Neural Network (CNN) is a deep learning Data Science Technique which is proven to be very effective in image classification with great Accuracy. Convnet is used by the famous companies like google and Facebook to develop the computer vision applications to recognize the objects in an image or moving object in videos.

CNN architecture is not so much difficult to understand. CNN processed the image with different convolutional phases and at the end it classifies the image with a label. An image is nothing but an array of pixels having height and width. If we see an image from the array perspective then a colour image consists three channels Red,Green,Blue (RGB) where as a greyscale image has only one channel in which each pixel represents with a value from 0-255 where 0 corresponds to white and other are dark as per intensity of colour.

The most important component of a Convnet model is the convolutional layer. During convolutional phase the size of the image is reduced keeping the necessary feature of the image intact and the irrelevant noise is removed. The purpose of this is to improve the performance of the computation weights and generalization. The image matrix is divided into small pieces to extract the most essential elements within each piece.

Convnet mainly has four components. CNN components in Figure 11.

Convolution- A mathematical technique for feature map creation.

ReLU- Rectified Linear Unit which is an activation function.

MaxPooling- It reduces the dimensionality of the feature maps.

Fully connected Layer – Used to classify the images.

Figure 11. CNN

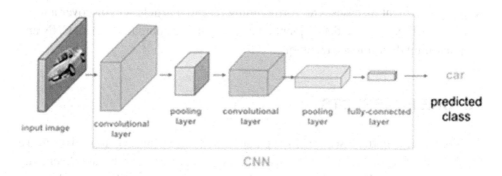

- **Some past work done in this field**

Number of the authors has given their method and techniques for the Disease identification in the crops. The work of some the authors are as Kulkarni (2012) used Artificial neural network for the classification of the plant diseases and Gabor filter also. Argenti (1990) gives the idea of co-occurrence matrix for classification. Sanjay (2013) in the same row gives the colour co-occurrence method. Mrunalini (2011) implements K-means algorithm and some pattern recognition techniques. Wang (2012) suggested some feature extraction techniques by using Gabor filter and PCA (Principal Component Analysis). Rathod (2016) implements the image processing techniques. Ghaiwat (2014) uses the multiple techniques for better results like ANN, PNN, SVM and Fuzzy logics.

CONCLUSION

Tremendous progress has been seen from past decades in the automation field of science and technology things are getting smarter and most of the work has been automated either it is the field of Medical or any Industry or the automation work is under process for rest of the field. We have proposed the techniques for an automated system which will be able to detect the plan leaf diseases in a more efficient manner by using the image processing.

This Report represents techniques involved in the detection of plant diseases these techniques are like Image classification and image segmentation and their sub categories. It also presents a comprehensive view on the various researches done in contemporary domain of Crop diseases. The collection of analysis is done dealing with various plant diseases. Our forthcoming research article will discover a more efficient methodology to detect plant diseases by using computer vision, CNN and deep learning data science techniques.

FUTURE PROSPECTS

A lot of scope is in the research of the plant diseases from future perspective. And a lot of research is going on presently to tackle the problem of these diseases occurring in the plant tremendously due to changing climatic conditions. So, researchers are working on more efficient technology to identify the disease timely and the effective measures can be taken to avoid the losses in production and consequentially to the economy. In today's scenario almost everyone is having one smart Android phone which has the very vast capabilities to use these techniques from the future point of view. One android app can be developed to take the picture of diseased plan leaf and on the basis of disease identification number of solutions can be advised to the user to save the entire crop. And on the same concept one web App can also be made to make the process faster and cheaper.

REFERENCES

Argenti, F. (1990). Fast Algorithms For Texture Analysis Using Co-Occurrence Matrices. *IEEE Proceedings, 137*(6), 443-44. 10.1049/ip-f-2.1990.0064

Badnakhe, M. R., & Deshmukh, P. R. (2011). K-Means Clustering And Artificial Intelligence In Pattern Recognition For Crop Diseases. *International Conference on Advancements in Information Technology, 20*, 134-138.

Choras, R. S. (2007). *Image Feature Extraction Techniques and Their Applications for CBIR and Biometrics Systems. International Journal Of Biology And Biomedical Engineering.*

Deshpandey, B. (n.d.). *Decision Tree Digest.* Retrieved from https://tanthiamhuat. files.wordpress.com/2015/04/decision-trees-digest.pdf

Ghaiwat, S.N. (2014). Leaf Diseases Using Image Processing Techniques: a review. *International Journal Recent Advance Engineering Technology, 2*(3), 512.

Haralick, R. M., &Linda, G. (1992). Computer and Robot Vision (vol. 1). Boston, MA: Addison-Wesley.

Kamavisdar, P., Saluja, S., & Agrawal, S. (2013). A Survey on Image Classification Approaches and Techniques. *International Journal of Advanced Research in Computer and Communication Engineering, India, 2*(1), 1005–1009.

Kowalczyk, A. (2017). *Support vector machine succinctly.* Syncfusion.

Kulkarni, A. H. (2015). Applying Image Processing Technique To Detect Plant Diseases. *International Journal of Engine Research, 2*(5), 3661–3664.

Lucas, G. B., Campbell, C. L., & Lucas, L. T. (1992). *Causes of Plant Diseases. In Introduction to Plant Diseases.* Springer. doi:10.1007/978-1-4615-7294-7

Rathod, A.N. (2013). Image Processing Techniques For Detection Of Leaf Disease. *International Journal Advance Research Computer Science & Software Engineering, 3*(11).

Sanjay, B. (2013). Agricultural Plant Leaf Disease Detection Using Image Processing. *International Journal of Advance Research in Electrical, Electronics and Instrumentation Engineering, 2*(1), 599–602.

Sonka, M., Hlavac, V., & Boyle, R. (1998). *Image Processing, Analysis and Machine Vision.* PWS Publishing.

Wang, H. (2012). Image Recognition of Plant Diseases. *5th International Congress on Image and Signal Processing,* 894-90.

Chapter 6
Wing of 5G IoT and Other Services

Prabhat Singh
ABES Engineering College, Ghaziabad, India

Harsh Khatter
ABES Engineering College, Ghaziabad, India

Sunil Kumar
Amity University, Noida, India

ABSTRACT

The day-to-day advancements have brought the biggest challenge to network providers as it has become difficult to keep up the traditional networks with the ever-advancing technologies for them. It also result as a motivation for vendors to grow by developing, innovating, deploying, and migrating in their services, upgrading to new hardware and infrastructure, as well as hiring newly trained people, which requires a large amount of money and time to implement. It results to a need of a new network architecture who has a capability of supporting future technologies along with solving all sorts of issues known as the network proposal by software. For meeting highly increasing demands, various proposals of load balancing techniques come forward in which highly dedicated balancers of loads are being required for ever service in some of them, or for every new service, manual recognition of device is required. In the conventional network, on the basis of the local information in the network, load balancing is being established.

DOI: 10.4018/978-1-7998-4685-7.ch006

INTRODUCTION

Since ancient times, communication is the most basic needs of everyone's life to communicate between two people. It in early start was started from talk only. It's very important to have a proper understandable communication for creating appropriate relations and solve our issues effectively. This communication hasn't seen much development for a very long time until 1950-1960s. As in 1950-1960s, the major evolution comes through the development of telephones and mobile known for first generation of communication (1G) for long distance interactions.

From that day, the evolutionary growth in communication never seen back. This growth has come to present in which we are using 4G, i.e., Fourth generation of communication. Which shows us the path to the Fourth generation of industrial revolution in the market and have given us the ray of light towards new boundaries to achieve. But still 4G is not capable to support the targets that have been shown by it to us (Kumar et al., 2015b).

Due to which, our present generation is moving forward to 5G technologies, i.e. also called as fifth generation of communication. Which have the capabilities to achieve the targets of which fourth generation of communication needs for working and grow.

5G Communication

5G is the fifth generation of wireless communications technologies supporting cellular data networks. Large scale adoption began in 2019 and today virtually every telecommunication service provider in the developed world is upgrading its infrastructure to offer 5G functionality. 5G communication requires the use of communications devices (mostly mobile phones) designed to support the technology. The 5G frequency bandwidth is being divided into three bands:

1. **Millimeter waves -** the fastest 5G band
2. **Mid band**
3. **Low band –** the slowest 5G band

Low-band uses a similar frequency range as the predecessor, 4G. 5G millimeter wave is the fastest, with actual speeds often being 1–2 Gbit/s down. Frequencies are above 24 GHz reaching up to 72 GHz which is above the extremely high frequency band's lower boundary. The reach is short, so more cells are required. Millimeter waves have difficulty traversing many walls and windows, so indoor coverage is limited. All the 5G wireless devices in a cell communicate by radio waves with a local antenna arrayand low power automated transceiver (transmitter and receiver) in the cell, over frequency channels assigned by the transceiver from a pool of frequencies that are reused in other cells.

Figure 1. 5G communication

All the 5G wireless devices in a cell communicate by radio waves with a local antenna array and low power automated transceiver (transmitter and receiver) in the cell, over frequency channels assigned by the transceiver from a pool of frequencies that are reused in other cells. The local antennas are connected with the telephone network and the Internet by a high bandwidth optical fiber or wireless backhaul connection. As in other cell networks, a mobile device crossing from one cell to another is automatically "handed off" seamlessly to the new cell. Which make it a highly reliable network communication system along with interconnected devices with high speed frequency bandwidths.(Kumar et al., 2015c)

Figure 2. Features of 5G communication technologies

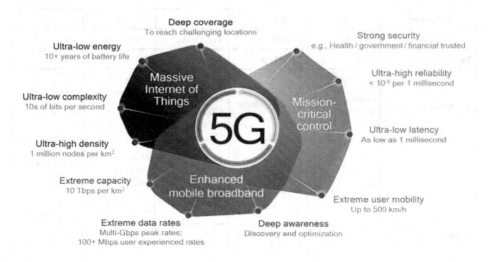

Features of 5G Communication Technology

The features of 5G technology made it the medium to cope up with the evergreen focus of real time work processing as well as made this technology to open up the new boundaries for us to achieve and focus in our technological development.

The features of 5G communication which made it possible are as follows: (Figure 1)

a) Real time connectivity
b) Capabilities to connect to Critical and massive machine technology
c) Highly reduced latency
d) Highly densed network communication stability
e) High speed data transfer
f) Strong Cyber security, etc.

Table 1. Comparison between Communication Generations

Technology	1G	2G / 2.5G	3G	4G	5G
Deployment	1970/1984	1980/1999	1990/2002	2000/2010	2019-
Bandwidth	2kbps	14-64kbps	2mbps	200mbps	>1gbps
Technology	Analog Cellular	Digital Cellular	Broadband width/ CDMA/ ip technology	Unified ip and seamless combo of LAN/ WAN/ WLAN/ PAN	4G + WWWW
Services	Mobile Telephony	Digital voice, short messaging	Integrated high quality audio, video and data	Dynamic information access, variable devices	Dynamic information access, variable devices with AI capabilities
Multiplexing	FDMA	TDMA/CDMA	CDMA	CDMA	CDMA
Switching	Circuit	Circuit/ circuit for access network and air interface	Packet except for air interface	All packet	All packet
Core Network	PSTN	PSTN	Packet Network	Internet	Internet
Handoff	Horizontal	Horizontal	Horizontal	Horizontal and Vertical	Horizontal and Vertical

Figure 3. **Comparison between Communication Generations**

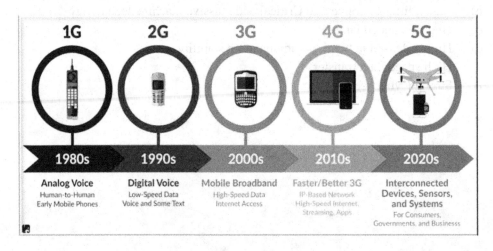

Figure 4.

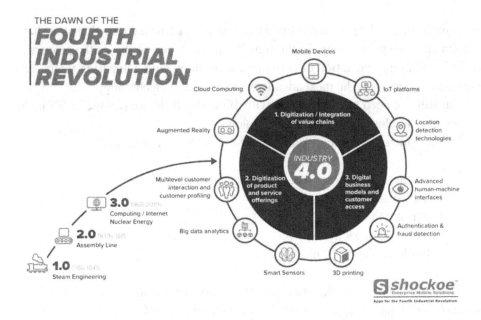

Why we Need 5G Technology?

As we know, we have talked about 5G technologies and its features but we haven't focused on the most basic questions that comes to mind when we started talking about 5G, i.e., why we need 5G when 4G is in developing phase and is evolving day by day with evolving technologies.

Its answer is simple which is being known as real time processing. Despite of evergreen growing speed the maximum speed offered by 4G is quite low along with high latency in comparison to the respects of 5G(Kumar et al., 2017a).

Secondly, the fourth generation of industrial revolution is the revolution in terms called as Cyber Physical Systems whose focus is the inter self-dependent connectivity of our cyber based technologies in a network to create an Artificial mind network of the objects. For which, high speed and dependable network is required which can't be supported by 4G as it can lag at some level. Due to which the development and introduction is needed.

The advantage of 5G over 4G is defined only comparing the capabilities of both of them and when we came to compare them we came to know that despite of initial stages of 5g and advantage of already developed and growing phases of 4G, 5G is more capable to achieve the objectives of fourth generation of industrial development.

Comparison Between 5G With Other Technologies

We have introduced 5g in market but we also need to know the growth that we have seen in previous generations. So through, Table-1, we can easily see the properties of each and every generation of communication along with comparing them. And we find out that 5G is the most advance communication technology.

But still, we need to compare 4G with 5G in details as we can see in 5G is the technology developed through 4G technologies.

Due to which, the comparison between 4g and 5g is as follows:

- 5G is a unified platform that is more capable than 4G
- 5G uses spectrum better than 4G
- 5G is faster than 4G
- 5G has more capacity than 4G
- 5G has lower latency than 4G

Through Table 2, it is clear to us the 5G is 10 times capable to 4G technologies which makes it highly capable to meet the demands of Fourth Generation of industrial Revolution.

Targets of 5G Communication Technologies

As 5G communication brought into existence because of the real time processing along with the world in which all of our objects and technologies achieved earlier comes to connect each other as one(Kumar et al., 2017b).

These objects include vehicles, mobiles, TVs and all other electronic items with cloud network.

Because of which 5G technologies have a target to achieve the connectivity and make them capable to work efficiently with cloud.

The technologies that needs to be targeted are as follows:

1. IoT (Internet of Things)
2. Cloud computing
3. VR and AR
4. Vehicle Management
5. Better Medical Support

Figure 5. Targets of 5G in Fourth Generation of Industrial Revolution

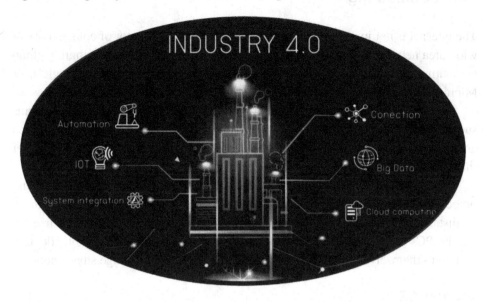

IOT – Internet of Things

The **Internet of things** (**IoT**) is a system of interrelated computing devices, mechanical and digital machines provided with unique identifiers (UIDs) and the ability to transfer data over a network without requiring human-to-human or human-to-computer interaction.

- It evolved due to the convergence of multiple technologies, real-time analytics, machine learning, commodity sensors, and embedded systems.
- In a household with low-latency 5G connectivity, today's so-called "smart devices" that are essentially smartphone-class computers could be replaced with dumb terminals that get their instructions from nearby edge computing systems.
- Machine-to-machine communications (M2M) enables scenarios where devices such as manufacturing robots can coordinate with one another for construction, assembly, and other tasks, under the collective guidance of an M2M hub at the 5G base station.

Cloud Computing

The internet is not just the conduit for content, but the facilitator of connectivity in wide-area networks (WAN). 5G wireless offers the potential for distributing cloud computing services much closer to users than most of Amazon's, Google's, or Microsoft's hyperscale data centers.

5G hugely impacts the performance of mobile and remote devices. Remote systems such as location tracking apps, home automation systems, and voice assistants, which are based on sensors, will use 5G to transfer a huge amount of data ten times faster than 4G networks.(Kumar et al., 2015d)

This is the edge computing scenario you may have heard about: Bringing processing power forward, closer to the customer, minimizing latencies caused by distance. If latencies can be eliminated just enough, applications that currently require PCs could be relocated to smaller devices -- perhaps even mobile devices that, unto themselves, have less processing power than the average smartphone.

VR and AR

Virtual reality (**VR**) is a simulated experience that can be similar to or completely different from the real world. Applications of virtual reality can include entertainment (i.e. video games) and educational purposes (i.e. medical or military training) (Punhani et al., 2019).

Augmented reality (AR) is an interactive experience of a real-world environment where the objects that reside in the real world are enhanced by computer-generated perceptual information, sometimes across multiple sensory modalities, including visual, auditory.

5G would allow for higher flexibility in use cases. AR is commonly used on smartphones or tablets in museums to present additional content for exhibits, or for interior design, allowing shoppers to virtually place furniture in a room to see how it matches. With 5G, the ability to use AR in live, outdoor environments away from reliable Wi-Fi signals can influence the types of interactions and integrations that developers can build(Kumar et al., 2014).

Vehicle Management

Vehicles are a very common parts of our life as we are completely dependent on it. But in India, we usually face a lot of issues on points of its maintenance as well as servicing, which may result to unnecessary problems like delay in servicing, in-between vehicle part damage, overheating, etc.

Figure 6. Vehicle Management in Fourth Generation of Industrial Revolution

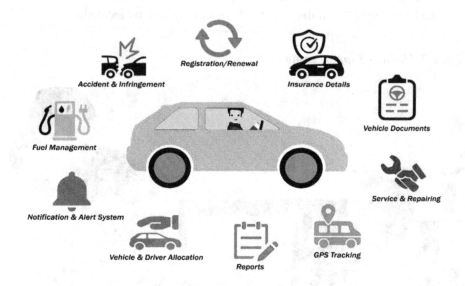

The solution is simple but hard to implement for which our vehicle system has to be capable of reporting every bit of its information to the company... And company will take care and analyze the vehicle reporting and informs the owner of the vehicle to reach the nearest service center as soon as possible. And without any delay the company already sent the required parts to that center for minimum delay in servicing (Kumar et al., 2015a).

It can help to maximize the utilization capacity of our vehicles as well as unnecessary delays too but for it we need fast network which works without permission and have a capacity to work on real time(Kumar et al., 2013). These things is present in 5G networking.

It also brings a door open to the possibilities of further development in vehicles like driverless cars, etc.

Medical Support

The availability of low-latency connectivity in rural areas would revolutionize critical care treatment for individuals nationwide.

No longer would patients in small towns be forced to upend their lives and relocate to bigger cities, away from the livelihoods they know and love, just to receive the level of care to which they should be entitled.

As recent trials in Mississippi are proving, connectivity at 5G levels enables caregivers in rural and remote areas to receive real-time instruction and support from the finest surgeons in the world, wherever they may be located.

Figure 7. Medical Support using 5G

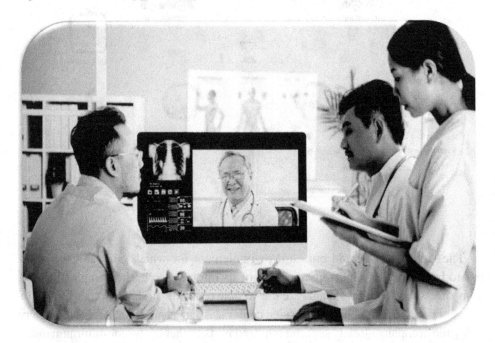

Disadvantages of 5G Technologies

Along with great benefits, Technologies are also encoded with some disadvantages too. Similarly, 5G also has some disadvantages too which are as follows:

- Signal connectivity falls in closed rooms because of which the multiple routers and connectors are needed to maintain the connectivity.
- Technology is still under process and research on its viability is going on.
- The speed, this technology is claiming seems difficult to achieve (in future, it might be) because of the incompetent technological support in most parts of the world.
- Many of the old devices would not be competent to 5G, hence, all of them need to be replaced with new one — expensive deal.
- Developing infrastructure needs high cost.
- Security and privacy issue yet to be solved.

Figure 8. Concern Areas in 5G Technology

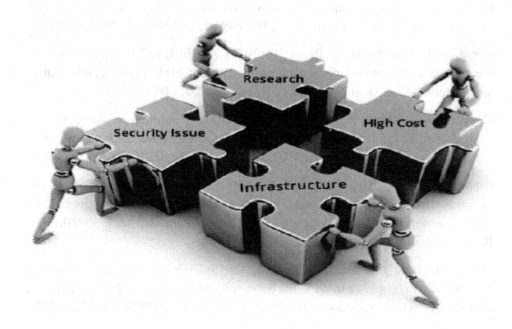

CONCLUSION

Through this paper, we have get knowledge about the various needs, facilities, advantages and disadvantages associated with the 5G communication technologies, along with communication development over ages and the type of technologies associated with it such as IoT, Cloud Computing, etc. This will help to us to design a dynamic self-adjustable network system of SDN to maximize the output and efficiency of the network. So, through this, in our future work, we are focusing on the same to design the SDN based dynamic network system along with the testing of its efficiency and reliabilities.

REFERENCES

Balabanov, G., & Mirtchev, M. (2014). Dynamic queue management of partial shared buffer with mixed priority for QoS guarantee in LTE uplink. Elektrotechnica & Elektronica (E+E), 49, 1–2.

Balabanov, G., & Mirtchev, S. (2008). A priority traffic models in wideband mobile networks. *Proceedings of XLIII International Scientific Conference on Information, Communication and Energy Systems and Technologies—ICEST 2008, 1*, 470–473.

Batalla, J. M., Kantor, M., & Mavromoustakis, C. X. (2015). A novel methodology for efficient throughput evaluation in virtualized routers. *2015 IEEE International Conference on Communications (ICC)*, 6899–6905. 10.1109/ICC.2015.7249425

Bernardo, V., Curado, M., & Braun, T. (2014). An IEEE 802.11 energy efficient mechanism for continuous media applications. Sustainable Computing: Informatics and Systems, 4(2), 106–117. doi:10.1016/j.suscom.2014.04.001

Ciobanu, R. I., Marin, R. C., & Dobre, C. (2015). Opportunistic dissemination using context-based data aggregation over interest spaces. *2015 IEEE International Conference on Communications (ICC)*, 1219–1225. 10.1109/ICC.2015.7248489

Cippitelli, E., Gasparrini, S., & Gambi, E. (2015). Time synchronization and data fusion for RGB-depth cameras and inertial sensors in AAL applications. *2015 IEEE International Conference on Communication Workshop (ICCW)*. 10.1109/ICCW.2015.7247189

Dias, J. A., Rodrigus, J. J., & Kumar, N. (2015). A hybrid system to stimulate selfish nodes to cooperate in vehicular delay-tolerant networks. *IEEE International Conference on Communications (ICC)*, 5910–5915. 10.1109/ICC.2015.7249264

Garcia, N. M., Garcia, N. C., & Sousa, P. (2014). TICE.Healthy: A perspective on medical information integration. *2014 IEEE-EMBS International Conference on Biomedical and Health Informatics (BHI)*, 464–467. 10.1109/BHI.2014.6864403

Garcia, N. M., & Rodrigues, J. J. P. (2015). *Ambient Assisted Living*. CRC Press. doi:10.1201/b18520

Goleva, R., Atamian, D., & Mirtchev, S. (2015). Traffic analyses and measurements: technological dependability. In G. Mastorakis, C. Mavromoustakis, & E. Pallis (Eds.), *Resource Management of Mobile Cloud Computing Networks and Environments* (pp. 122–173). Information Science Reference. doi:10.4018/978-1-4666-8225-2.ch006

Goleva, R., Stainov, R., & Savov, A. (2014). Reliable platform for enhanced living environment. In *Mobile Networks and Management, First COST Action IC1303 AAPELE Workshop Element 2014, in Conjunction with MONAMI 2014 Conference, Wurzburg, 24 Sept 2014*. Springer. 10.1007/978-3-319-16292-8_23

Goleva, R., Stainov, R., & Savov, A. (2015). Automated ambient open platform for enhanced living environment. In S. Loshkovska & S. Koceski (Eds.), *ICT Innovations 2015, Advances in Intelligent Systems and Computing, ELEMENT 2015* (Vol. 399, pp. 255–264). Springer. doi:10.1007/978-3-319-25733-4_26

Grguric, A., Huljenic, D., & Mosmondor, M. (2015). AAL ontology: from design to validation. *2015 IEEE International Conference on Communication Workshop (ICCW)*, 234–239. 10.1109/ICCW.2015.7247184

Han, G., Jiang, J., Sun, N., & Shu, L. (2015). Secure communication for underwater acoustic sensor networks. *IEEE Communications Magazine*, *53*(8), 54–60. doi:10.1109/MCOM.2015.7180508

Jarschel, M., Zinner, T., Hossfeld, T., Tran-Gia, P., & Kellerer, W. (2014). Interfaces, attributes, and use cases: A compass for SDN. *IEEE Communications Magazine*, *52*(6), 210–217. doi:10.1109/MCOM.2014.6829966

Kryftis, Y., Mavromoustakis, C. X., & Mastorakis, G. (2015). Resource usage prediction algorithms for optimal selection of multimedia content delivery methods. *2015 IEEE International Conference on Communications (ICC)*, 5903–5909. 10.1109/ICC.2015.7249263

Kumar, S., Ranjan, P., & Ramaswami, R. (2014). Energy optimization in distributed localized wireless sensor networks. *International conference ICICT-2014.*

Kumar, S., Ranjan, P., Ramaswami, R., & Tripathy, M. R. (2015a). Energy aware distributed protocol for heterogeneous wireless sensor network. *International Journal of Control and Automation, 8*(10), 421-430. . doi:10.14257/ijca.2015.8.10.38

Kumar, S., Ranjan, P., Ramaswami, R., & Tripathy, M. R. (2015b). An NS3 Implementation of physical layer based on 802.11 for utility maximization of WSN. *IEEE International Conference CICN.*

Kumar, S., Ranjan, P., Ramaswami, R., & Tripathy, M. R. (2015c). A Utility Maximization Approach to MAC Layer Channel Access and Forwarding. *PIERS Draft Proceedings.*

Kumar, S., Ranjan, P., Ramaswami, R., & Tripathy, M. R. (2015d). EMEEDP: Enhanced multi-hop energy efficient distributed protocol for heterogeneous wireless sensor network. *International conference CSNT-2015.*

Kumar, S., Ranjan, P., Ramaswami, R., & Tripathy, M. R. (2017a). Energy Efficient Multichannel MAC Protocol for High Traffic Applications in Heterogeneous Wireless Sensor Networks. Recent Advances in Electrical & Electronic Engineering, 10(3), 223-232. doi:10.2174/2352096510666170601090202

Kumar, S., Ranjan, P., Ramaswami, R., & Tripathy, M. R. (2017b). Resource efficient clustering and next hop knowledge based routing in multiple heterogeneous wireless sensor networks. *International Journal of Grid and High Performance Computing, 9*(2), 1–20. doi:10.4018/IJGHPC.2017040101

Kumar, S., Rao, A. L. N., & Ramaswami, R. (2013). Localization Technique in Wireless Sensor Network Using Directionally Information. *International conference at AKGEC Ghaziabad.*

Mirtchev, S., & Goleva, R. (2009). Discrete time single server queueing model whit a multimodal packet size distribution. *Proceedings of a Conjoint Seminar "Modelling and Control of Information Processes"*, 83–101.

Punhani, Faujdar, & Kumar. (2019). Design and Evaluation of Cubic Torus Network-on-Chip Architecture. *International Journal of Innovative Technology and Exploring Engineering, 8*(6).

Wu, D., He, J., Wang, H., Wang, C., & Wang, R. (2015). A hierarchical packet forwarding mechanism for energy harvesting wireless sensor networks. *IEEE Communications Magazine, 53*(8), 92–98. doi:10.1109/MCOM.2015.7180514

Yang, Q., & Wang, H. (2015). Toward trustworthy vehicular social networks. *IEEE Communications Magazine, 53*(8), 42–47. doi:10.1109/MCOM.2015.7180506

Yu, C., Chen, C. Y., & Chao, H. C. (2015). Verifiable, privacy-assured, and accurate signal collection for cloud-assisted wireless sensor networks. *IEEE Communications Magazine, 53*(8), 48–53. doi:10.1109/MCOM.2015.7180507

Chapter 7
Priority Encoding–Based Cluster Head Selection Approach in Wireless Sensor Networks

Pooja Chaturvedi

 https://orcid.org/0000-0001-5207-2696
School of Management Sciences, Varanasi, India

Ajai Kumar Daniel
Madan Mohan Malaviya University of Technology, Gorakhpur, India

ABSTRACT

Wireless sensor networks have gotten significant attention in recent times due to their applicability in diverse fields. Energy conservation is a major challenge in wireless sensor networks. Apart from energy conservation, monitoring quality of the environmental phenomenon is also considered a major issue. The approaches that addressed both these problems are of great significance. One such approach is node scheduling, which aims to divide the node set into a number of subsets such that each subset can monitor a given set of points known as targets. The chapter proposes a priority coding-based cluster head selection approach as an extension of the energy efficient coverage protocol (EECP). The priority of the nodes is determined on the basis of residual energy (RE), distance (D), noise factor (N), node degree (Nd), and link quality (LQ). The analytical results show that the proposed protocol improves the network performance by reducing the overhead by a factor of 70% and hence reduces the energy consumption by a factor of 70%.

DOI: 10.4018/978-1-7998-4685-7.ch007

INTRODUCTION

Wireless sensor network is an autonomous network consisting of a number of sensor nodes observing an environmental phenomenon through the collaborative communication. The wireless sensor networks are also exposed to various constraints in terms of bandwidth, storage and processing capabilities. In a sensor network the nodes are often deployed unattended for long duration and frequent recharging of battery is not always possible. Hence energy conservation approaches are of great significance Akylidiz (2002), Yick (2008).

The coverage problem is also a major research field in the context of WSNs Rourke (1987), Gregg (1998), Gage (1992). The coverage problem defined as the duration until the given point of interest is within the sensing area of at least one sensor node. The coverage problem is usually affected by a number of factors such as node deployment random or deterministic and homogeneous/heterogeneous, presence of obstacles in the terrain, sensing and communication ranges etc. The coverage problem is usually studied from three point of view: area coverage which ensures the coverage of each point within a target region, point/target coverage which implies the coverage of a set of specified points and barrier coverage are used to determine the trajectory of the moving intruder (Mulligan (2010), Thai (2008).

The organization of the paper is as follows: related work in section 2, network model and design issues in section 3, problem formulation in section 4, proposed pattern based clustering approach in section 5, experimental results in section 6 and section 7 concludes the paper.

RELATED WORKS

Minimizing the energy consumption of the sensor network is a major research challenge. There are various energy efficient approaches proposed in the literature such as energy efficient routing, clustering, data aggregation etc. The energy efficient routing algorithms are basically concerned with the determination of optimal routes along which the energy consumption is least and network performance is enhanced. The clustering approaches aim to divide the set of nodes into a number of clusters such that the similarity within the cluster is usually greater than between the clusters. In each cluster usually a CH is selected which is responsible for the data collection and aggregation on the sensed data by the cluster members. However if a same node is selected as a CH then it will exhaust it's energy sooner. So dynamic clustering are also considered. The data aggregation based approaches aim to reduce the number of bits required to transmit a data packet. The pioneer clustering approach is considered as Low Energy Adaptive Clustering Hierarchy (LEACH) protocol for the static network Heinzelman (2000). The LEACH protocol operates in rounds and each round is divided into two phases as: setup phase and steady state phase. The setup phase consists of the determination of CHs which will remain constant till the network lifetime. The steady phase consists of sensing and communication functionalities. For the cluster head selection, each node generates a random number between 0 to 1 and it is compared with the predefined threshold value in the Equation 1:

$$Th(x) = \begin{cases} \dfrac{pr}{1 - pr\left[r \bmod \left(\dfrac{1}{pr} \right) \right]}, & \text{if } x \notin CH' \\ 0, & \text{otherwise} \end{cases} \tag{1}$$

Where pr is the percentage of the CHs, r is the round number and CH' is the number of nodes which are not selected as CHs in the previous $\dfrac{1}{pr}$ number of rounds. The scalability of the LEACH protocol is low as it considers CH as fixed. There are various variations proposed in the literature as in which aims to enhance the performance of the LEACH protocol Rehman (2019), Mhatre (2004), Ahmed (2013), Deng (2011), Kim (2006), Sarma 2010, Anitha (2013).

The different approaches for clustering has also been considered in the literature such as in authors have proposed region based clustering which aims to divide the target region into number of regions. The CH selection process has also been investigated on the basis of several parameters such as residual energy, distance between the CH and the base station, centrality, node degree, survivability factor etc. Few approaches have also considered the clustering process for heterogeneous nodes such as normal and advanced nodes Singhal (2014), Maurya (2014), Maurya (2014), Maurya (2014).

Coverage is another major research challenge. Target coverage problem consist of monitoring a set of predefined target for as long as possible with the objective of maximizing the network lifetime while considering the resource constraints. The target coverage problem can be defined into various ways in the literature such as energy efficient target coverage; which aims to minimize the energy consumption in the process of target coverage, connected target coverage; which aims to provide coverage of the targets such that there is always a path from the sensor nodes towards the base station. The target coverage approaches can be classified into three approaches: sensing range adjustment based approaches, geometrical construct based approaches, deployment based approaches and node scheduling based approaches. The sensing range adjustment based approaches aim to adjust the sensing range of the nodes depending on the residual energy of the node. The geometrical construct based approaches aim to utilize the Voronoi diagrams and Delanauy triangulation based approaches to identify the least covered areas and maximize the coverage of the region of interest. The deployment based approaches aim to determine the optimal location of dispatch and deployment of the sensor nodes such that coverage is maximized and the deployment cost is reduced. The node scheduling based approaches aims to put the redundant sensor nodes in least energy consuming state. The redundant sensor nodes are those sensor nodes which provide coverage to those areas/points which can be observed by neighboring nodes. These approaches schedule the nodes to exist between two working state as active/ sleep state. This approach puts the nodes in sleep state depending on some criteria to reduce the energy consumption and hence improve the network performance as compared to the approach in which all the nodes are activated simultaneously. There are various scheduling approaches proposed in the literature as in (Carbunar (2006)-Wang (2006). In Cardei (2005), authors have determined a number of disjoint set cover to address the target coverage problem in which a node can participate in only one set cover. The authors have formulated the target coverage problem as integer linear programming problem. The authors have also proved that the determination of optimal number of set covers such that network lifetime is maximized is NP hard. In Cardei (2005), authors have improved the Disjoint Set cover (DSC) problem as Maximum Set Cover problem (MSC) by allowing the sensor nodes to participate in any number of set covers restricted with the initial battery level of the nodes. It has been found from the literature that the distributed approaches for node scheduling approaches are considered more efficient rather than the centralized approach. The distributed and localized algorithm operates on the basis of the information collected through nearby neighbors whereas the centralized algorithms rely for the decision making on the central node.

Several coverage problem approaches also emphasize on the relationship between the sensing and the communication range of the sensor nodes as in Tian (2002). In this authors have proved that a convex region having k coverage is said to be connected if the communication range of the sensor nodes is twice the sensing range. Several approaches have studied the target coverage problem as Q-coverage problem where target point is expected to have different levels of coverage. The various factors which influence the coverage computation approaches are as: deployment, sensing model, coverage level, algorithm, and connectivity and QoS requirements. The deployment of the network may be either random or deterministic. In the random deployment strategies the nodes are deployed at random locations which results in the sparse/ dense covered regions in the target area. The sparsely deployed network often results in coverage hole which implies that there are regions which are not covered by any sensor node. The deterministic deployment approaches aim to deploy the nodes at predetermined points. The deterministic deployment may be grid based triangular or hexagonal deployment. These deployment techniques are practically not feasible. The sensor node in the sensor network is usually modeled as a circular disk and the node is placed at the center of the disk. The area of this disk represents the sensing range of the sensor node. The sensing model defines the detection capability of the sensor node based on distance of the target point from the sensor node. The sensing model may be either Boolean, Probabilistic or Exponential. In the Boolean sensing model the sensor node can detect the events within its sensing range with full probability and with 0 probability outside it. In the probabilistic sensing model the sensing model decays as a probabilistic function with the increasing distance. In the exponential sensing model, the sensing capability of the node is represented as an exponential function which decays exponentially with the increase in the distance. Coverage level of a target region is usually represented as the number of nodes which are able to monitor entire area or specific point. K-coverage means every point of the target region is covered by k number of sensor nodes. Coverage problem ensures the monitoring of the target region for as long as possible whereas connectivity problems are concerned with the assurance of the path from the sensor nodes towards the base station.

Research Gap and Motivation

The existing literature lacks the consideration of QoS requirement while addressing the target coverage problem. Area coverage problem has been widely studied in the literature. Further most of the coverage approaches in the literature considers the Boolean coverage model which represents the absolute values of coverage extent. The closest work related to our work is in Taghikhaki (2013), in which the trust based probabilistic coverage protocol (TBCA) for target coverage is proposed. This paper aims to maximize the number of set covers on the basis of trust values and coverage probabilities. However in this work only communication trust is considered. So in order to enhance the performance of TBCA we have incorporated the aggregated trust values on the basis of direct trust, indirect trust and recommendation trust in Energy Efficient Coverage Protocol (EECP) Chaturvedi (2015). The EECP protocol determines the number of set covers on the basis of probability of event detection, trust worthiness of the nodes and the contribution of the nodes. The results show that the proposed protocol enhances the network performance in terms of network performance, reliability and energy conservation.

The motivation of this work is to develop a node scheduling strategy to provide the target coverage while considering the QoS requirements and also consider the realistic coverage model as an extension of EECP protocol. In EECP, authors have proposed a hybrid node scheduling strategy to determine a number of set covers to be activated periodically as determined by the base station. Set cover is a subset of the nodes which can monitor all the targets while considering the required confidence level by considering the coverage probability and trust values of the nodes. In the scheduling based approach only a subset of node is activated while other nodes are kept in low energy consuming state/sleep state. This approach has been proved to be effective in overcoming both the problems of coverage and energy conservation. In the proposed protocol we aim to reduce the overhead involved in the calculation of the trust values of the nodes by dividing the nodes into a number of clusters where cluster head (CH) is responsible for determining the trust values of the nodes Jiang (2014), Lim (2010), Saaty (1990). The number of bits used to determine the CH is reduced by using the proposed encoding based approach, hence energy consumption is reduced and network lifetime is prolonged.

Network Model and Design Issues

The target coverage problem objective is to maximize the network lifetime in terms of duration of observation of targets such that each target is monitored with required quality and for the longest possible time. For a sensor network consisting of *sn* sensor nodes and *tr* distinct targets to monitor, following assumptions have been considered:

1. The sensor nodes and targets are deployed randomly in the two dimensional region.
2. The communication and sensing region of the nodes is considered as circular and the sensor nodes are placed at the center of the sensing region.
3. The nodes in the network are homogeneous and have the same initial energy.
4. The base station, nodes and targets are considered to be as static.
5. Each node possesses the location information of every node and target node.
6. The probabilistic coverage model for the detection of an event for each is considered. It implies that the detection probability of the sensor node is not in Boolean (0/1) form but it decreases exponentially with the distance.

For example consider a network of 4 targets as $tr = \{tr_1, tr_2, tr_3, tr_4\}$ and 3 sensor nodes as $sn = \{sn_1, sn_2, sn_3\}$. If the nodes can monitor the targets as $sn_1 = \{tr_1, tr_3\}$ and $sn_2 = \{tr_2, tr_1\}$, $sn_3 = \{tr_2, tr_3, tr_4\}$, then we obtain two set covers as $c_1 = \{sn_1, sn_3\}$ and $c_2 = \{sn_2, sn_3\}$. If the initial energy of the nodes is 1J then the network lifetime is 1 time unit if all the nodes are activated simultaneously. But if we schedule the nodes in the set covers such that at a time only one set cover is active then the network lifetime is computed as 2 time units.

PROBLEM FORMULATION

For a network of *sn* sensor nodes and *tr* targets the objective of the node scheduling protocol is to maximize the network lifetime of the network which depends on the activation duration of the set covers. Let the number of set covers are determined as C and the activation duration of the set covers are at1, at2,....atC. Then the target coverage problem is formulated as:

$$\max \sum_{i=1}^{C} at_i \tag{2}$$

such that

$$P_{obs}(j) \geq th \quad \forall j \in tr \tag{3}$$

and

$$\sum_{i \in C} A_{jk} \times at_i \leq 1 \tag{4}$$

which implies that the observation probability of each target is greater than the required coverage threshold (*th*) and the activation duration of a node in all the set covers is less than the initial battery level of the node. The observation probability of a target *j* with respect to a set of nodes *nc* is determined as:

$$P_{obs}(j) = 1 - \prod_{k \in nc} \left(1 - P_{obs}^{jk}\right) \tag{5}$$

where $nc_j = \{l$ such that $cvpr > 0$ and nc_j is active$\}$ where $l \in sn$ and *cvpr* represents the coverage probability of the node. A_{jk} is a boolen variable which represents the active status of the nodes as:

$$A_{jk} = \begin{pmatrix} 1, \text{ if node j can monitor a target and is in active state} \\ 0, \text{ if node j cannot monitor a target and is in sleep state} \end{pmatrix} \tag{6}$$

The observation probability of a target by a node is determined as:

$$P_{obs}^{jk} = \text{cov}(j,k) \times t_k \tag{7}$$

Where $\text{cov}(j,k)$ represents the coverage probability of target j with respect to node k and t_k is trust value of the node k.

The coverage probability is determined as:

$$\text{cov}(k,j) = \begin{cases} 0, & \text{if } r_{sn} + r_e \leq dis\left(sn_k, tr_j\right) \\ e^{-\mu\alpha^\beta}, & \text{if } r_{sn} - r_e \leq dis\left(sn_k, tr_j\right) \leq r_{sn} + r_e \\ 1, & \text{if } r_{sn} - r_e \geq dis\left(sn_k, tr_j\right) \end{cases} \tag{8}$$

Where $dis\left(sn_k, tr_j\right)$ represents the distance of the node sn_k and the target tr_j

Energy Model

The sensor network consists of a number of tiny low devices known as Motes/sensor nodes. The sensor node consists of sensing unit, processing unit and communication unit. Some additional components are also present in the sensor nodes as power management, localization unit. The sensor node is responsible for performing the sensing of the data from the environment, processing and communicating towards the base station. The communication of the sensed data from the sensor nodes towards the base station is usually performed in collaboration between the nodes. In performing these tasks sensors consume energy. Based on different tasks the sensor node may exist in different states as sensing, idle and sleep state. It has been found that the sensor nodes consume highest energy during the communication activity. Energy models are used for determining the energy consumption of the nodes in different tasks and states Heinzelman (2000).

The energy consumption of node i is determined as:

$$RE_i = E_i - e_i \tag{9}$$

Where E_i is the initial energy of the node, e_i is the consumed energy of the node in the last communication and RE_i is the residual energy of the node.

The total energy consumption of the node is determined as the summation of energy consumed during sensing, processing, receiving and transmitting activities.

$$e_i = \left(e_s \times (n_o) + e_p \times (n_o + n_r) + e_t \times (n_o + n_r) \times \alpha_g + e_r \times (n_r)\right) \times d_b \tag{10}$$

Where e_s, e_p, e_t and e_r are the energy consumed in the sensing, processing, transmitting and receiving activities respectively for a data packet of d_b bits and no and nr are the number of originated and relayed data packets respectively. α_g is the aggregation ratio of the data packets.

The energy consumption during the transmission of d_b data bits for a distance *dis* is determined as:

$$e_{t_{ij}} = e_{telec} \times d_b + e_{tamp} \times d_b \times dis \tag{11}$$

$$e_{t_{ij}} = \begin{cases} d_b \times e_{elec} + d_b \times \varepsilon_f \times (dis)^2 & \text{if } dis < d_{th} \\ d_b \times e_{elec} + d_b \times \varepsilon_{mp} \times (dis)^4 & \text{if } dis \geq d_{th} \end{cases} \tag{12}$$

Where e_{elec} and e_{amp} are the electronic and amplifier energy required for transmitting d_b data bit packets at a distance dis. d_{th} represents the threshold distance. ε_f and ε_{mp} represents the free space and multipath fading constants.

PROPOSED PROTOCOL

The proposed protocol for target coverage works in rounds where each round is divided into phases: setup phase, sensing phase and transmission phase as shown in the Fig.1.

Figure 1. Phases of the Proposed Protocol

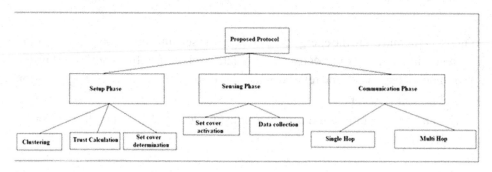

The setup phase is further divided into phases as: clustering, trust calculation and set cover determination. In the clustering phase the nodes are divided into a number of clusters using the proposed approach. In the trust calculation the trust value of the node for the target monitoring is determined on the basis of direct trust, indirect trust and recommendation trust. In the set cover determination phase the nodes are divided into a number of set covers which are scheduled by the base station to perform the sensing operation. The sensor nodes collect the data from the environmental phenomenon in the sensing phase. In the data transmission phase, the nodes transfer the sensed data towards the base station.

The various parameters used for the CH election are defined as follows:

Residual energy (RE)

It represents the remaining energy of the node and is determined as:

$$RE_i = \frac{E_i - e_i}{r} \tag{13}$$

Where E_i is the initial energy of the node i, e_i is the energy consumption of the node i and r is the round number.

Distance (D)

It represents the distance of the base station from the node. The node having the smaller distance towards the base station is preferred.

Noise factor (N)

It represents the degree of unwanted signal in the received signal.

Node degree (N_d)

It represents the number of nodes within the communication range of the sensor node. If a node can directly communicate with 5 nodes then node degree is considered as 5. In densely connected network the node degree of a node tends to be larger as compared to the sparsely connected network.

Link Quality (LQ)

It represents the reliability of the network in terms of number of packets transmitted to the successfully received packets. The higher the number of successfully received packets higher will be link quality.

The flow chart of the proposed cluster head selection protocol is shown in the Fig.2.

In the above figure P_i is the encoded pattern value for the node i and B_i is the benchmark pattern advertised by the Base station.

In this paper we use the priority based approach to select the nodes to participate in the CH selection. The proposed clustering approach consists of three phases as: CH selection, cluster formation and the data transmission phase. In the initial phase all the nodes have same initial energy so every node constitutes a cluster head. For the subsequent stages the CH are determined on the basis of encoded priority.

CH SELECTION

The node's priority is determined on the basis of residual energy (RE), distance (D), Noise factor (N), Node degree (Nd) and Link Quality (LQ). Based on the threshold values the priority is assigned to each node as low, medium or high as shown in the Table 1.

The node status is determined using the three step process as: 1. Priority Encoding 2. Comparison 3. CH selection.

Figure 2. Flow Chart of the Proposed CH election Protocol

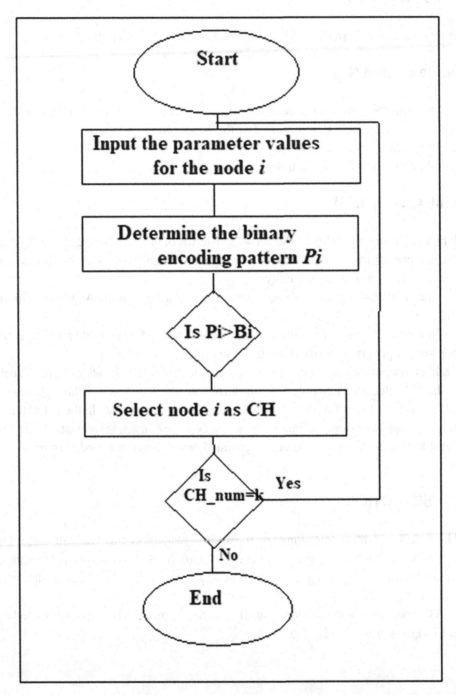

Table 1. Priority vs Threshold values

Threshold Value (%)	<40	40-60	60-80	>80
Priority	Low	Medium	High	Very High

Priority Encoding

In this phase the priority of node is encoded in binary form for each parameter, so as to reduce the number of bits needed to represent node's status as shown in the Table 2.

Table 2. Encoding table

Parameter	Priority	Priority	Priority	Priority
Residual Energy	Low	Medium	High	Very High
Noise Factor	Low	Medium	High	Very High
Node degree	Low	Medium	High	Very High
Distance	Very High	High	Medium	Low
Link Quality	Low	Medium	High	Very High
Binary Form	**00**	**01**	**10**	**11**

Comparison

In the second step the encoded priority is compared with the benchmark encoding provided by the base station. The benchmark is the highest encoded priority for that round. The values of benchmark encoding keeps changing as the network operate.

Cluster Head Selection

After the comparison of the encoded pattern of the nodes with the benchmark pattern, the node is elected as CH. This process is repeated until desired number of cluster heads is computed.

Table 3. Simulation Setup

Attribute	Value
Target area	100*100 square meter
Number of Nodes	20~100
Number of Targets	10
Sensing Range	5m
Communication Range	10m
Initial energy of the nodes	3J
Coverage Threshold Value	0.5
Energy Consumption Rate	0.3

Cluster Formation

After the determination of the CHs, the nodes are added to the clusters. The CHs broadcast their status to the neighboring nodes and the nodes join the CH whose distance from it is minimum.

Data Communication Phase

In this phase the CHs are responsible for the determination of trust values of the nodes based on the communication between the nodes. The aggregated trust value is determined using the direct trust value, recommendation trust and indirect trust. If the nodes are directly connected then the direct trust between the nodes is considered on the basis of Data Trust, Communication Trust and Energy Trust. If the nodes are connected via neighbors then the recommendation of the neighboring is also considered in determination of the trust values of the nodes. If there is no direct trust/ recommendation trust between the nodes then indirect trust is considered.

Table 4. Cluster members in different clusters

Cluster Id	Cluster Members	Cluster id	Cluster members
C1	{1, 3, 5,23,24}	C6	{17, 27, 45, 50}
C2	(2, 7, 14, 29, 30,44}	C7	{5,13,20, 27,35,43}
C3	(6, 12,15, 39, 40, 47}	C8	{11,19,24,37,46,}
C4	{3,10,21,26, 31,36}	C9	{4,18,34,38,41,}
C5	{8,16,22,28,32, 48}	C10	{9,25,33,42, 49}

Table 5. Parameter values of cluster members C5

Node/ Parameter	Residual Energy(RE)	Noise Factor (N)	Node Degree (Nd)	Distance (D)	Link Quality (LQ)
8	0.40	0.1	0.3	0.80	0.2
16	0.35	0.5	0.6	0.95	0.3
22	0.67	0.9	0.7	0.52	0.7
28	0.73	0.3	0.1	0.34	0.6
32	0.52	0.2	0.4	0.12	0.1
48	0.82	0.7	0.5	0.23	0.4

Table 6. Encoded pattern for cluster members in cluster 5

Node Id	Pattern
8	0000000100
16	0001100000
22	1011101000
28	1000000010
32	0100100000
48	1110010001

Table 7. Cluster heads in different clusters

Cluster Id	Cluster Head	Cluster Id	Cluster Head
C1	23	C6	17
C2	7	C7	5
C3	12	C8	37
C4	21	C9	34
C5	48	C10	42

After the completion of clustering phase the nodes are included in the set cover based on their coverage probability and trust values as in [9]. The base station determines a schedule according to which the nodes are activated.

Table 8. Comparison of overhead

Method	Overhead
EECP	1225
Proposed	100

EXPERIMENTAL RESULTS

Let us consider the network of 100*100 meter^2 dimension and 50 nodes are deployed to monitor 10 targets. The other simulation parameters are as shown in the Table 3.

Considering the expected number of cluster heads is similar to the number of targets monitored. Therefore, the number of clusters is 10. Let the number of nodes are equally distributed and randomly selected on the basic of different parameters in each cluster shown in Table 4:

Let us consider the cluster members C5 from Table 4 for different values parameters are as shown in Table 5:

Based on these parameters the pattern code for each node is represented as shown in Table 6:

If the benchmark pattern advertised for this round by the base station is 100001110 node 48 will be elected as the cluster head for the cluster c5.

Figure 3. Comparison of overhead vs. number of nodes

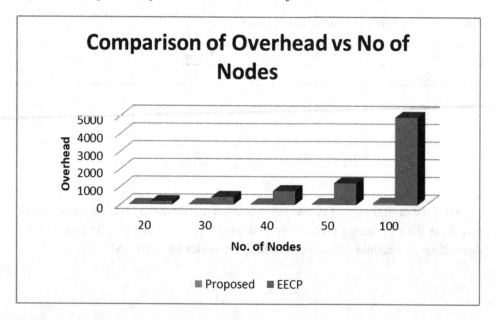

Table 9. Node coverage set for each target

Target	Nodes
P1	{C1,C2}
P2	{C4,C3}
P3	{C2,C4,C8}
P4	{C6, C4}
P5	{C9, C1}
P6	{C10, C4, C7}
P7	{C8, C5}
P8	[C7,C2}
P9	{C7,C3}
P10	{C5, C8, C9}

Similarly we can find the CH for the remaining clusters as shown in the Table 7:

For the determination of cluster heads each nodes transmits two control messages: one for informing the neighbor nodes, the pattern of the nodes and second is acknowledgment message. The overhead of selecting the cluster heads is as shown in Table 8:

Hence, the overhead in the cluster formation is reduced by a factor of 70% by using the proposed approach.

Table 10. Contribution of different cluster heads

Cluster Head	Contribution
C1	2
C2	3
C3	2
C4	3
C5	1
C6	1
C7	3
C8	3
C9	2
C10	1

Table 11. Residual energy of the cluster heads

Cluster Head	Residual energy
C1	0.6
C2	0.9
C3	1.8
C4	1.8
C5	2.1
C6	2.7
C7	0.6
C8	1.8
C9	2.4
C10	2.9

We have compared the overhead involved in CH selection by varying the number of nodes from 20 to 100 for the fixed number of targets as 10. The results are as shown in the Fig. 3.

We can observe from the Fig. that the overhead increases with the increasing number of nodes. The results show that the overhead is reduced significantly with the proposed approach as compared to EECP protocol.

Figure 4. Comparison of Residual Energy of Different CHs

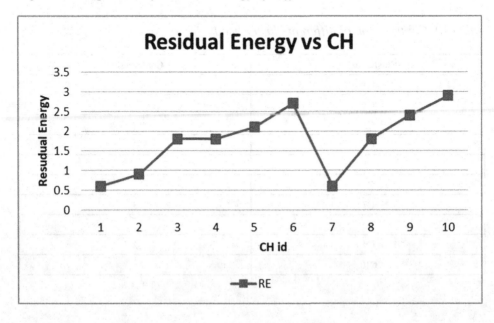

The CHs are grouped into a number of set covers such that all the targets are monitored. Based on the distance between the target and the sensor nodes the targets can be monitored as shown in the Table 9:

The contribution of various CH is as shown in the Table 10. It can be observed from the table that CHs C2, C4, C7 and C8 has the highest contribution as they can be included in 3 set covers.

The set covers determined in this case are 34. We have assumed the initial energy of the nodes as 3 J. The network lifetime on activating the set cover is determined as 20.5 time units.

The residual energy of the CHs are as in Table 11:

The comparison of the residual energy of the different CHs is as shown in the Fig. 4.

Based on the above figure, we can conclude that the node 1 and node 7 have least energy remaining whereas the node 10 has the highest residual energy as it has participated in the least number of set covers.

CONCLUSION AND FUTURE SCOPE

The paper proposed a priority based CH selection approach for the node scheduling based target coverage protocol for wireless sensor networks. The scheduling approach aims to maximize the network lifetime by dividing the set of nodes into a number of set covers which are activated alternatively such that network lifetime is maximized while providing the required coverage to all the targets. In this paper only the high priority nodes are participating in the cluster head selection. The priority of the nodes is determined on the basis of several parameters such as residual energy, distance, node degree, noise level and link quality. The base station generates a benchmark priority for every round against which the node's priority is compared. Based on the matching the node is permitted to participate in the CH selection process. The performance of the protocol in terms of overhead is also analyzed for varying the number of nodes from 20~100. The analytical results show that the proposed approach improves the network lifetime by reducing the network overhead by a factor of 70% and reducing the energy consumption by a factor of 70%.

The study of the effects of mobility of nodes and targets on the performance of the proposed protocol is our future work. In future we would also study the effect of heterogeneity in the proposed protocol.

REFERENCES

Ahmed, A., & Qazi, S. (2013). Cluster head selection algorithm for mobile wireless sensor networks. In *Open Source Systems and Technologies (ICOSST)* (pp. 120–125). IEEE. doi:10.1109/ICOSST.2013.6720617

Akyildiz, I. F., Su, W., Sankarasubramaniam, Y., & Cayirci, E. (2002). Wireless sensor networks: A survey'. *Computer Networks*, *38*(4), 393–422. doi:10.1016/S1389-1286(01)00302-4

Anitha, R. U., & Kamalakkannan, P. (2013). Energy efficient cluster head selection algorithm in mobile wireless sensor networks. *Computer Communication and Informatics (ICCCI), 2013 International Conference on*, 1-5.

Aurenhammer, F. (2001). Computational Geometry– Some Easy Questions and their Recent Solutions. *Journal of Universal Computer Science*, *7*(5).

Cărbunar, B., Grama, A., Vitek, J., & Cărbunar, O. (2006). Redundancy and coverage detection in sensor networks. *ACM Transactions on Sensor Networks*, *2*(1), 94–128. doi:10.1145/1138127.1138131

Cardei, M., & Du, D. Z. (2005). Improving wireless sensor network lifetime through power aware organization. *Wireless Networks*, *11*(3), 333–340. doi:10.100711276-005-6615-6

Cardei, M., Thai, M. T., Li, Y., & Wu, W. (2005). Energy-efficient target coverage in wireless sensor networks. In *Proceedings IEEE 24th Annual Joint Conference of the IEEE Computer and Communications Societies* (Vol. 3, pp. 1976-1984). IEEE. 10.1109/INFCOM.2005.1498475

Cardei, M., & Wu, J. (2006). Energy-efficient coverage problems in wireless ad-hoc sensor networks. *Computer Communications*, *29*(4), 413–420. doi:10.1016/j.comcom.2004.12.025

Chaturvedi, P., & Daniel, A. K. (2015). An energy efficient node scheduling protocol for target coverage in wireless sensor networks. *5th International Conference on Communication System and Network Technologies (CSNT-2015)*.

Chaturvedi, P., & Daniel, A. K. (2017). A novel sleep/wake protocol for target coverage based on trust evaluation for a clustered wireless sensor network', Int. J. *Mobile Network Design and Innovation*, *7*(3/4), 199–209. doi:10.1504/IJMNDI.2017.089301

Cheng, M., Ruan, L. & Wu, W. (2005). Achieving Minimum Coverage Breach under Bandwidth Constraints in Wireless Sensor Networks. *IEEE INFOCOM'05*.

Deng, S., Li, J., & Shen, L. (2011). Mobility-based clustering protocol for wireless sensor networks with mobile nodes. *IET Wireless Sensor Systems, 1*(1), 39-47. doi:10.1049/iet-wss.2010.0084

Gage, D. W. (1992). Command control for many-robot systems. *Proceedings of the Nineteenth Annual AUVS Technical Symposium*, 22–24.

Gregg, W. W., Esaias, W. E., Feldman, G. C., Frouin, R., Hooker, S. B., McClain, C. R., & Woodward, R. H. (1998). Coverage opportunities for global ocean color in a multimission era. *IEEE Transactions on Geoscience and Remote Sensing, 5*(5), 1620–1627. doi:10.1109/36.718865

Heinzelman, W. R., Chandrakasan, A., & Balakrishnan, H. (2000). Energy-efficient communication protocol for wireless micro-sensor networks. In *HICSS '00: Proceedings of the 33rd Hawaii International Conference on System Sciences-Volume 8*. IEEE Computer Society.

Howard, A., Matarić, M. J., & Sukhatme, G. S. (2002). Mobile Sensor Network Deployment using Potential Fields: A Distributed, Scalable Solution to the Area Coverage Problem. In H. Asama, T. Arai, T. Fukuda, & T. Hasegawa (Eds.), *Distributed Autonomous Robotic Systems 5*. Springer. doi:10.1007/978-4-431-65941-9_30

Jaggi, N., & Abouzeid, A. A. (2006, January). Energy-efficient connected coverage in wireless sensor networks. In *Proceedings of 4th Asian International Mobile Computing Conference* (pp. 77-86). Academic Press.

Jiang, J., Han, G., Wang, F., Shu, L., & Guizani, M. (2014). An efficient distributed trust model for wireless sensor networks. *IEEE Transactions on Parallel and Distributed Systems, 26*(5), 1228–1237. doi:10.1109/TPDS.2014.2320505

Kar, K., & Banerjee, S. (2003). *Node placement for connected coverage in sensor networks*. Academic Press.

Kim, D. S., & Chung, Y. J. (2006). Self-organization routing protocol supporting mobile nodes for wireless sensor network. Computer and Computational Sciences, 2006. doi:10.1109/IMSCCS.2006.265

Li, X. Y., Wan, P. J., & Frieder, O. (2003). Coverage in wireless ad hoc sensor networks. *IEEE Transactions on Computers, 52*(6), 753–763. doi:10.1109/TC.2003.1204831

Lim, H. S., Moon, Y. S., & Bertino, E. (2010). Provenance-based trustworthiness assessment in sensor networks. In *Proceedings of the Seventh International Workshop on Data Management for Sensor Networks* (pp. 2-7). Academic Press.

Maurya, S., & Daniel, A. K. (2014). Hybrid Routing Approach for Heterogeneous Wireless Sensor Networks Using Fuzzy Logic Technique. *Fourth International Conference on Advanced Computing & Communication Technologies*, 202-207, 10.1109/ACCT.2014.81

Maurya, S., & Daniel, A. K. (2014). An Energy Efficient Routing Protocol under Distance, Energy and Load Parameter for Heterogeneous Wireless Sensor Networks. *International Conference on Information Technology*, 161-166, 10.1109/ICIT.2014.63

Maurya, S., & Daniel, A. K. (2015). RBHR: Region-Based Hybrid Routing Protocol for Wireless Sensor Networks Using AI Technique. In *Proceedings of Fourth International Conference on Soft Computing for Problem Solving. Advances in Intelligent Systems and Computing, vol. 336.* Springer. 10.1007/978-81-322-2220-0_4

Mhatre, V., & Rosenberg, C. (2004). Design guidelines for wireless sensor networks: Communication, clustering and aggregation. *Ad Hoc Networks, 2*(1), 45–63. doi:10.1016/S1570-8705(03)00047-7

Mini, S., Udgata, S. K., & Sabat, S. L. (2013). Sensor deployment and scheduling for target coverage problem in wireless sensor networks. *IEEE Sensors Journal, 14*(3), 636–644. doi:10.1109/JSEN.2013.2286332

Mulligan, R., & Ammari, H. M. (2010). Coverage in wireless sensor networks: a survey. *Network Protocols and Algorithms, 2*(2).

O'Rourke, J. (1987). *Art Gallery Theorems and Algorithms.* Oxford University Press.

Rehman, E., Sher, M., Naqvi, S. H. A., Khan, K. B., & Ullah, K. (2019). Secure Cluster-Head Selection Algorithm Using Pattern for Wireless Mobile Sensor Networks. *Tehnicki Vjesnik (Strojarski Fakultet), 26*(2), 302–311.

Saaty, T. L. (1990). How to make a decision. The Analytical Hierarchy Process. *European Journal of Operational Research, 48*(1), 9–26. doi:10.1016/0377-2217(90)90057-I

Sarma, H. K. D., Kar, A., & Mall, R. (2010). Energy efficient and reliable routing for mobile wireless sensor networks. *2010 International Conference on Distributed Computing in Sensor Systems Workshops (DCOSSW 2010)*, 1-6. 10.1109/DCOSSW.2010.5593277

Shakkottai, S., Srikant, R., & Shroff, N. (2003). Unreliable Sensor Grids: Coverage, Connectivity and Diameter. *Proc. of Twenty-Second Annual Joint Conference of the IEEE Computer and Communications Societies*, 2, 1073-1083. 10.1109/INFCOM.2003.1208944

Shen, X., Chen, J., Zhi, W., & Sun, Y. (2006). Grid Scan: A Simple and Effective Approach for Coverage Issue in Wireless Sensor Networks. *Proc. Of IEEE International Communications Conference*, 8, 3480-3484. 10.1109/ICC.2006.255611

Singhal, S., & Daniel, A. K. (2014). Cluster head selection protocol under node degree, competence level and goodness factor for mobile ad hoc network using AI technique. *2014 Fourth International Conference on Advanced Computing & Communication Technologies (ACCT)*, 415-420. 10.1109/ACCT.2014.82

Taghikhaki, Z., Meratnia, N., & Havinga, P. J. (2013). A trust-based probabilistic coverage algorithm for wireless sensor networks. *Procedia Computer Science*, *21*, 455–464. doi:10.1016/j.procs.2013.09.061

Thai, M. T., Wang, F., Du, D. H., & Jia, X. (2008). Coverage problems in wireless sensor networks: Designs and analysis. *International Journal of Sensor Networks*, *3*(3), 191–200. doi:10.1504/IJSNET.2008.018482

Tian, D., & Georganas, N. D. (2002). A coverage-preserving node scheduling scheme for large wireless sensor networks. In *Proceedings of the 1st ACM international workshop on Wireless sensor networks and applications (WSNA '02)*. Association for Computing Machinery. 10.1145/570738.570744

Wang, G., Cao, G., & La Porta, T. F. (2006). Movement-assisted sensor deployment. *IEEE Transactions on Mobile Computing*, *5*(6), 640–652. doi:10.1109/TMC.2006.80

Wang, G., Cao, G., & La Porta, T. F. (2006). Movement-assisted sensor deployment. *IEEE Transactions on Mobile Computing*, *5*(6), 640–652. doi:10.1109/TMC.2006.80

Wang, G., Cao, G., & Porta, T. L. (2003). A Bidding Protocol for Deploying Mobile Sensors Network Protocols. *Proc. of 11th IEEE International Conference on Network Protocols*, 315 – 324. 10.1109/ICNP.2003.1249781

Wang, J., & Zhong, N. (2006). Efficient point coverage in wireless sensor networks. *Journal of Combinatorial Optimization, 11*(3), 291–304. doi:10.100710878-006-7909-z

Xu, X., & Sahni, S. (2007). Approximation algorithms for sensor deployment. *IEEE Transactions on Computers, 56*(12), 1681–1695. doi:10.1109/TC.2007.1063

Ye, Zhong, Cheng, Lu, & Zhang. (2003). PEAS: A Robust Energy Conserving Protocol for Long-lived Sensor Networks. In *Proceedings of the 23rd International Conference on Distributed Computing Systems (ICDCS '03)*. IEEE Computer Society.

Yick, J., Mukherjee, B., & Ghoshal, D. (2008). Wireless sensor networks survey. *Computer Networks, 52*(12), 2292–2330. doi:10.1016/j.comnet.2008.04.002

Zhou, Z., Das, S., & Gupta, H. (2004, October). Connected k-coverage problem in sensor networks. In *Proceedings. 13th International Conference on Computer Communications and Networks* (pp. 373-378). IEEE.

Zou, Y., & Chakrabarty, K. (2004). Sensor deployment and target localization in distributed sensor networks. *ACM Transactions on Embedded Computing Systems, 3*(1), 61–91. doi:10.1145/972627.972631

KEY TERMS AND DEFINITIONS

Clustering: Clustering is the process of process of dividing the sensor nodes into a number of clusters such that intra cluster similarity is higher and inter cluster is lower. There are various parameters such as residual energy, distance from the base station and node degree etc. to choose the cluster head. Clustering approaches are of great significance from the energy efficiency perspective. The major task of the cluster head is to perform the data collection from the cluster members and transfer it to the base station after performing data aggregation. Aggregation is usually done to reduce the data packets by performing certain operations such as minimum, maximum, average etc.

Coverage: Coverage is considered as a quality of service parameter which determines how well and for how long the region of interest can be monitored by the sensor nodes. A region of interest is said to be monitored by a sensor node if it is within the sensing range of at least one sensor node. Depending on the number of nodes which can monitor a given point in the target region coverage is defined as 1-coverage, 2-coverage and k coverage. Mission critical applications may require, higher degree of coverage. Coverage is categorized as three types: area coverage which intends to cover entire target region. Target/ Point coverage approaches aim to monitor a specific set of points. The barrier coverage problems are basically used in identifying the penetration points within the target region and are classified as Maximum Breach Path and Maximum Support Path.

Encoding: Encoding is a process of transforming the information into a format which requires less number of bits to represent it.

Energy Efficient: The energy efficiency is usually determined as the difference between the initial energy of the network and energy consumed during the operation of the network. The approaches which minimize the energy consumption in the network are said to be energy efficient. There are various approaches which provide energy efficiency to the sensor network such as clustering approaches, routing protocols etc.

Network Lifetime: The network lifetime of the network is defined as the duration in which the network can perform the desired functionality. Network lifetime may be defined in different ways depending on the application such as in the clustering approaches the network lifetime is defined as the time when all the nodes in the network dies. In area coverage problem it is defined as the duration till the complete target region is monitored by at least one sensor node. In the target coverage problem the network lifetime is defined as the time duration till all the specified set of targets/ points is monitored by at least one sensor node.

Node Scheduling Approach: The nodes in the sensor network can exist in either active, idle or sleep state. In the active state node is involved in the collection of the data from the environmental phenomenon. In the idle phase node is only sensing the environment and performs no communication operation. In the sleep state the node is not performing any operation. It has been observed that the sensor nodes consume least energy in sleep state. So the redundant nodes in terms of coverage may be put into sleep state such that energy consumption is reduced and network lifetime is maximized. The objective of node scheduling approach is to divide the set of nodes into a number of subsets such that it subset can provide coverage to the specified set of points. The set covers thus obtained are activated periodically by the base station. The network lifetime is such case is proportional to the number of set covers obtained. The higher the number of set covers higher will be the network lifetime.

Quality of Service: Quality of service represents the quality of the functionalities provided by the sensor network. It may be represented in terms of coverage, delay, throughput, reliability and energy efficiency.

Trust: Trust is a quality of service parameter which reflects the trust worthiness of the nodes. If the trust value of a node is higher, then the node is assumed to provide the desired functionality correctly. If a node shows misbehavior in communicating with peer nodes such as dropping packets or misrouting the data packets then the node trust worthiness is lower.

Wireless Sensor Network: Wireless sensor network is defined as autonomous network which consists of a number of sensor nodes and a central node known as Base Station. The sensor network main function is providing the observation capability to the network. The nodes in the network are usually battery powered and it is not easily feasible to recharge or replace the battery. The nodes are responsible for collecting the information from the environment and transfer it to the central node for further processing. The communication in the node is usually done in either single or multi hop fashion.

Chapter 8

Improvement and Reduction of Clustering Overhead in Mobile Ad Hoc Network With Optimum Stable Bunching Algorithm

Manish Bhardwaj
KIET Group of Institutions, India

Neha Shukla
KIET Group of Institutions, India

Arti Sharma
KIET Group of Institutions, India

ABSTRACT

In MANET, every hub is fit for sending message (information) progressively without prerequisite of any fixed framework. Portable hubs oftentimes move in/out from the system powerfully, making arrange topology unsteady in portable specially appointed system (MANET). Therefore, it turns into an incredibly moving errand to keep up stable system. In this chapter, the authors have proposed an upgraded stable bunching calculation that will give greater soundness to the system by limiting the group head changes furthermore, diminishing grouping overhead. In proposed optimum stable bunching calculation (OSBC), another hub is presented which goes about as a reinforcement hub in the bunch. Such reinforcement hub goes about as group head, when real bunch head moves out (or passed on) from the bunch. Last mentioned, the group head reelect another reinforcement hub. This training keeps

DOI: 10.4018/978-1-7998-4685-7.ch008

arrange accessibility without aggravation. Further, the need of group head and reinforcement hub is determined dependent on the hub degree and the rest of the battery life for portable hubs.

INTRODUCTION

A portable impromptu organize (MANET) is an independent framework less organize in which gathering of versatile hubs (i.e., portable, sensor, palmtop, PC) powerfully speaks with one another through remote medium inside their own transmission extend (utilizing single bounce or numerous jumps) through middle of the road hubs (Bhardwaj & Ahlawat, 2017a). The framework less nature of versatile specially appointed system causes visit change in the topology of system because of dynamic versatility of portable hubs, correspondence the board, what's more, production of a steady system are the most testing undertakings in MANET. Bunching is a conceivable answer for location these current difficulties. With the assistance of bunching, hubs are composed into various gatherings that make the system progressively strong, solid, and adaptable (Bhardwaj & Ahlawat, 2019).

The MANET can be sent without prerequisite of any further extra cost and time. In a MANET, each portable hub assumes a job of switch alongside its activity as an customary host. MANET still has a few difficulties like restricted data transfer capacity, constrained battery control for each portable hub, and successive topology changes in light of the fact that of hub development (Bhardwaj & Ahlawat, 2017b; Bhardwaj & Ahlawat, 2017c). To rundown such unpredictable and dynamic condition difficulties of versatile specially appointed arrange, different grouping calculations have been proposed in the proficient (Jin, 2005). A few directing conventions have been proposed in the writing to deal with the one jump and multihops, self-sorting out system in view of proactive, receptive, and half and half conventions (). Steering conventions are classes in three classes which are Proactive, Reactive Active and Mixture Protocol. Proactive convention remains actuate all the time in system even there is no information to transmit and keeps course data accessible all the time from source to goal. Though, in responsive directing conventions, course data is accessible on solicitation. This decreased power utilization in receptive conventions. Cross breed convention chips away at the head of proactive and responsive convention.

For the enormous systems, level directing structure requires unreasonable data. So as to survive such issue, various leveled structure (grouping) assumes a significant job in MANET decreasing system overhead, expanding reusability of transmission capacity, giving steadiness to the bunch structure, diminishing battery control utilization of versatile hub, and decreasing bunching just as in intracluster correspondence (Pathak & Jain, 2013).

Bunching is tied in with isolating a gathering of versatile hubs into various virtual consistent gatherings in a MANET. Each group is proficient to associate with other group utilizing bunch entryway to give availability for a system. Each group comprises of different portable hubs, for example, bunch head, group part, and group passage, and they perform various jobs in group at the hour of information correspondence in versatile specially appointed system. Each bunch head is a unique versatile hub in a bunch which goes about as nearby facilitator inside the bunch. In a group, just a single versatile hub goes about as bunch head at once. Fundamental obligations of bunch head incorporate information sending from source hub to goal versatile hub, intracluster transmission, furthermore, dealing with all part hubs of a bunch. Bunch individuals in a bunch are treated as should be expected versatile hubs which can speak with one another through bunch head. A bunch entryway is group part which is utilized to associate at least two groups with the goal that each group can get to its neighbour group to send or get information from other neighbouring group.

It is clear that MANET is dynamic in nature; because of such nature, execution of system diminishes as the size of system increments. Such issue can be decreased by presenting bunching, for such arranges. Grouping expands adaptability of remote system and diminishes organize overhead (Spyropoulos et al., 2010). Bunching likewise gives spatial reuse of asset to build the system limit. The equivalent recurrence code can be utilized if two bunches are most certainly not neighbours (not inside a similar radio range).

In (Ping, 2006), concentrated metaheuristic dependent on "tabu search" and a disseminated heuristic dependent on "subterranean insect state" are connected to lessen calculation overhead in remote sensor arrange (WSNs). Vitality Efficient, Deferral Aware, and Lifetime-Balancing (EDAL) take care to limit the framework lifetime for person hub. It lessens the measure of traffic created in the system by compressive detecting. The present scientific categorization is of crafty steering conventions for disturbance tolerant systems (DTNs). In (Suchismita & Kumar, 2009) crafty directing arrangements, number of highlights which are utilized to ordered DTNs as per portability, ability, and network of hubs. It additionally portrays pioneering directing conventions for DTN and essential pioneering directing structure squares Figure 1.

Figure 1. Cluster head Selection

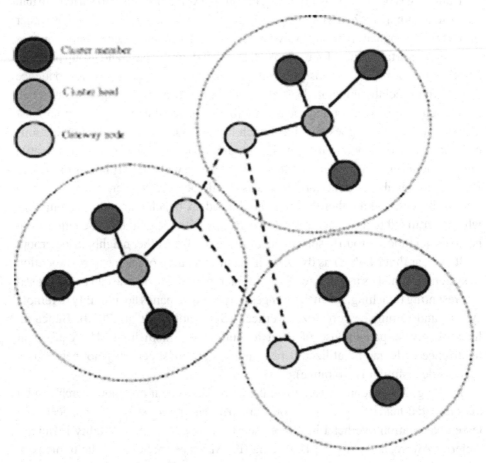

Vitality utilization for versatile hub is a very significant issue in MANET since it diminishes arrange availability when portable hub passes on because of battery waste. In (Chlamtac & Conti, 2003) the best next jump, portable hub is chosen dependent on vitality effectiveness to give organize availability. Choosing the best hubs will lessen the way change from source to goal and diminished system overhead. Ideal bunching and throughput are chronicled in progressive participation in versatile specially appointed arrange. The careful throughput for different numbers of stages can likewise be accomplished. The ideal bunch size is capable to limit throughput for all stages. The progressive plan does not handle direct scaling.

A weight-based bunching calculation is depicted to oversee versatile hubs and keeping up the neighborhood topology inside the system. Every versatile hub computes its weight by utilizing weight work furthermore, contrasts its weight and other portable hubs which are neighbor hubs inside two jumps to make the bunch head. The hub with the most elevated weight will be chosen as the bunch head and the remaining versatile hubs will be considered as group individuals.

In this paper, neighboring portable hub has higher need to gather into a similar group, which lessens number of bunch, improved group soundness furthermore, diminished bunching overhead. In (Yu & Chong, 2005) different bunch heads, determination plans have been proposed for WSNs and MANET. The principle goals of such plans are to choose productive group head for a bunch with the goal that dynamic topology changes might be diminished as bunch head moves from the group or bites the dust as a result of battery seepages. Subsequently, an answer is required which chooses a solid (stable) bunch head.

In grouping calculations (Yanjun & Cao, 2015), steering data is common with bunch head and group portal. This decreases the all out number of transmission for directing data and proficiently oversees steering table in a system. A bunch structure expands adaptability of system and vitality utilization (Meghanathan, 2009) and diminishes arrange overhead.

In (Ryu & Song, 2001), present a steering calculation that handles versatility of hubs and grouped remote system, by an able passage choice that is in charge of burden adjusting abilities. Virtual chains of importance of groups are utilized to investigate the logical nearness of hubs. The convention additionally makes use of a piece based connection quality estimator which consents to pick the most fitting entryways with burden adjusting furthermore, disengagement predication capacity in each bunch. In (Hussain & Abdullah, 2013), N-layer discrete power control plan is configuration to improve bigger transmission limit and spatial reuse factor in a group with N-layers.

In (Ephremides & Wieselthier, 1987), issue identified with non-uniform burden circulation in portable specially appointed system is studded also, proposed light-weighted unique channel designation what's more, agreeable burden adjusting calculation based on bunch. Burden adjusting and dynamic channel assignment strategy diminished grouping overhead and message passing. A molecule swarm streamlining (PSO) is utilized to lessen organize overhead and message drop while keeping up message conveyance proportion. Focal points of bunching: In contrast with the conventional arrange, bunching has numerous focal points. A few of them are as per the following:

- Bunching permits better execution of the convention for the Medium Access Control (Macintosh) layer by improving the spatial reuse, throughput, versatility, and power utilization.
- Efficient treatment of portability the board improve steering at system layer and decline transmission overhead. Every hub stores less data identified with

system topology and spares vitality of versatile hub and data transfer capacity for multipath directing calculation in versatile specially appointed organize.

Inconveniences of bunching: An enormous what's more, level system is overseen in MANET utilizing grouping topology. Grouping required development also, upkeep cost in contrast with other topology.

Some symptoms of grouping are as per the following:

- In MANET, portable hubs moves much of the time; this prompts change organize topology in all respects rapidly powerfully. In light of dynamic development of versatile hub and passing of portable hub, revamping of bunch structure is required. This necessities trade messages inside a group that expends data transfer capacity and vitality of versatile hub. Group head and entryway hub advances (deal with) the message for bunch part, so control utilization of such hubs is higher contrasted with group part hubs.This causes re-appointment of bunch head furthermore, group passage.

RELATED WORK

Writing study of grouping calculations incorporates numerous research papers on versatile impromptu organizes. Some of conventions identified with our proposed calculation are as pursues beneath.

Most reduced ID (LID) calculation was proposed by Ephremides, Wieselthier, and Baker (Karaoglu & Heinzelman, 2015). In this calculation, each versatile hub is appointed a exceptional irregular non-negative ID number, which goes about as central factor for status of versatile hub in MANET. Working of LID calculation is as per the following beneath:

- Every hub in group communicates and its ID to its close by hubs gets the equivalent from its neighbor hubs.
- If a portable hub got IDs from the whole neighbor hub, the hub with higher ID among its neighbor chooses as group head among its everything prompt neighbors.
- All hubs who have not gotten all neighbors' IDs become the individual from the recently chose head.
- This technique is rehashed till every one of the hubs are appointed with the status of a bunch head or bunch part.

Figure 2. (a) Information interchange between nodes. (b) Selection of node 1 as Cluster Head

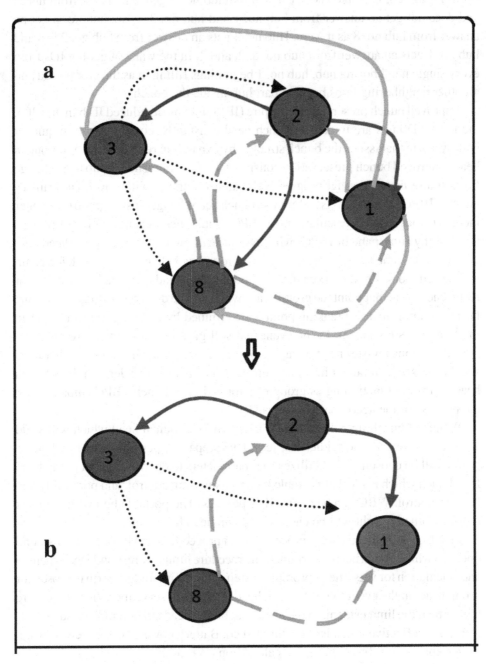

In Figure 2a, all hubs (i.e., 1, 2, 3, and 8) communicate their IDs to one another. From Figure 2b, it is likewise clear that the hub no. 8 gets an answer from hub 3 and does not get an answer from hub no. 1 and hub no. 3. Also, hub no. 2 got an answer from hub no. 8 as it were. Hub no. 3 gets an answer from hub no. 2 just and hub no. 1 gets an answer from hub no. 8, 2, and 3. In the wake of getting IDs from every single neighboring hub, hub no. 1 beginnings filling in as the group head and all other neighboring hubs become part hub inside the bunch.

Improved bunch preservation conspire (IBPC): In most reduced ID bunch (LIC), the lower ID hubs are treated as bunch head constantly, coming about in quicker battery waste that issues the bunch strength by expanding re-appointment for bunch head. Improved bunch preservation conspire (IBPC) diminished group head change furthermore, causes arrange progressively stable in contrast with Cover. The primary target of IBPC calculations is to diminish bunch head changes inside group to conquer inconvenience of LID calculation. In IBPC, bunch head changes are deferred up to a worthy timespan. In IBPC, whenever at least two than two bunch heads are closer inside same recurrence; at first, the group head changes will be deferred up to deferred clock. On the off chance that both group heads are still inside a similar recurrence go, at that point the group head switch will be deferred up to most extreme farthest point (greatest breaking point is determined by isolating transmission run multiple times by speed). In the event that still group head changes are required, the calculations register need of each group head; the bunch head with higher need will be chosen as a bunch head, and different needs to surrender its job as bunch head and starts functioning as group part for a similar bunch. IBPC chips away at the premise of the accompanying advances.

Weighted bunching calculation (WBC): An ideal bunch head which will yield high throughput and low idleness, less data preparing per hub, and low battery power will be chosen. WBC utilizes four parameters to choose an ideal group head for a bunch which is level of portable hub, transmission control, and portability and battery control. WBC can be depicted as pursues. The portable hub with the most reduced joined weight will be chosen as group head for a bunch.

In WBC, group head choice procedure isn't proceeding and it conjures all around once in a while; bunch head determination procedure limits correspondence expenses and calculation for versatile impromptu systems. Predefined edge worth is chosen for group head, in the event that if a bunch head attempts to serve more hubs which are higher than the limit esteem. In the event that bunch head still attempts in such case, framework effectiveness might be diminished. Battery power is effectively utilized.

An epic weight-based grouping calculation (WBGC):

WBGC works in three distinct stages which are preclustering, bunch arrangement, and bunch support.

- In preclustering stage, all hubs ascertain their hub degree and transmission capacity prerequisite furthermore, develop a parcel called node_info (). To register hub degree (number of neighboring hubs), the portable hub communicates a HI bundle. All the close by hubs that can hear HI bundle record the source hub's location as its neighbor hub. At that point, the hub can figure the absolute number of neighbors by tallying the quantity of HI parcels that it hears. A table is kept up by every hub to store nearby data which can be utilized in future correspondence.

- Each hub can evaluate its data transfer capacity necessity dependent on its normal information transmission necessity. The hub at that point conveys its transfer speed prerequisite to every one of its neighbors who are expectedly shaping group. These data later utilized for bunch head choice. While choosing bunch head (CH), if a hub has intense interest for data transfer capacity, at that point it suggests that it has its own assignment to do and subsequently will get less time to pass other information. Author detail a strategy to choose a CH with the criteria that too high transmission capacity prerequisite has less likelihood of that hub to be chosen as bunch head as the job of bunch head itself requests much transfer speed.

- In bunch arrangement stage, when hubs get node_info () parcel, at that point it ascertains joined load for every hub and the hub with higher joined weight will chose as bunch head.

- In WBC, bunch support stage utilizes IBPC calculation to limit the CH determination cost by deferring the procedure up as far as possible. It won't promptly change the CH as and when two CH come nearer. In the event that two bunch heads are inside the equivalent recurrence run, after greatest rundown, need of each bunch head is determined in view of the most extreme level of a hub furthermore, the rest of the battery control. Higher need hub progresses toward becoming group head and lower need hub will go about as individual from group. In the event that both group heads have a similar need factor, at that point LIC calculation is utilized to choose a bunch head.

PROPOSED OPTIMUM STABLE BUNCHING CALCULATION

Author propose "an optimum stable bunching calculation for portable specially appointed systems (OSBC)" which is an augmentation of a novel weight-based bunching calculation. The principle point of the proposed convention is to shape a stable (solid) bunch for portable advertisement hoc arrange. In proposed calculation, bunch head changes are diminished to make bunch head more stable and continue for longer period which diminished bunching overhead and makes organize progressively tough for such organize. Every portable hub contains node_info bundles which contains data related to portable hub. node_info is communicated to all its neighbors during grouping.

Before talking about inside and out insights regarding the proposed calculation, Author give some essential and plan theory of our proposed calculations. The accompanying presumptions are thought about before bunching strategy happens.

- One portable hub can join precisely one group at a time.
- Data directed just by means of bunch head to individuals and through door.
- All versatile hubs (old/new) share its open data (i.e., battery control, status) to the bunch head before sending joining demand.
- Backup hub is made by the group head and can go about as group head if bunch head moves (kicked the bucket) from inside the group. Initially, status of different portable hubs is as per the following under:

Group head = 1, bunch part = 0, and reinforcement hub = 2.

Working of proposed an optimum stable bunching calculation for portable specially appointed systems (OSBC) is as pursues underneath:

Each group contains four sorts of portable hubs which are bunch head, group part, reinforcement hub, and bunch door. In the proposed calculation, beginning bunch head arrangement is done utilizing weighted bunching calculation (WBC) and bunch support will be finished by our proposed calculations.

In bunch arrangement process, the hub with the most reduced consolidated weight will be chosen as group head and the second most reduced joined weight will be going about as reinforcement hub for the bunch. In OSBC, bunch head is in charge of assets sharing hub for all individuals in a bunch, group portal hub is in charge of intercluster correspondence, furthermore, reinforcement hub can go about as a bunch head for a bunch without real group head to maintain a strategic distance from bunching overhead and additional message correspondence inside the bunch. Later on, recently chose bunch head will choose new back hub utilizing weighted grouping calculation. The working of the proposed calculation is portrayed as pursues:

- If two group heads are in a similar bunch, at that point bunch head changes will be betrayed up to postpone time. In the event that they are still in the same transfer speed, at that point group head changes will be deferred up to most extreme limit.
- Priority of old bunch head, new group head, and reinforcement hub is determined which depends on hub degree and battery life.
- Based on need if new bunch head need is higher than old bunch head, at that point new bunch head will stay as group head what's more, old bunch

head need will be looked at with reinforcement hub need. On the off chance that old bunch head need is higher than reinforcement hub, at that point old bunch head will progress toward becoming reinforcement hub furthermore, reinforcement hub will go about as group part inside the bunch; generally, old group head will go about as bunch part and the status of reinforcement hub will remain the equivalent.

- Priority factor of bunch head, reinforcement hub, what's more, recently arrived bunch head is determined by including total of level of hub and the remaining battery life.
- Maximum point of confinement is determined by isolating transmission go multiple times by speed.

Proposed here is an improved stable grouping calculation for portable impromptu organizes (OSBC) that can portray as pursues:

```
OSBC_CALCULATION ()
{
IF (old_CH received Hi msg from New_CH)
      Delay_timer=Delay_peroid
End IF
Highest_Range= (Transmission Range/2) *Speed
Hi_interval= transmission_time
Cluster head Modification delayed by delay_timer
IF (old_CH have same radio range as New_CH)
  WHILE(delay_time<=Highest_range)
    Old_CH_TH=Highest_degree_OLDCLUSTERHEAD+Battery_life
    New_CH_TH=Highest_degree_NEWCLUSTERHEAD+Battery_life
    BN_TH=Highest_degree_BN+Battery_life
      IF(New_CH_TH>Old_CH_TH)
        New_CH=1
         IF(Old_CH_TH>BN_TH)
           Old_CH=2
        BN=0
        Else
          Old_CH=0
          BN=2
        EndIF
        ElseIF(NEw_CH_TH<Old_CH_TH && New_CH_TH>BN_TH)
            New_CH=2
            BN=0
```

```
            Old_CH=1
        Else
            New_CH=0
        Exit (0)
        EndIF
    delay_time=delay_time+Hi_interval
    END WHILE
    End IF
}
```

In the event that new group head need is not exactly old bunch head need and new group head need is more prominent than reinforcement hub need, at that point new group head will go about as reinforcement hub and reinforcement hub will go about as group part and old group head stays as bunch head for group and else new group head will go about as group part inside group.

Table 1. Simulations Metrics

Simulation Metrics	Data
Network Nodes	80
Area of Simulation	1000*1000 m
Time of Simulation	40-180 sec
Pause Time	2-30 sec
Node Speed	2-10 mps
Transmission Range	20-250 m

SIMULATION ARRANGEMENT AND EXECUTION ASSESSMENT

The proposed OSBC for portable specially appointed systems is recreated utilizing system test system (NS). Hub development generator is utilized to create different hub developments following by arbitrary way point model. Number of hubs, interruption time, most extreme speed, and field setup and reproduction time are given to development generator as information parameter.

It is difficult to create programming which contains different systems administration segments like switches, organize topology, and different system calculations. System test system sets aside cash and time to finish such task. Network Simulator-3 (ns-3) is utilized to reenact stage for systems administration and instructive reason. It gives different models for how parcel information system functions. It includes with set of inbuilt libraries which may consolidate together with some other outer programming.

Reproduction is completed in two stages. In the initial step, interruption time (portability) changes and in the subsequent advance changes the speed. For reproduction reason, couple of standard parameters and their individual qualities are given in Table 1.

Proposed OSBC calculation is contrasted and existing WBC and IBPC as far as number of bunch head changes, number of bunch part changes, and bunching overhead for proposed OSBC conspire.

SIMULATION STUDY

Proposed OSBC is reproduced for N number of hubs on a reproduction zone 500×500 m. Every portable hub is allowed to move toward all path during reproduction. Figure 3 demonstrates the exhibition of proposed OSBC in terms of number of bunch head changes as reenactment time variety. As recreation time expands number of bunch head changes are diminished. From the Figure 3, it is seen that our proposed OSBC is limiting group head changes as contrasted and ICSM and WBC.

Figure 3. No. of Cluster Head changes vs Simulation Time

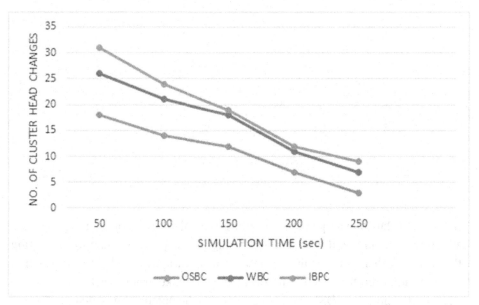

Figure 4. No. of Cluster Head changes vs Node Speed

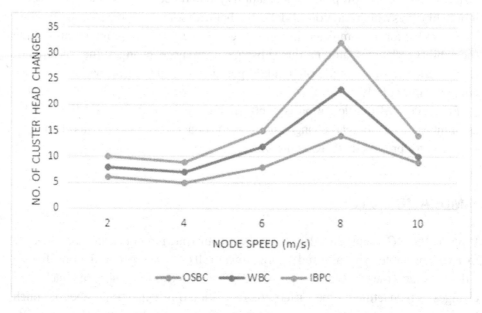

Figure 5. No. of Cluster Member changes vs Simulation Time

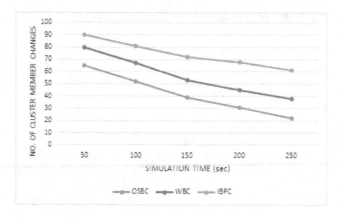

As versatile hub moves quicker inside the group, plausibility of changing in bunch head, group part, and reinforcement will be higher. As portable hub moves starting with one bunch then onto the next group, such condition expanded transformation of group head or reinforcement hub for a bunch to make group practical. In Figure 4, execution of proposed OSBC is appeared; from the outcome, it is clear that group head changes rely upon the development of versatile hubs and its development speed.

From the figure, obviously bunch head change relies upon interruption time for portable hub. At introductory of delay time, group head changes are insignificant.

Figure 6. No. of Cluster Member Changes vs Pause Time

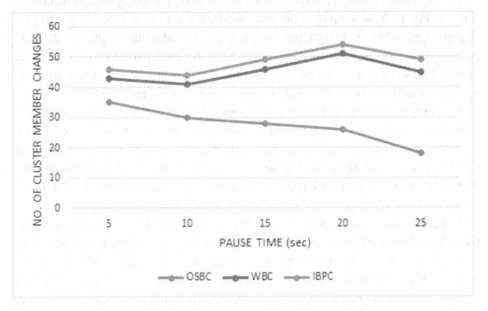

Figure 7. Cluster Overhead vs Simulation Time

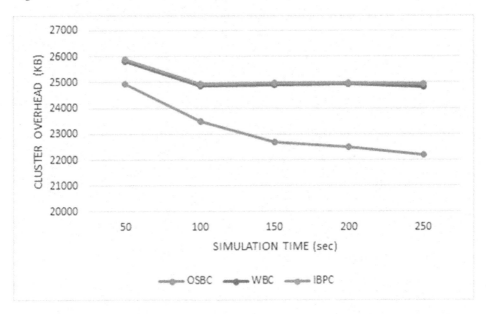

Be that as it may, when interruption time expanded, plausibility of group head changes moreover expanded. This makes shaky system. Near study demonstrates that our proposed calculation performs better as far as less bunch head changes as interruption time expanded.

Figure 5 demonstrates the quantity of bunch part changes against reenactment time. In Figure 5, as reproduction time builds, the all out number of group part changes diminishes. From the reproduction result, it is clear that our proposed OSBC calculation performs better by lessening number of bunch part changes for a group against reenactment time. When reproduction time expands, bunch part changes are diminished and execution of OSBC is better against IBPC and WBC.

From Figure 6, it is obvious that proposed OSBC constantly diminishes bunch part changes as respite time increments. At first, in the middle of 5 to 10 interruption time, bunch part changes are diminished in IBPC, WBC, what's more, our proposed OSBC. It is obvious from the Figure 6 that at the point when interruption time increments from 10 to 20 m/s, the rate of bunch part changes is expanded in IBPC and WBC however in proposed OSBC, it keeps on being in diminishing organize.

Bunching overhead is significant issue in portable specially appointed system. The procedure of trade of messages for choosing bunch head (reinforcement hub) from a group builds the bunching overhead. To lessen such bunching overhead, another calculation is proposed which limits bunching overhead, by making group head a progressively steady bunch. In Figure 7, in OSBC, bunching overhead is constantly diminished however in IBPC and WBC, grouping overhead changes are low.

Figure 8. Cluster Overhead vs Node Speed

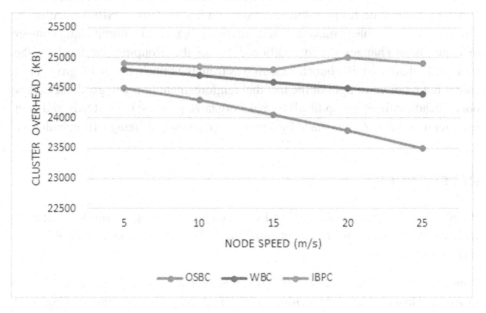

Figure 8, for the proposed calculation, demonstrates the execution of grouping overhead over versatile hub speed. As the outcome demonstrates that at first, for proposed calculation, grouping overhead is higher however as portable hub speed expands, bunch overhead starts diminishing, as contrasted and IBPC and WBC for MANETs (Table 2).

CONCLUSIONS

To close, it very well may be unmistakably expected that there is a legitimate activity of important issue on MANET in the field of grouping calculations. As indicated by the writing survey from the past articles, numerous calculations and plans are proposed for grouping and race of group head in portable specially appointed systems. The present inquire about interest dissects a proposed calculation named "an optimum stable bunching calculation for versatile advertisement hoc systems (OSBC)" to limit group head change what's more, make bunch progressively steady and lessens grouping overhead. In the calculation proposed, an additional portable hub (which is known as reinforcement hub) is presented which will function as a subsequent bunch head inside the group, to make bunch a progressively dependable and reliable one.

As indicated by the exploratory outcomes that proposed a streamlined stable bunching calculation for portable advertisement hoc systems (OSBC) calculation, it won't just be capable to make a system increasingly stable by diminishing number of bunch head changes yet in addition decrease the grouping overhead. In the proposed calculation, if a bunch head moves from the bunch, the quick group head race is not required in light of the fact that reinforcement hub will go about as new bunch head (without group head) to make organize progressively steady and later on, a reinforcement hub is made by the new group head, utilizing LID calculation.

REFERENCES

Bhardwaj, M., & Ahlawat, A. (2017a). Reduce energy consumption in ad hoc network with wireless power transfer concept. *International Journal of Computational Theory and Application, 10.*

Bhardwaj, M., & Ahlawat, A. (2017b). Enhance Lifespan of WSN Using Power Proficient Data Gathering Algorithm and WPT. *DEStech Transactions on Computer Science and Engineering.*

Bhardwaj, M., & Ahlawat, A. (2017c). Optimization of Network Lifetime with Extreme Lifetime Control Proficient Steering Algorithm and Remote Power Transfer. *DEStech Transactions on Computer Science and Engineering.*

Bhardwaj, M., & Ahlawat, A. (2019). Evaluation of Maximum Lifetime Power Efficient Routing in Ad hoc Network Using Magnetic Resonance Concept. *Recent Patent on Engineering., 13*(3), 256–260.

Chlamtac, I., & Conti, M. (2003). Mobile ad hoc networking: Imperatives and challenges. *Ad Hoc Networks, 1,* 13–64.

Ephremides, A., & Wieselthier, J. E. (1987). A design concept for reliable mobile radio networks with frequency hoping signaling. *Proceedings of the IEEE, 75*(1), 56–73.

Hussain, K., & Abdullah, A. H. (2013). Cluster head election schemes for WSN and MANET: A survey. *World Applied Sciences Journal, 23*(5), 611–620.

Jin, W. (2005). A load-balancing and energy-aware clustering algorithm in wireless ad-hoc networks; Embedded and Ubiquitous Computing EUC 2005 Workshops. *Lecture Notes in Computer Science, 3823,* 1108–1117.

Karaoglu, B., & Heinzelman, W. (2015). Cooperative load balancing and dynamic channel allocation for cluster-based mobile ad hoc networks. *IEEE Transactions on Mobile Computing, 14*(5), 951–963.

Lai, Y. C., Lin, P., & Liao, W. (2011). A region-based clustering mechanism for channel access in vehicular ad hoc networks. *IEEE Journal of Selective Areas Communication, 29*(1), 83–93.

Li, D., & Gross, J. (2011). Robust clustering of ad-hoc cognitive radio networks under opportunistic spectrum access. *Proc. IEEE International Conference Communication.* DOI: 10.1109/icc.2011.5963426

Liu, C. H., & Rong, B. (2015). Optimal discrete power control in poisson-clustered ad hoc networks. *IEEE Transactions on Wireless Communications, 14*(1), 138–151.

Meghanathan, N. (2009). Survey and taxonomy of unicast routing protocols for mobile ad hoc networks. *International Journal of Applied Graph Theory and Wireless Sensor Network, 1*(1), 1–21.

Palma, C. (2013). Scalable multi-hop routing in wireless networks. *EURASIP Journal on Wireless Communications and Networking,* 86.

Pathak, S., & Jain, S. (2013). A survey: On unicast routing protocols for mobile ad hoc network. *International Journal of Emerging Technology and Advanced Engineering, 3*(1), 2250–2459.

Perkins, C. E. (2000). *Ad hoc networking.* Addison-Wesley.

Ping, Y. Y. B. (2006). A multipath energy-efficient routing protocol for ad hoc networks. In *2006 International conference on communications, circuits and systems proceedings* (vol. 3). IEEE.

Ryu, J. H., & Song, S. (2001). New clustering schemes for energy conservation in two-tiered mobile ad-hoc networks. *Proc. IEEE ICC\'01, 3,* 862–866.

Spyropoulos, T., Rais, B. N. R., & Turletti, T. (2010). Routing for disruption tolerant networks: Taxonomy and design. *Wireless Networks, 16,* 2349–2370. doi:10.100711276-010-0276-9

Suchismita, C., & Kumar, R. (2009). A survey on one-hop clustering algorithms in mobile ad hoc networks. *Journal of Network and Systems Management, 17,* 183–207.

Ulema, M., & Nogueira, J. M. (2006). Management of wireless ad hoc networks and wireless sensor networks. *Journal of Network and Systems Management, 14*(3), 327–333.

Vasilakos, A. V., Li, Z., & Simon, G. (2015). Information centric network: Research challenges and opportunities. *Journal of Network and Computer Applications*, *52*, 1–10.

Yanjun, Y. Y., & Cao, Q. V. (2015). EDAL: An energy-efficient, delay-aware, and lifetime-balancing data collection protocol for heterogeneous wireless sensor networks. *IEEE/ACM Transactions on Networking*, *23*(3), 810–823.

Yu, J. Y., & Chong, P. H. J. (2005). A survey of clustering schemes for mobile ad hoc networks. *IEEE Communications Surveys and Tutorials*, *7*(1), 32–48.

Chapter 9

The Role of Dynamic Network Slicing in 5G:
IoT and 5G Mobile Networks

Kaushal Kumar
A. P. J. Abdul Kalam Technical University, Lucknow, India

Ajit Kumar Singh
R . V. Institute of Technology, Bijnor, India

Sunil Kumar
Amity University, Noida, India

Pankaj Sharma
Sharda University, India

Jaya Sharna
SRM University, Modinagar, India

ABSTRACT

Energy and speed are very important parts in this fast-growing world. They also play a crucial role in economy and operational considerations of a country, and by environmental concerns, energy efficiency has now become a key pillar in the design of communication networks. With the help of several of base station and millions of networking devices in the fifth generation of wireless communications, the need of energy efficient devices and operation will more effective. This chapter focused on following areas to enhance efficiency, which incorporate EE improvement utilizing radio access techniques like synchronously remote endurance and force move. In this research paper, the authors have searched various methods or techniques that are working with 5G wireless networks and got techniques that can address to increase speed with the help of 5G wireless network. It discusses energy-efficiency techniques that can be useful to boost user experience on 5G wireless network and also discusses the problems that can arrive in and addressed in future.

DOI: 10.4018/978-1-7998-4685-7.ch009

INTRODUCTION

Energy and speed is very important part in this fast growing world and it's demand increasing day by day in the universe, it's also play a crucial role in economy and operational considerations of a country, and by environmental concerns energy efficiency has now become a key pillar in the design of communication networks. With the help of several of base station and millions of networking devices in fifth generation of wireless communications, the need of energy efficient devices and operation will more effective. Our focused on following areas to enhance efficiency which incorporate EE improvement utilizing radio access techniques like synchronously remote endurance and force move.

In this research paper, I have searched various methods or techniques that are working with 5G wireless networks and got techniques that can address to increase speed with the help of 5G wireless network.

Energy efficiency techniques that can be useful to boost user experience on 5G wireless network and also discusses the problems that can arrive in and addressed in future.

With evolution of network technology, there is corresponding need for optimizing of energy consumption is also growing. Among all the user, mobile user is among the top consumer of the energy in the world and the rate of consumption of energy is increasing day by day at rapid rate with the organization of 4G it increase so think when there is deployment of 5G than the consumption of energy will be at the peak and it will top the chart in all categories like a user, consumption of energy (Kumar et al., 2017). The design of 5G is especially build on the energy efficiency technique to be the key pillar of the 5G wireless communication. The base station is the main consumer of energy than come the user. Thus not only according to the operators but also the point of consumers, the energy efficiency is going to be the key factor in economic point of view also. So it's an urgent need to bring energy efficiency in the day to day life not only economic point view but also for natural point of view because right now we are dependent on natural resources for energy and the natural resources are degrading day by day because of the consumption of them is increasing due to population. So now mainly the mobile phones should be more energy efficient due to increase in demand of the mobile phones and should have good battery life because the main problem in devices is the battery draining fast so we have to design the battery like it take less energy to get charged and give backup for long time because due to this fast growing world we need more time to complete our work, less time to charge our devices (Punhani et al., 2019). With the development of 5G network the value of wireless network has been realized more now. The main concern is to improve energy efficiency of the gadgets without compromising on the user experience "Energy Efficiency conventionally is defined as the measure of number of bits transmitted per joule of energy consumed" (Kumar et al., 2015a)."

ECONOMIC CONCERN:

In economic concern, the main concern is that if the devices will not be energy efficient than they consume more power than the consumer will have to pay more money so the budgets of the consumer will be change. So the devices has to be energy efficient that the user don't have to pay high bill and the remaining amount can be used in further investment option so that they can earn more money.

ENVIRONMENT CONCERN:

Current wireless communication network are predominantly fuel by customary carbon-based energy sources. At present, data and correspondence innovation frameworks are liable for 5% of the world's CO_2 outflows, yet this rate is expanding as quickly as the quantity of associated gadgets. Besides, it is anticipated that 75% of the data and correspondence innovation segment will be remote by 2020, hence inferring that remote interchanges will turn into the basic part to address similarly as diminishing data and correspondence innovation related CO_2 outflows is concerned."

ENERGY EFFICIENT TECHNIQUES

To make 5G network more energy efficient and more useful we can use various techniques that can make 5G network best network till date. These techniques are further divided into three categories which makes our work easier to understand them. So the techniques are follows:

- Energy Efficient Architecture
- Energy Efficient Resource Management
- Energy Efficient Radio Technology"
-

ENERGY EFFICIENT ARCHITECHURES

The optimising the cell size is estimated to maximize the total network capacity and minimise the cost of deployment under the different level of user capacity demands. That's why large cell is used rather than small cell so that we can maximize the network capacity and the cost of small cell is high in comparison to large cell. Small cell are low powered cell where as large cell are high powered cell. Small cell have range from 10 metres to a few kilometres where as large cell are opposites. The important point in architecture is about overlay sources how we can give user speed actual speed of 5G what they actually deserve for what they are paying. So there are three ways. The ways are as follows:-

1. MICRO CELL
2. PICO CELL
3. FEMTO CELL

MICRO CELL

Microcells are basically little poles that can be install to existing physical framework in zones where it's unrealistic to introduce a full-size versatile tower or considerably progressively standard portable radio wires that are found on housetops of tall buildings.

Microcells don't occupy a lot of room so can be joined to road furniture, for example, light posts, transport covers or the side of a structure. Mobile operators would then be able to give extra ability to cover an enormous number of clients in a jam-packed territory –, for example, an open square, strip mall or football arena.

A scope of up to 2km is conceivable, notwithstanding if the microcell is utilizing high range, for example, mmWave, actually structures and different articles will block the signal. Also the quantity of clients may surpass the limit of the microcell.

Figure 1.

PICO CELL

Picocells can be seen as a trade off between the high limit, high range microcell and the short range, basic femtocell. Like microcells, picocells are overseen by the administrator, which is liable for arrangement, power and backhaul.

Anyway they are less expensive to work and are littler, which takes into consideration progressively adaptable position. The range is littler than a microcell, commonly around 200 meters, just like the limit.

Picocells are appropriate for indoor and outside network and not at all like femtocells, various cells can be utilized in a solitary area. This implies clients are given off starting with one passageway then onto the next as they move around a structure – great in the event that you are anticipating an approach the path from your work area to the kitchen.

From multiple points of view picocells are a trade off choice. They are more costly than a femtocell however offer more noteworthy limit and upkeep is the duty of the administrator as opposed to the person.

Figure 2.

FEMTO CELL

Femtocells are another sort of micro infrastructure with a pivotal contrast. While administrators are liable for the arrangement, support and execution of microcells, femtocells are introduced and run by an individual client or business.

They are pitched as a simple to approach to improve indoor inclusion at home or in the workplace, albeit late advancements, for example, Voice-over-Wi-Fi (VoWi-Fi), which permit clients to make and get brings on their cell phone over a nearby remote system, may have decreased their allure.

Moreover, femtocells just help a predetermined number of clients and have a far restricted range than microcells and picocells – regularly around 10 meters. Femtocells additionally will in general work in confinement, which means it's hard to utilize complex exhibit arrangements that administrators may endeavor with different types of microinfrastructure.

Figure 3.

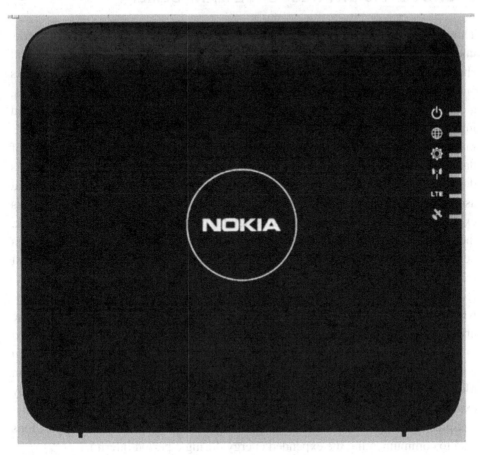

Notice:

In any case, femtocells are a basic, less expensive alternative for private ventures who need to improve indoor inclusion. For instance, an office should let staff utilize their cell phones during working hours however doesn't need these gadgets interfacing with a corporate system. Or on the other hand maybe a country bar needs to guarantee benefactors can ring for a taxi home on a Friday night. What's more, the business doesn't need to trust that the administrator will improve the circumstance.

ENERGY EFFICIENT RESOURCE MANAGEMENT"

This method is to structure the equipment for wireless communications frameworks unequivocally representing its energy utilization, and to receive major structural changes, for example, the cloud-based execution of the radio access organize. As energy efficient has developed as a key presentation marker for future 5G systems, a change in outlook from throughput -upgraded to energy-productivity enhanced interchanges has started (Kumar et al., 2015b). A communications framework's radio assets should never again be exclusively advanced to augment the measure of data that is dependably transmitted, however or maybe the measure of data that is dependably transmitted per joule of expended energy. Contrasted with conventional asset distribution plots, this requires the utilization of novel numerical instruments explicitly custom fitted to energy proficiency augmentation. From a physical outlook, the proficiency with which a framework utilizes a given asset, is the proportion between the advantage acquired by utilizing the asset, and the relating caused cost (Kumar et al., 2015c). Applying this general definition to correspondence over a remote connection, the expense is spoken to by the measure of devoured energy, which incorporates the emanated energy, the energy misfortune because of the utilization of non-perfect influence speakers, as well as the static energy disseminated in all other equipment squares of the framework (for example signal up and down conversion, recurrence synthesizer, separating tasks, computerized to-simple and an a log to-advanced transformation, and cooling activities). In the writing it is normally expected that the transmit intensifiers work in the straight area, and that the static equipment energy is autonomous of the emanated energy. These two suppositions lead to communicating the expended energy during a period interim T as "

"$E = T\,(\mu p + Pc)$ [Joule]"

Where in p is the transmitted force, $\mu = 1/\eta$, with η the productivity of the transmit power enhancer, and Pc incorporates the static lower dispersed in all other circuit squares of the transmitter furthermore, collector.

Figure 4.

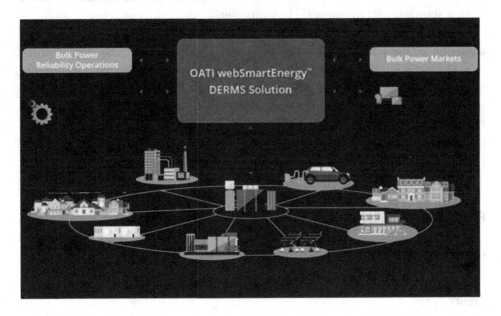

ENERGY EFFICIENT RADIO TECHNOLOGY

The third technique is to work communications frameworks by gathering energy from the earth. This applies to both inexhaustible and clean energy sources like sun or wind energy, and to the radio signal present over the air.As of late because of more noteworthy interest of energy productivity in remote communications, there is a great deal of enthusiasm of coordinating energy gathering advancements in remote communications framework. The most up and coming innovation is WPT (wireless power transfer) where nodes charge their batteries from electromagnetic radiations. Solid signals increment power move and yet they likewise increment the measure of obstruction. This strategy can be generally valuable in the wireless sensor networks (Kumar et al., 2015d).

In place of sensor nodes or for the up and coming innovation of Internet of Things in which the control signals will be utilized to charge the passage. The future systems will defeat its issues of way misfortune with the utilization of MIMO, little cells also, mm waves (Kumar et al., 2014). The component utilized for this object is a Rectenna which changes over microwave energy to coordinate current. This is accomplished by parting of the got sign to two symmetrical signals. "This technique refers to harvesting energy from the radio signals over the air, thus enabling the recycling of energy that would otherwise be wasted (Kumar et al., 2013) (Punhani et al., 2019) (Fasolo et al., 2007). In this context, interference signals provide a natural source of electromagnetic-based power."

The main problem in the plan of communications frameworks fuel by energy gathering is the irregular measure of energy accessible at some random time (Intanagonwiwat et al., 2003). This is because of the way that the accessibility of ecological energy sources (for example sun or wind) is innately a stochastic procedure, and represents the issue of energy blackouts. Dissimilar to customarily fuel systems, communications frameworks fuel by energy gathering must consent to the alleged energy causality requirement, for example the energy utilized at time t can't surpass the energy reaped up to time t (Mottola, 2011) (Zhao et al., 2008).

RELATED WORK

Concept of 5G Technology:

Figure 5.

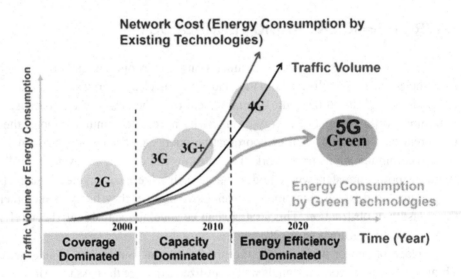

THEORITICAL FRAMEWORK:

Key terms of 5G Technology (Li et al., 2011)[16]:"

1. 5G is a completed wireless communication with almost no limitation; somehow people called it REAL wireless world "

2. Additional features such as Multimedia Newspapers, also to watch T.V programs with the clarity as to that of an HD T.V."

3. We can send Data much faster than that of the previous generations.

4. 5G will bring almost perfect real world wireless or called "WWWW: World Wide Wireless Web

5. Real wireless world with no more limitation to access and zone issues.

6. Wearable devices with AI capabilities.

7. Internet protocol version 6 (IPv6), where a visiting care-of mobile IP address is assigned according to location and the connected network.

8. One unified global standard.

9. Pervasive networks providing ubiquitous computing: The user can simultaneously be connected to several wireless access technologies and seamlessly move between them (See Media independent handover or vertical handover, IEEE 802.21, also expected to be provided by future 4G releases). These access technologies can be a 2.5G, 3G, 4G or 5G mobile networks, Wi-Fi, PAN or any other future access technology. In 5G, the concept may be further developed into multiple concurrent data transfer paths."

Key Points:

1. 5G technology offers high resolution for crazy cell phone user and bi- directional large bandwidth shaping.

2. The advanced billing interfaces of 5G technology make it more attractive and effective.

3. 5G technology also providing subscriber supervision tools for fast action.

4. The high quality services of 5G technology based on Policy to avoid error.

5. 5G technology is providing large broadcasting of data in Gigabit which supporting almost 65,000 connections.

6. 5G technology offers a transporter class gateway with unparalleled consistency.

7. The traffic statistics by 5G technology makes it more accurate.

8. Through remote management offered by 5G technology a user can get a better and faster solution.

9. The remote diagnostics also a great feature of 5G technology.

10. The 5G technology is providing up to 25 Mbps connectivity speed.

11. The 5G technology also supports virtual private network.

12. The new 5G technology will take all delivery services out of business prospect

13. The uploading and downloading speed of 5G technology touching the peak.

RESULT

After doing all the research surveys observation I concluded that 5G is the future of the network which is going to be the fastest network on earth which we will going to be used by the each and every people on the planet earth. Not only speed but also it will tell about the energy efficiency which will help us in recovering our natural resources and use of the reusable resources like solar energy wind energy water energy will increase so, 5G will be going to be like a gold which will help us to shine in networking as well as energy sector. It will help us to save our planet and our economy too.

REFERENCES

Fasolo, E., Rossi, M., Widmer, J., & Zorzi, M. (2007). In Network Aggregation Techniques for Wireless Sensor Networks: A Survey. *IEEE Wireless Communications, 14*(2), 70–87. doi:10.1109/MWC.2007.358967

Intanagonwiwat, C., Govindan, R., Estrin, D., Heidemann, J., & Silva, F. (2003, February). Directed Diffusion for Wireless Sensor Networking. *IEEE/ACM Transactions on Networking, 11*(1), 2–16. doi:10.1109/TNET.2002.808417

Kumar, S., Ranjan, P., & Ramaswami, R. (2014). Energy optimization in distributed localized wireless sensor networks. *International conference ICICT-2014.*

Kumar, S., Ranjan, P., Ramaswami, R., & Tripathy, M. R. (2015a). Energy aware distributed protocol for heterogeneous wireless sensor network. *International Journal of Control and Automation, 8*(10), 421-430. . doi:10.14257/ijca.2015.8.10.38

Kumar, S., Ranjan, P., Ramaswami, R., & Tripathy, M. R. (2015b). An NS3 Implementation of physical layer based on 802.11 for utility maximization of WSN. *IEEE International Conference CICN.*

Kumar, S., Ranjan, P., Ramaswami, R., & Tripathy, M. R. (2015c). A Utility Maximization Approach to MAC Layer Channel Access and Forwarding. *PIERS Draft Proceedings.*

Kumar, S., Ranjan, P., Ramaswami, R., & Tripathy, M. R. (2015d). EMEEDP: Enhanced multi-hop energy efficient distributed protocol for heterogeneous wireless sensor network. *International conference CSNT-2015.*

Kumar, S., Ranjan, P., Ramaswami, R., & Tripathy, M. R. (2017). Resource efficient clustering and next hop knowledge based routing in multiple heterogeneous wireless sensor networks. *International Journal of Grid and High Performance Computing*, *9*(2), 1–20. doi:10.4018/IJGHPC.2017040101

Kumar, S., Rao, A. L. N., & Ramaswami, R. (2013). Localization Technique in Wireless Sensor Network Using Directionally Information. *International conference at AKGEC*.

Li, H., Wu, C., Hua, Q. S., & Lau, F. C. M. (2011). Latency-minimizing data aggregation in wireless sensor networks under physical interference model. *Ad Hoc Networks*, *12*, 52–68. doi:10.1016/j.adhoc.2011.12.004

Mottola, L. (2011). *MUSTER: Adaptive Energy-Aware Multisink Routing in Wireless Sensor Networks. IEEE Transactions on Mobile Computing, 10(12)*.

Özdemir, S., Nair, P., Muthuavinashiappan, D., & Sanli, H. O. (2006). Energy-efficient secure pattern based data aggregation for wireless sensor networks. *Computer Communications, 29*(4), 446–455.

Punhani, A., Faujdar, N., & Kumar, S. (2019). Design and Evaluation of Cubic Torus Network-on-Chip Architecture. *International Journal of Innovative Technology and Exploring Engineering, 8*(6).

Shan, M., Chen, G., Luo, D., Zhu, X., & Wu, X. (2014). Building maximum lifetime shortest path data aggregation trees in wireless sensor networks. *ACM Transactions on Sensor Networks*, *11*(1), 11–18. doi:10.1145/2629662

Zhao, M., Ma, M., & Yang, Y. (2008). Mobile Data Gathering with Space-Division Multiple Access in Wireless Sensor Networks. IEEE INFOCOM Proceedings, 1957-1965. doi:10.1109/INFOCOM.2008.185

Chapter 10
Network Slicing and the Role of 5G in IoT Applications

Ashish Sharma
Lebanese French University, Iraq

Sunil Kumar
Amity School of Engineering and Technology, Amity University, India

ABSTRACT

The research and development along the 5th generation are moving with extreme speed around the global world. In this paper, the authors are going put light on the concepts of network slicing architecture of the 5G network at multi-level stages. The network slicing concept is another challenge faced by the 5G network. Further, the broad description of 5G architecture and analysis on infrastructure design and applications of network slicing in terms of 5G are done. This technique plays a major part in 5G technology deals with virtualization and software-defined technology. Due to low latency and its explosive growth, it is a technology to look into the deep knowledge it inculcates within. The chapter also focuses on the applications that the industry is looking into, and it has made a large impact on the user's life. With quantitative examples to show, this research will give a proper estimation for network slicing networking.

DOI: 10.4018/978-1-7998-4685-7.ch010

INTRODUCTION

With cellular communication automation development, the conventional single network model is unable to meet the needs of users, and the demand for evolved assistance is growing at a faster rate.

Now for the solution to this problem, 5G came into existence. The 4G growing levels and launch of 5G are driving innovation in industry and markets. There is going to be a tremendous amount of usage on the spectrum side in the case of 5G.the network slicing is a key concept of this technology, wherein commonly shared assets can be used by access providers (Sallent et al., 2017).

This will also result in higher levels of network softwarization, which will eventually provide latest and revolutionary network assistance.

Each slice independently tailors the web runs according to demands of markets, industries and traffic models. Network slicing in 5G controls the logical networks to be generated on peak of a usually shared material network. The networks are tailored by means of slicing to meet the specific needs of applications, utilities, gadgets, customers or operatives (Ordonez-Lucena et al., 2017).

Figure 1. Network Slicing concepts

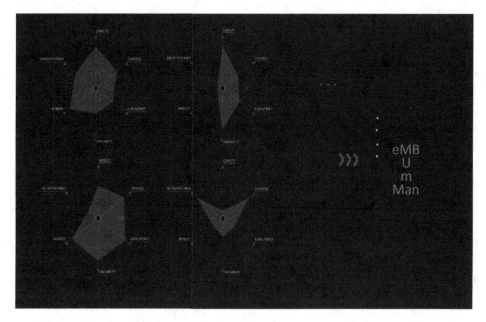

Figure 2. Industrial Applications of 5G

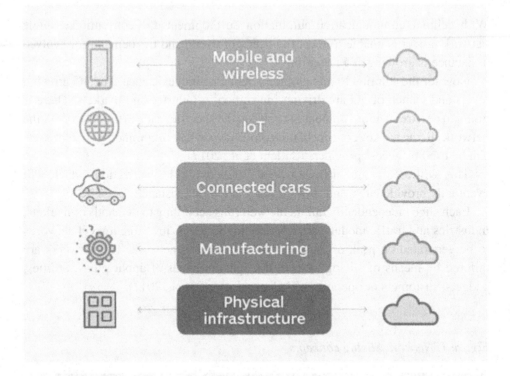

With 5G being initialized, the need to enable the co-existence of multiple services over the same network is also important. The new infrastructure scheme is developed due to this which provide the guaranteed service that receive its proper service level regardless of the status of other services. This calls for comprehensive service orchestration measures and techniques involving network slicing which is called the key factor of 5G which is not trivial in today's networks. With 5G network slicing, industry in India both online and offline are heavily dependent on SDN (Software Defined Network) and NFV (Network Function Virtualisation) which we will elaborate in the coming pages (Zhang et al., 2017).

Slice of the management function contacts with organic series business operations, virtual resource platform and network management system, for different sections of the demand side (such as vertical industry users, virtual operators and other business users) special logic network to provide with secure isolation, highly controlled.

BRIEF INTRODUCTION OF 5G AND NETWORK SLICING

5G typically stands for the fifth generation of cellular mobile communication. It is the successor of 4G, i.e. the 4th generation of wireless communication. 5G works on being the most capable version of wireless communication yet in terms of performances to deliver high end user experience. Some of its features include high data transfer rates, reliable communication and low latency. It also could be stated as opportunity for the economy to grow by growing business and empowering citizens (Afolabi et al., 2018).

5G wireless communication carries the version that comes with up-scaled data rates with low latency and an improvement in quality service as perceived by the user in comparison to 4G networks. With 5G impact on technological part the industries have been heavily investing in the experiment rated to 5G. As mobile operators are pushing hard for themselves to work with upcoming 5G. Network slicing is an important part 5G architecture lifecycle. The 5G architecture will reliance on network slicing will enable the operator to use certain part of 5G network for respective use. Network slicing key that enables to deploy function at particular aspect this saves large amount of data loss and also make the network strong (Kumar et al., 2017a).

As India plans to start 5G services in coming years, operators will try to adopt the new network architecture slicing under which virtualisation will be one of the most critical aspects. 5G network slicing provide flexibility of network and bandwidth, automation and programmability enabling providers to monetise their whole range of cloud services, which are linked to 5G, smart phone, IOT, AI and more (Kumar et al., 2017b).

Network slicing is nothing but dividing single physical network into multiple logical virtual networks, to achieve the right resource allocation and process optimization, and to share network infrastructure with multiple network slices, so as to improve the utilization rate of cyber source, to provide the best support for different users who use different service. Further virtualized and centralized use in network slicing will only take place with the help of key elements driving the adaptation of SDN and NFV. SDN and NFV technologies are complementary.

Figure 3. Process of Automated Deployment

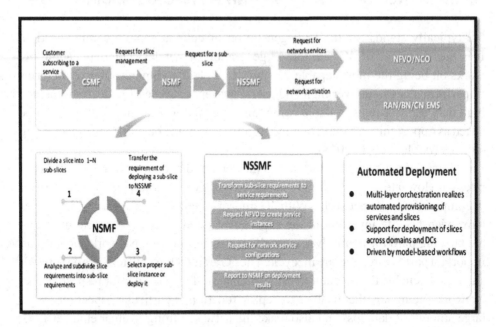

FEATURES FOR 5G

5G has a wide number of applications when it comes to their features. But here we will take a look at some of the major ones:

- First and foremost, the most important one is **faster speeds**. 5G uses an extra band of spectrum in the existing frequency range. This results in approx. 100x more speed and data transfer rates than 4G. At peak speeds. Downloading an HD movie used to take 10 minutes can now be done in just 9 seconds. This could mean a lot more time for a lot more features.
- Another major one is **low latency (Punhani et al., 2019)**. Latency represents the time that a signal takes to go from one point to another. 5G has reduced this speed to almost nothing and this results in faster responses and development of more machine-to-machine communication possible.
- It also provides **increased bandwidth**, meaning 5G can create larger parts of data to be transmitted than those which were possible with 4G. Along with low latency, this ultimately provides a faster and smooth user experience.
- **Availability and coverage** are some features that some countries like India are still working upon. But more developed countries like USA and Japan have already adapted to this technology.

Figure 4. Features of 5G

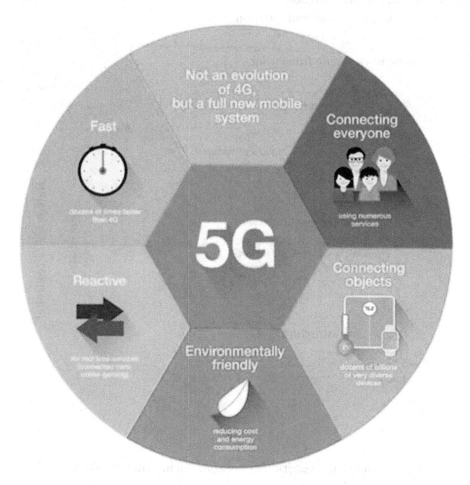

- 5G was predicted to be developed by 202, but was already completed and in use by 2018. This resulted in various new technologies like Augmented Reality (AR) and Virtual Reality (VR) to grown. Streaming of 4K resolution videos and better communications are now enabled.

NETWORK SLICING ARCHITECTURE FOR 5G NETWORK

There are many different types and proposal of network slicing architecture, so we can just describe a common architecture that shows the general elements of every solution as single result in the framework.

Basically, the network slicing architecture divided into two main blocks-

1-The actual slice implementation
2-The slice management and configuration

Figure 5. 5G network slicing framework

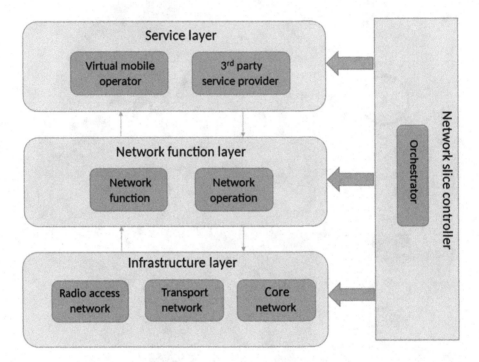

This diagram shows the generic 5G network slicing framework in which the following steps takes place.

First block is mainly designed as a multitier that consist of 3 layers:

1. Service layer
2. Network function layer
3. Infrastructure layer

And the final block.

The **Second block** that acts as a centralized network that depicts as network slice controller, which manages the working among the layers as mentioned above in the diagram.

A brief description of the layers are as follows:

Service Layer: This layer interface directly with the network business entities along with that they share the physical network that results in single point of service requirement.

Network Function Layer: This layer plays the role of creation of each layer, keeping in mind for every network slice according to service provided at that point, specifically for the requests which are coming from the upper layer. Multiple network functions are placed above the virtual network layer with respect to make a chain together that helps to create an end to end network slice instance, so that the characteristic can be reflected for network requested by the service (Kumar et al., 2015a).

To increase lifeline of resource by using it with full efficiency and making it capable to share same network function instantly via different network slices at the stake of an increase in the complexity of operation management.

Infrastructure Layer: This layer shows the main physical network topology like core network and transport network that depend mostly upon network slice being multiplexed and with aim of providing physical network function to the host that comprise of each slice.

There is a heterogeneous set of infrastructure components like devices enabling network connectivity like as routers, data centers for storage and computation capacity resource, and root stations for radio bandwidth related resources.

Network slice controller: This slice controller defines the network orchestrator whose function is to have automated configuration, coordination, and management of computer software and system, which communicate with different functionalities that are performed by respective layer to constantly handle request of each slice.

There are some tasks of slice controller that provide an effective coordination-

1. End to end service management
2. Virtual resource definition
3. Slice life cycle management

Figure 6. 5G Network Slicing

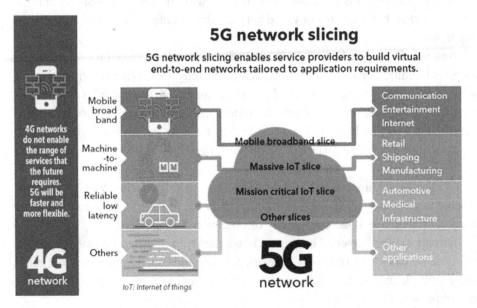

Figure 7. 5G Switch

EVOLUTION OF 5G

The shift from 4G to 5G is one of the most technological advancements yet in wireless communication. Its development resulted in massive changes for both customers and industries. What makes it better than 4G is that it makes use of an extra spectrum in the existing LTE frequency range. This creates an additional powerful network to 4G. LTE that stands for Long Term Evolution was first introduced along 4g in its early stages. This means that early stages of 4G could be said as the first generation of LTE (Kumar et al., 2015b).

Along with 5G, the precision of telecommunication was mark-able improved. This was made possible because of large bandwidth and low latency features. This meant that larger signals can now travels and that too at significantly better rate. It also makes use of shorter antennas than 4G which allows shorter antennas to be used. Also, even though with shorter antennas 5G still manages to connect up to 1000 more devices than 4G per meter making it even more user friendly and interconnected.

HOW 5G CAN CHANGE YOUR LIFE?

The use of 5G is still not made available to use for users all over the world but its applications could be already thought of and it is amazing seeing how it can revolutionize our lifestyles (Kumar et al., 2015c).

- It can change the way we watch sports. Features like using sensor in cricket balls or soccer balls, in wickets or goalposts, at the boundaries to make cameras automatically point it towards them. This could revolutionize the way we watch sports forever.
- If cities are made 5G enables then they can process their request quicker. Instant updates by government and to officials could be provided. For example, fused streetlights, or clogged sewages, etc.
- Patients could be treated quicker. With 5G and evolving technologies like AI, the doctors can diagnose patients quicker without patient coming to the clinic or any other healthcare center. Patients will also be able to self-diagnose themselves.
- Features like work from home will be implemented more and more as video chats will become prominent and more content would be shared across platforms.
- Features like driverless cars will be made possible using extensive combination of 5G with AI. As of now, the major problem for driverless cars is the huge response time. With better connections, this problem could be overcome.

But also, to make these tasks possible certain developments have to be made that we will study about in the next portion of the report. These include problems like increasing traffic density in urban areas and network coverage.

Figure 8. SDN Components

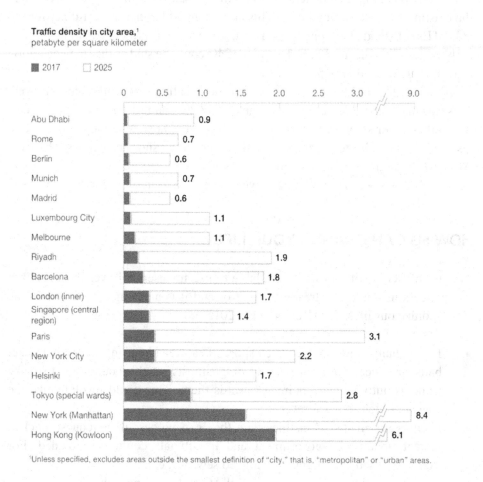

Traffic density in city area,[1]
petabyte per square kilometer

■ 2017   □ 2025

Abu Dhabi	0.9
Rome	0.7
Berlin	0.6
Munich	0.7
Madrid	0.6
Luxembourg City	1.1
Melbourne	1.1
Riyadh	1.9
Barcelona	1.8
London (inner)	1.7
Singapore (central region)	1.4
Paris	3.1
New York City	2.2
Helsinki	1.7
Tokyo (special wards)	2.8
New York (Manhattan)	8.4
Hong Kong (Kowloon)	6.1

[1]Unless specified, excludes areas outside the smallest definition of "city," that is, "metropolitan" or "urban" areas.

ROLE OF NETWORK SLICING IN NEXT GENERATION TECHNOLOGIES

The introduction of cutting-edge and advanced technologies in slice cutting architecture such as IOT, AI and many more has always contributed to the need for building digital infrastructure.

IOT (INTERNET OF THINGS)

IOT is viewed as a key enabler for driving digital transformation for unlocking a number of operational efficiencies. With the help of slice cutting network architecture, IOT will be able to perform these on wider levels (Kumar et al., 2015d).

Slice cutting architecture will allow IOT cloud computing services and delivery models to be embraced by organizations across the country for their numerous benefits which include better collaboration, higher data availability, flexibility, greater business agility and higher cost savings.

TTBS already has an IOT slice cutting practice focused on location-based services like fleet management, asset tracking, workforce tracking etc.

Industry believes that IOT using slice cutting architecture in market will grow exponentially and industry will continue to strengthen IOT services as per customer's requirements (Kumar et al., 2014).

AI (ARTIFICIAL INTELLIGENCE)

AI technology gives organizations the ability to develop new business models and also to undergo digital transformation, thereby offering endless benefits such as real time interaction with machines, better inventory management, better resource allocation etc.

AI with slice cutting architecture will be able to automate and simplify data analysis of any type, this can clearly offload the work from human staff and increase productivity. While AI is still typically based in data centres, real time connectivity to AI application requires a ubiquitous connection that is provided by 5G slice cutting architecture. As machines and objects communicate directly with each other, real value of data is getting generated, enabling automation and ultimately faster and better decision making by the help of AI and slice cutting architecture.

SDN (SOFTWARE DEFINED NETWORK)

When coupled with virtualisation, SDN can provide significant improvement in terms of agility and effective resource utilisation.

The mass development and massive network management and optimization are improved by using SDN and by reducing the number of solution variants. All these are possible due to the increased flexibility of the disaggregated solution.

SDN enables best efficient service orchestration and supports network slicing across different network domains (Kumar et al., 2013).

SDN architecture is the initialization of various automation and resource optimization tools. Such tools increase operational efficiency while deploying, maintaining and optimizing networks and services and also to ensure customer quality of experience.

SDN applications automate monitoring and analytics and optimizes phases, and utilizes big data tools to analyse the massive amount of data gathered from network elements. This helps to address network bottlenecks proactively and quickly define the root cause of a service failure.

Figure 9. SDN Architecture

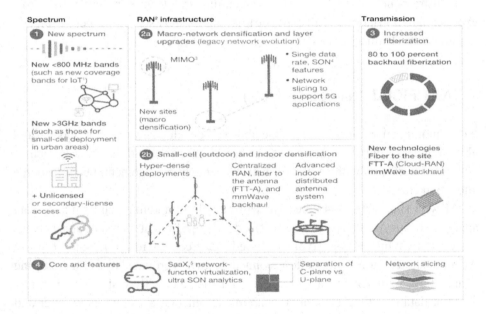

NFV (NETWORK FUNCTION VIRTUALISATION)

NFV gives operators the flexibility to dynamically increase or decrease the network capacity on needed basis. The outlay of physical networking equipment and overhead costs are reduced by a huge amount with NFV deployment.

Enterprises across various verticals are using NFV to deploy a centralised management framework for automating all securing network services like firewall, security rules and load balancers.

NFV is helping operators move traditional network functions out of the physical hardware and run them as virtual network functions by logically dividing them.

With NFV telecom service providers can rapidly launch innovative network services. The technology provides them the flexibility to scale up or down depending on the varying business demands.

NFV critically optimises the actual network services that manages the data flow.

Figure 10. NFV

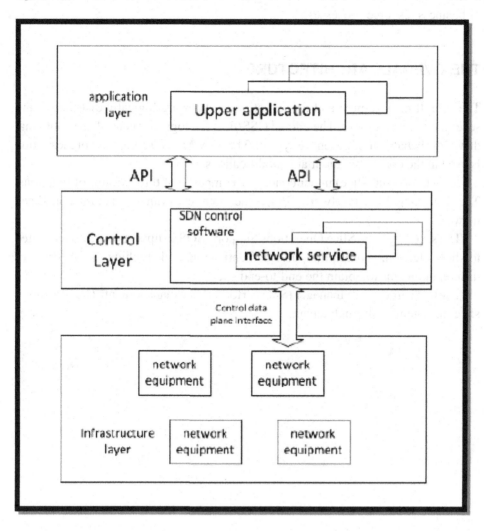

MANO (MANAGEMENT AND ORCHESTRATION)

MANO is an orchestration module for NFV. It consists of following entities: virtualised infrastructure manager (VIM), virtual network function management (VNFM) and ORCHESTRATOR.

It is mainly responsible for the dynamic configuration of the infrastructure and functions of the complete network. To complete the virtualization layer, the hardware resource layer management and layout, is responsible for the mapping between virtual network and hardware resources and OSS / BSS implementation of business resource processes.

THE OVERALL ARCHITECTURE

The overall management and orchestration of slices are logically distributed into several functional blocks. The Global OSS/BSS is a logically centralised entity that drives the behaviour of the entire system. The NFV MANO compliant orchestration is used in the concept without any modifications.

A slice (or a sub-slice) in our concept is composed of three groups of functions. The first group, Sliced Network (SN), is the same set of functions of the non-sliced network.

The second group, Slice Operations Support (SOS), supports operations related to slice selection, subscription, user authentication, and stitching of sub-slices of different domains to obtain the end-to-end slice.

The third group slice manager (SM) performs slice management. The SM allows slice management through tenant.

Figure 11. Interfaces of Network

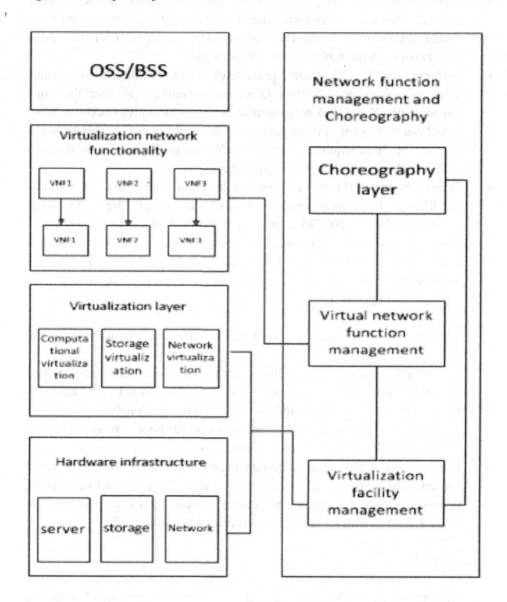

CHALLENGES AND FUTURE SCOPE

There are challenges that have come into lime light. In this para we focus upon some main research Base problems and also on some future directions in the field of 5G network slicing.

- **Security-** There are many existing open interfaces in network slicing. They give edge towards to network program issues to bring on new potential attacks to software network. These are the major problems that have created huge barriers on the way to initiate 5G network.
- **Performance-** The 5G system are made of several virtual network, various radio technology and different QoS requirement all are over the same infrastructure. When QoS measurement and network analysis becomes more complicated then we have to deploy the network slices. For this situation intensive study is required to provide solutions to the problem underlined with consideration of both time and money.
- **Standardization-** This process mainly focuses on vertical and it is still in its initial phase. There are many researchers conducted on the topic of network slicing including 5G NORMA, NGMN, 3GPP and 5GPP.In all these research papers the one of the best necessary requirements of 5G communication system is Network slicing. At this stage network slicing development focuses on to dealing with various new concepts, new architecture and make it more futuristic and upgraded.

In addition to these, there are some inevitable costs that have to be overcome along.

- To enable faster transmissions, **fibre-only transmissions** have to be enabled or else the requirements for the capacity latency issues would not be achieved.
- Mobile operator will need to **update their systems and hardware** capable of 5G to cope up with the growth. Standard measures have to be kept in mind, but also to look out for alternative approaches, like revenue models.
- **Core networks also need to be converged** as they also require increased capacity and functionality. These function upon IT advances like software defined networking and hence need to be upgraded. This can also be made possible as it provides features for re-configurability and agility.

SUMMARY

- Network slicing has become one of the most representative network service capabilities available in 5G networks. SDN and NFV have become the main technical support network section, through business scene they demand for network customized cutting and realizing network flexibility, and optimize business processes and data routing, makes use of cyber source to achieve the optimization.
- At the same time, it can also meet the dynamic needs of users, so that the network has the ability to dynamically allocate resources, and more flexibly

adapt to the real-time business and needs of users. Although network slicing has great potential, the problems we face are still much larger.

CONCLUSION

In this paper, we have studied and talked on the topic of multistage analysis of network slicing architecture for 5G mobile network. Keeping in mind on network slicing and architecture of 5G .We have also addressed some challenges and in the field of network slicing for the future direction.

5G is a key to the future technology, which provides very high speed data transfer rate. At this time, we all are using the 4G but in future we can use the 5G technology.

So overall I observe that the there is a great future for 5G network and network slicing which will enable business customers to select the features required by their applications which also helps to improve the condition and efficiency of the network and the experiences of customers

5G will be a revolutionary innovation in mobile communications technology that meets people's needs for quality of life and delivers ubiquitous low latency, low power, and high-security networks. The 5G network slicing is precisely the 5G multiplex structure indispensable method. As technologies such as software-defined networking and virtualization continue to evolve, the value and implications of web-based slicing are emerging. Although many achievements have been made in the exploration and work of network slicing, the execution of network slicing is still faced with number of challenges in network slicing, partial scenes and functional specifications. Further research is always needed for that purpose.

REFERENCES

Afolabi, Taleb, Samdanis, Ksentini, & Flinck. (2018). Network Slicing and Softwarization: A Survey on Principles, Enabling Technologies, and Solutions. *IEEE Communications Surveys & Tutorials, 20*(3), 2429-2453. doi:10.1109/COMST.2018.2815638

Kumar, S., Ranjan, P., & Ramaswami, R. (2014). Energy optimization in distributed localized wireless sensor networks. *International conference ICICT-2014.*

Kumar, S., Ranjan, P., Ramaswami, R., & Tripathy, M. R. (2015a). Energy aware distributed protocol for heterogeneous wireless sensor network. *International Journal of Control and Automation, 8*(10), 421-430.

Kumar, S., Ranjan, P., Ramaswami, R., & Tripathy, M. R. (2015b). An NS3 Implementation of physical layer based on 802.11 for utility maximization of WSN. *IEEE International Conference CICN.*

Kumar, S., Ranjan, P., Ramaswami, R., & Tripathy, M. R. (2015c). A Utility Maximization Approach to MAC Layer Channel Access and Forwarding. *PIERS Draft Proceedings.*

Kumar, S., Ranjan, P., Ramaswami, R., & Tripathy, M. R. (2015d). EMEEDP: Enhanced multi-hop energy efficient distributed protocol for heterogeneous wireless sensor network. *International conference CSNT-2015.*

Kumar, S., Ranjan, P., Ramaswami, R., & Tripathy, M. R. (2017a). Energy Efficient Multichannel MAC Protocol for High Traffic Applications in Heterogeneous Wireless Sensor Networks. Recent Advances in Electrical & Electronic Engineering, 10(3), 223-232. doi:10.2174/2352096510666170601090202

Kumar, S., Ranjan, P., Ramaswami, R., & Tripathy, M. R. (2017b). Resource efficient clustering and next hop knowledge based routing in multiple heterogeneous wireless sensor networks. *International Journal of Grid and High Performance Computing,* 9(2), 1–20. doi:10.4018/IJGHPC.2017040101

Kumar, S., Rao, A. L. N., & Ramaswami, R. (2013). Localization Technique in Wireless Sensor Network Using Directionally Information. *International conference at AKGEC.*

Ordonez-Lucena, J., Ameigeiras, P., Lopez, D., Ramos-Munoz, J. J., Lorca, J., & Folgueira, J. (2017, May). Network slicing for 5g with sdn/nfv: Concepts, architectures, and challenges. *IEEE Communications Magazine,* 55(5), 80–87. doi:10.1109/MCOM.2017.1600935

Punhani, A., Faujdar, N., & Kumar, S. (2019). Design and Evaluation of Cubic Torus Network-on-Chip Architecture. *International Journal of Innovative Technology and Exploring Engineering,* 8(6).

Sallent, O., Perez-Romero, J., Ferrus, R., & Agusti, R. (2017). On radio access network slicing from a radio resource management perspective. IEEE Wireless Communications, 2–10. doi:10.1109/MWC.2017.1600220WC

Zhang, H., Liu, N., Chu, X., Long, K., Aghvami, A., & Leung, V. C. M. (2017). *Network Slicing Based 5G and Future Mobile Networks: Mobility, Resource Management, and Challenges.* Academic Press.

Compilation of References

Abdelwahab, S., Hamdaoui, B., Guizani, M., & Rayes, A. (2014). Enabling smart cloud services through remote sensing: An Internet of Everything enabler. *IEEE Internet Things Journal, 1*(3), 276–288. doi:10.1109/JIOT.2014.2325071

Ahmad, I., Liyanage, M., Shahabuddin, S., Ylianttila, M., & Gurtov, A. (2018). Design Principles for 5G Security. *A Comprehensive Guide to 5G Security*, 75–98.

Ahmed, A., & Qazi, S. (2013). Cluster head selection algorithm for mobile wireless sensor networks. In *Open Source Systems and Technologies (ICOSST)* (pp. 120–125). IEEE. doi:10.1109/ICOSST.2013.6720617

Akyildiz, I. F., Su, W., Sankarasubramaniam, Y., & Cayirci, E. (2002). Wireless sensor networks: A survey'. *Computer Networks, 38*(4), 393–422. doi:10.1016/S1389-1286(01)00302-4

Akyildiz, I. F., Wang, P., & Lin, S.-C. (2015). *SoftAir: Software de-fined networking architecture for 5G wireless systems. In Computer Netwworkins*. Elsevier.

Al-Fuqaha, A., Guizani, M., Mohammadi, M., Aledhari, M., & Ayyash, M. (2015). Internet of things: A survey on enabling technologies protocols and applications. *IEEE Communications Surveys and Tutorials, 17*(4), 2347–2376.

Ali-Ahmad, H., Cicconetti, C., De la Oliva, A., & Mancuso, V. (2013). SDN-based network architecture for extremely dense wireless networks. IEEE SDN for Future Networks and Services (SDN4FNS).

Ameigeiras, P., Ramos-Muñoz, J., Schumacher, L., Prados-Garzon, J., Navarro-Ortiz, J., & López-Soler, J. M. (2015). Link-level access cloud architecture design based on SDN for 5G networks. *IEEE Network*. Advance online publication. doi:10.1109/MNET.2015.7064899

Anitha, R. U., & Kamalakkannan, P. (2013). Energy efficient cluster head selection algorithm in mobile wireless sensor networks. *Computer Communication and Informatics (ICCCI), 2013 International Conference on*, 1-5.

Araújo, I. L., Santos, I. S., Filho, J. B. F., Andrade, R. M. C., & Neto, P. S. (2017). Generating test cases and procedures from use cases in dynamic software product lines. *Proceedings of the 32nd ACM SIGApp Symposium on Applied Computing*.

Argenti, F. (1990). Fast Algorithms For Texture Analysis Using Co-Occurrence Matrices. *IEEE Proceedings, 137*(6), 443-44. 10.1049/ip-f-2.1990.0064

Atzori, L., Iera, A., & Morabito, G. (2010). The Internet of Things: A survey. *Computer Networks, 54*(15), 2787–2805. doi:10.1016/j.comnet.2010.05.010

Atzori, L., Iera, A., & Morabito, G. (2016). The internet of things: A survey. *Computer Networks, 54*(15), 2787–2805.

Aurenhammer, F. (2001). Computational Geometry– Some Easy Questions and their Recent Solutions. *Journal of Universal Computer Science, 7*(5).

Badnakhe, M. R., & Deshmukh, P. R. (2011). K-Means Clustering And Artificial Intelligence In Pattern Recognition For Crop Diseases. *International Conference on Advancements in Information Technology, 20*, 134-138.

Bahga, A., & Vijay, M. (2015). *Internet of Things - A Hands-on Approach*. Universities Press.

Basta, A., Kellerer, W., Hoffmann, M., Morper, H. J., & Hoffmann, K. (2014). Applying NFV and SDN to LTE Mobile Core Gateways, the Functions Placement Problem. *ACM Proceedings of the 4th Workshop on All Things Cellular: Operations, Applications, Challenges, All Things Cellular '14, 33*–38.

Bojanova, I. (2015). *What Makes Up the Internet of Things? Computing Now*. https://www.computer.org/web/sensing-iot/content?g=53926943&type=article&urlTitle=what-are-the-components-of-iot-

Brief, O. N. F. Solution. (2015). *Open Flow enabled SDN and Network Functions Virtualization*. On-line at https://www.opennetworking.org/images/stories/downloads/sdnresources/solution briefs/sb-sdn-nvf-solution.pdf

Buyya, R., Yeo, C. S., Venugopal, S., Broberg, J., & Brandic, I. (2009). Cloud computing and emerging IT platforms: Vision, hype, and reality for delivering computing as the 5th utility. *Future Generation Computer Systems. Elsevier, 25*(6), 599–616.

Cărbunar, B., Grama, A., Vitek, J., & Cărbunar, O. (2006). Redundancy and coverage detection in sensor networks. *ACM Transactions on Sensor Networks, 2*(1), 94–128. doi:10.1145/1138127.1138131

Cardei, M., & Du, D. Z. (2005). Improving wireless sensor network lifetime through power aware organization. *Wireless Networks, 11*(3), 333–340. doi:10.100711276-005-6615-6

Cardei, M., Thai, M. T., Li, Y., & Wu, W. (2005). Energy-efficient target coverage in wireless sensor networks. In *Proceedings IEEE 24th Annual Joint Conference of the IEEE Computer and Communications Societies* (Vol. 3, pp. 1976-1984). IEEE. 10.1109/INFCOM.2005.1498475

Cardei, M., & Wu, J. (2006). Energy-efficient coverage problems in wireless ad-hoc sensor networks. *Computer Communications, 29*(4), 413–420. doi:10.1016/j.comcom.2004.12.025

Chaturvedi, P., & Daniel, A. K. (2015). An energy efficient node scheduling protocol for target coverage in wireless sensor networks. *5th International Conference on Communication System and Network Technologies (CSNT-2015).*

Chaturvedi, P., & Daniel, A. K. (2017). A novel sleep/wake protocol for target coverage based on trust evaluation for a clustered wireless sensor network', Int. J. *Mobile Network Design and Innovation, 7*(3/4), 199–209. doi:10.1504/IJMNDI.2017.089301

Cheng, M., Ruan, L. & Wu, W. (2005). Achieving Minimum Coverage Breach under Bandwidth Constraints in Wireless Sensor Networks. *IEEE INFOCOM'05.*

Choras, R. S. (2007). *Image Feature Extraction Techniques and Their Applications for CBIR and Biometrics Systems. International Journal Of Biology And Biomedical Engineering.*

Christos, S., Psannis, K., Kim, B., & Gupta, B. (2016). Secure integration of IoT and cloud computing. In *Future Generation Computer Systems.* Elsevier.

Condoluci, M., Dohler, M., Araniti, G., Molinaro, A., & Sachs, J. (2016, February). Enhanced Radio Access and Data Transmission Procedures Facilitating Industry-Compliant Machine-Type Communications over LTE-Based 5G Networks. *IEEE Wireless Communications, 23*(1), 56–63. doi:10.1109/MWC.2016.7422406

Costa-Requena, J. (2015). SDN and NFV Integration in Generalized Mobile Network Architecture. *European Conf. Networks and Communications*, 1-6. 10.1109/EuCNC.2015.7194059

Culler, D. (2003). 10 emerging technologies that will change the world. *Technology Review*, 33–49.

Demestichas, P., Georgakopoulos, A., Karvounas, D., Tsagkaris, K., Stavroulaki, V., Lu, J., Xiong, C., & Yao, J. (2013). 5G on the Horizon: Key Challenges for the Radio-Access Network. *Vehicular Technology, 8*(3), 47–53. doi:10.1109/MVT.2013.2269187

Deng, S., Li, J., & Shen, L. (2011). Mobility-based clustering protocol for wireless sensor networks with mobile nodes. *IET Wireless Sensor Systems, 1*(1), 39-47. doi:10.1049/iet-wss.2010.0084

Deshpandey, B. (n.d.). *Decision Tree Digest.* Retrieved from https://tanthiamhuat.files.wordpress.com/2015/04/decision-trees-digest.pdf

Diop, A., Qi, Y., Wang, Q., & Hussain, S, (2013). An advanced survey on secure energy-efficient hierarchical routing protocols in wireless sensor networks. *Int J Computer Sci Issues, 10*, 490–500.

Docomo, N. T. T. (2015). *5G radio access: Requirements, concepts technologies.* White paper.

Dong, T., Churchill, E. F., & Nichols, J. (2016). Understanding the challenges of designing and developing multi-device experiences. *Proceedings of the 2016 ACM Conference on Designing Interactive Systems*, 62–72.

Ericsson. (2015). *5G radio access.* White paper.

European Commission. (2011). *HORIZON 2020, The EU framework program for Research and Innovation.* Available: http://ec.europa.eu/programmes/horizon2020/

Evans, D. (2011). *The internet of things: How the next evolution of the internet is changing everything*. CISCO White Paper. https://www.cisco.com/web/about/ ac79/docs/innov/IoT_IBSG_0411FINAL.pdf

Gage, D. W. (1992). Command control for many-robot systems. *Proceedings of the Nineteenth Annual AUVS Technical Symposium*, 22–24.

Ghaiwat, S.N. (2014). Leaf Diseases Using Image Processing Techniques: a review. *International Journal Recent Advance Engineering Technology, 2*(3), 512.

Gregg, W. W., Esaias, W. E., Feldman, G. C., Frouin, R., Hooker, S. B., McClain, C. R., & Woodward, R. H. (1998). Coverage opportunities for global ocean color in a multimission era. *IEEE Transactions on Geoscience and Remote Sensing, 5*(5), 1620–1627. doi:10.1109/36.718865

Gubbi, J., Buyya, R., Marusic, S., & Palaniswami, M. (2013). Internet of Things (IoT): A vision architectural elements and future directions. *Future Generation Computer Systems, 29*(7), 1645–1660. doi:10.1016/j.future.2013.01.010

Gubbi, J., Buyya, R., Marusic, S., & Palaniswami, M. (2013). Internet of Things (IoT): A vision, architectural elements, and future directions. *Future Generation Computer Systems, 29*(7), 1645–1660.

Gubbi, J., Buyya, R., Marusic, S., & Palaniswami, M. (2013). Internet of Things (IoT): A vision, architectural elements, and future directions. *Future Generation Computer Systems, 29*, 1645–1660.

Gudipati, A., Perry, D., Li, L. E., & Katti, S. (2013). Soft RAN: Software Defined Radio Access Network. *Proceedings of the Second ACM SIGCOMM Workshop on Hot Topics in Software Defined Networking, HotSDN '13*, 25–30.

Guermazi, A., & Abid, M. (2011). An efficient key distribution scheme to secure data-centric routing protocols in hierarchical wireless sensor networks. *Proc ComputSci*, 208–15.

Gupta, R. (2016). ABC of Internet of Things: Advancements, Benefits, Challenges, Enablers and Facilities of IoT. *IEEE Symposium on Colossal Data Analysis and Networking (CDAN)*.

Haralick, R. M., &Linda, G. (1992). Computer and Robot Vision (vol. 1). Boston, MA: Addison-Wesley.

Heinzelman, W. R., Chandrakasan, A., & Balakrishnan, H. (2000). Energy-efficient communication protocol for wireless micro-sensor networks. In *HICSS '00: Proceedings of the 33rd Hawaii International Conference on System Sciences-Volume 8*. IEEE Computer Society.

Howard, A., Matarić, M. J., & Sukhatme, G. S. (2002). Mobile Sensor Network Deployment using Potential Fields: A Distributed, Scalable Solution to the Area Coverage Problem. In H. Asama, T. Arai, T. Fukuda, & T. Hasegawa (Eds.), *Distributed Autonomous Robotic Systems 5*. Springer. doi:10.1007/978-4-431-65941-9_30

Huawei. (2013). *5G a technology vision*. White paper.

IOT-UK. (2017). *Satellite technologies for IoT applications.* Report produced by IoT UK.

Jaggi, N., & Abouzeid, A. A. (2006, January). Energy-efficient connected coverage in wireless sensor networks. In *Proceedings of 4th Asian International Mobile Computing Conference* (pp. 77-86). Academic Press.

Jangra, A., Goel, N., Priyanka, & Bhati, K. (2010). Security Aspects in Mobile Ad Hoc Networks (WSNs): A Big Picture. *International Journal of Electronics Engineering*, 189-196.

Jansen, W. A. (2011). Cloud hooks: Security and privacy issues in cloud computing. *Proc. 44th Hawaii Int. Conf. Syst. Sci. (HICSS)*, 1-10. 10.1109/HICSS.2011.103

Jiang, J., Han, G., Wang, F., Shu, L., & Guizani, M. (2014). An efficient distributed trust model for wireless sensor networks. *IEEE Transactions on Parallel and Distributed Systems*, *26*(5), 1228–1237. doi:10.1109/TPDS.2014.2320505

Jin, X., Li, L. E., Vanbever, L., & Rexford, J. (2013). SoftCell: Scalable and Flexible Cellular Core Network Architecture. *Proceedings of CoNEXT*, *2013*, 163–174.

John, W., Pentikousis, K., Agapiou, G., Jacob, E., Kind, M., Manzalini, A., Risso, F., Staessens, D., Steinert, R., & Meirosu, C. (2013). Research Directions in Network Service Chaining. IEEE SDN forFuture Networks and Services (SDN4FNS).

Joseph, D. A., Tavakoli, A., & Stoica, I. (2008). A policy-aware switching layer for data centers. *Proceedings of the ACM SIGCOMM*, 51–62. 10.1145/1402958.1402966

Kamavisdar, P., Saluja, S., & Agrawal, S. (2013). A Survey on Image Classification Approaches and Techniques. *International Journal of Advanced Research in Computer and Communication Engineering, India*, *2*(1), 1005–1009.

Kar, K., & Banerjee, S. (2003). *Node placement for connected coverage in sensor networks.* Academic Press.

Karakus, M., & Durres, A. (2017). Quality of Service (QoS) in Software Defined Networking (SDN): A survey. *Journal of Network and Computer Applications*, *80*, 200-218.

Karakus, M., & Durres, A. (2017). Quality of Service (QoS) in Software De-fined Networking (SDN): A survey. *Journal of Network and Computer Applications, 80*, 200-218.

Keoh, S. L., Kumar, S., & Tschofenig, H. (2014). Securing the Internet of Things: A standardization perspective. *IEEE Internet Things J.*, *1*(3), 265–275. doi:10.1109/JIOT.2014.2323395

Khan, Khan, Zaheer, & Khan. (2012). Future internet: The Internet of Things architecture possible applications and key challenges. *Proc. IEEE 10th Int. Conf. Frontiers Inf. Technol.*, 257-260.

Kim, D. S., & Chung, Y. J. (2006). Self-organization routing protocol supporting mobile nodes for wireless sensor network. Computer and Computational Sciences, 2006. doi:10.1109/IMSCCS.2006.265

Kim, H., & Feamster, N. (2013). Improving network management with software defined networking. *IEEE Communications Magazine*, *51*(2), 114–119. doi:10.1109/MCOM.2013.6461195

Koshizuka, N., & Sakamura, K. (2010). Ubiquitous ID: Standards for ubiquitous computing and the internet of things. *IEEE Pervasive Computing*, *9*(4), 98–101.

Kowalczyk, A. (2017). *Support vector machine succinctly*. Syncfusion.

Kulkarni, A. H. (2015). Applying Image Processing Technique To Detect Plant Diseases. *International Journal of Engine Research*, *2*(5), 3661–3664.

Lafuente, G. (2015). The big data security challenge. *Network Security*, *20*(1), 12–14. doi:10.1016/S1353-4858(15)70009-7

Lee, J., Uddin, M., Tourrilhes, J., Sen, S., Banerjee, S., Arndt, M., Kim, K.-H., & Nadeem, T. (2014). Mesdn: Mobile extension of SDN. *ACM Proceedings of the Fifth International Workshop on Mobile Cloud Computing; Services*, 7–14.

Lesjak, C., Ruprechter, T., Haid, J., Bock, H., & Brenner, E. (2014). *A secure hardware module and system concept for local and remote industrial embedded system identification. In Proceeding Emerging Technology Factory Automation*. ETFA.

Lim, H. S., Moon, Y. S., & Bertino, E. (2010). Provenance-based trustworthiness assessment in sensor networks. In *Proceedings of the Seventh International Workshop on Data Management for Sensor Networks* (pp. 2-7). Academic Press.

Li, W., Meng, W., & Kwok, L. F. (2016). A survey on openflow based soft-ware defined networks: Security challenges and countermeasures. *Journal of Network and Computer Applications*, *68*, 126–139. doi:10.1016/j.jnca.2016.04.011

Li, X. Y., Wan, P. J., & Frieder, O. (2003). Coverage in wireless ad hoc sensor networks. *IEEE Transactions on Computers*, *52*(6), 753–763. doi:10.1109/TC.2003.1204831

Lucas, G. B., Campbell, C. L., & Lucas, L. T. (1992). *Causes of Plant Diseases. In Introduction to Plant Diseases*. Springer. doi:10.1007/978-1-4615-7294-7

Machado, H., & Shah, K. (2017). *Internet of Things (IoT) impacts on supply chain*. APICS Houston Student Chapter. http://apicsterragrande.org/images/articles/Machado _Internet_of_ Things_impacts_on_Supply_Chain_Shah_Machado_Second_Place_Grad.pdf

Mahalle, P. N., Anggorojati, B., Prasad, N. R., & Prasad, R. (2013). Identity authentication and capability based access control (IACAC) for the Internet of Things. *Journal Cyber Security Mobility*, *1*(4), 309–348.

Masoudi, R., & Ghaffari, A. (2016). Software defined networks: A survey. *Journal of Network and Computer Applications*, *67*, 1–25. doi:10.1016/j.jnca.2016.03.016

Maurya, S., & Daniel, A. K. (2015). RBHR: Region-Based Hybrid Routing Protocol for Wireless Sensor Networks Using AI Technique. In *Proceedings of Fourth International Conference on Soft Computing for Problem Solving. Advances in Intelligent Systems and Computing, vol. 336.* Springer. 10.1007/978-81-322-2220-0_4

Maurya, S., & Daniel, A. K. (2014). An Energy Efficient Routing Protocol under Distance, Energy and Load Parameter for Heterogeneous Wireless Sensor Networks. *International Conference on Information Technology,* 161-166, 10.1109/ICIT.2014.63

Maurya, S., & Daniel, A. K. (2014). Hybrid Routing Approach for Heterogeneous Wireless Sensor Networks Using Fuzzy Logic Technique. *Fourth International Conference on Advanced Computing & Communication Technologies,* 202-207, 10.1109/ACCT.2014.81

McKeown, N., Anderson, T., Balakrishnan, H., Parulkar, G., Peterson, L., Rexford, J., Shenker, S., & Turner, J. (2008). OpenFlow: Enabling innovation in campus networks. *Computer Communication Review, 38*(2), 69–74. doi:10.1145/1355734.1355746

McKinley. (2020). *Big Data, AI, IoT & Cloud Computing: Futuristic Approach?* https://www. techbooky.com/big-data-ai-iot-cloud-computing/

Mhatre, V., & Rosenberg, C. (2004). Design guidelines for wireless sensor networks: Communication, clustering and aggregation. *Ad Hoc Networks, 2*(1), 45–63. doi:10.1016/S1570-8705(03)00047-7

Mineraud, J., Mazhelis, O., Su, X., & Tarkoma, S. (2015). *A gap analysis of Internet-of-Things platforms.* Available: http://arxiv.org/abs/1502.01181

Mini, S., Udgata, S. K., & Sabat, S. L. (2013). Sensor deployment and scheduling for target coverage problem in wireless sensor networks. *IEEE Sensors Journal, 14*(3), 636–644. doi:10.1109/ JSEN.2013.2286332

Misra, S., & Dias Thomasinous, P. (2010). A simple, least-time, and energy-efficient routing protocol with one-level data aggregation for wireless sensor networks. *Journal of Systems and Software, 83*(5), 852–860. doi:10.1016/j.jss.2009.12.021

Modirkhazeni, A., Ithnin, N., & Ibrahim, O. (2010). Secure multipath routing protocols in wireless sensor networks: a security survey analysis. *Proceedings of the2nd international conference on network application protocols and services,* 22833. 10.1109/NETAPPS.2010.48

Mulligan, R., & Ammari, H. M. (2010). Coverage in wireless sensor networks: a survey. *Network Protocols and Algorithms, 2*(2).

Naudts, B., Kind, M., Westphal, F., Verbrugge, S., Colle, D., & Pickavet, M. (2012). Techno economic Analysis of Software Defined Networking as Architecture for the Virtualization of a Mobile Network. *Workshop on Software Defined Networking (EWSDN), 2012 European,* 67–72. 10.1109/EWSDN.2012.27

Nguyen & Kim. (2015). Proposal and evaluation of SDN-based mobile packet core networks. *Journal on Wireless Communications and Networking,* 172.

Nguyen, Do, & Kim (2016). *SDN and Virtualization-Based LTE Mobile Network Architectures: A Comprehensive Survey*. DOI doi:10.100711277-015-2997-7

Nia, M., Mozaffari-Kermani, M., Sur-Kolay, S., Raghunathan, A., & Jha, N. K. (2015). Energy-efficient long-term continuous personal health monitoring. *IEEE Transaction on Multi-Scale Computing System, 1*(2), 85–98. doi:10.1109/TMSCS.2015.2494021

Nokia Networks. (2014). *Looking ahead to 5G: Building a virtual zero latency gigabit experience*. White paper.

O'Rourke, J. (1987). *Art Gallery Theorems and Algorithms*. Oxford University Press.

Osseiranet, A. (2014). IEEE: Scenarios for 5G mobile and wireless communications: The vision of the METIS project. *IEEE Communications Magazine, 52*(5), 26–35. doi:10.1109/MCOM.2014.6815890

Pallavi, S., & Jayashree, D. (2017). Remote sensing of greenhouse parameters based on IoT. *International Journal of Advanced Computational Engineering and Networking, 5*(10).

Paper, W. (2018) *Internet of Things (IoT), Technology, economic view and technical standardization*. Version 1.0, July 2018, Agence pour la Normalisation et l'Economie de la Connaissance (ANEC).

Pentikousis, K., Wang, Y., & Hu, W. (2013). MobileFlow: Toward Soft-ware-Defined Mobile Networks. *IEEE Communications Magazine*.

Peterson, L., & Roscoe, T. (2006). The design Principles of PlanetLab. *Operating Systems Review, 40*(1), 11–16. doi:10.1145/1113361.1113367

Quadri, I. S. A., & Sathish, P. (2017). IoT based home automation and surveillance system, *International Conference on Intelligent Computing and Control Systems (ICICCS)*.

Qualcomm Technologies, Inc. (2014). *Qualcomm's 5G vision*. White paper.

Rathod, A.N. (2013). Image Processing Techniques For Detection Of Leaf Disease. *International Journal Advance Research Computer Science & Software Engineering, 3*(11).

Rehman, E., Sher, M., Naqvi, S. H. A., Khan, K. B., & Ullah, K. (2019). Secure Cluster-Head Selection Algorithm Using Pattern for Wireless Mobile Sensor Networks. *Tehnički Vjesnik (Strojarski Fakultet), 26*(2), 302–311.

Rossana, M. C., Andrade, R. M., Carvalho, I. L. de A., Oliveira, K. M., & Maia, M. E. F. (2017). What changes from ubiquitous computing to internet of things in interaction evaluation? *International Conference on Distributed, Ambient, and Pervasive Interactions, DAPI 2017 (vol. 10, 291, pp 3-21)*. Academic Press.

Rost, P., Banchs, A., Berberana, I., Breitbach, M., Doll, M., Droste, H., Mannweiler, C., Puente, M. A., Samdanis, K., & Sayadi, B. (2016, May). Mobile network architecture evolution toward 5G. *IEEE Communications Magazine, 54*(5), 84–91. doi:10.1109/MCOM.2016.7470940

Roy, S., Bose, R., & Sarddar, D. (2015). A fog-based DSS model for driving rule violation monitoring framework on the internet of things. *International Journal of Advanced Science and Technology*, 23-32.

Rutvij, H., & Jhaveri. (2012). *A Novel Approach for GrayHole and BlackHole Attacks in Mobile Ad-hoc Networks*. IEEE.

Saaty, T. L. (1990). How to make a decision. The Analytical Hierarchy Process. *European Journal of Operational Research*, 48(1), 9–26. doi:10.1016/0377-2217(90)90057-I

Said, O., & Tolba A. (2016). Performance evaluation of a dual coverage system for internet of things environments. *Mobile Information Systems*. doi:10.1155/2016/3464392

Said, S. B. H., Sama, M. R., Guillouard, K., Suciu, L., Simon, G., Lagrange, X., & Bonnin, J.-M. (2013), New control plane in 3GPP LTE/EPC architecture for on-demand connectivity service. *Proceedings of second IEEE International Conference on Cloud Networking (CLOUDNET)*, 205–209. 10.1109/CloudNet.2013.6710579

Salmani, H., & Tehranipoor, M. M. (2016). Vulnerability analysis of a circuit layout to hardware Trojan insertion. *IEEE Transactions on Information Forensics and Security*, 11(6), 1214–1225. doi:10.1109/TIFS.2016.2520910

Sama, M., Ben Hadj Said, S., Guillouard, K., & Suciu, L. (2014). Enabling network programmability in LTE/EPC architecture using OpenFlow. *12th International Symposium on Modelling and Optimization in Mobile, Ad Hoc, and Wireless Networks (WiOpt)*, 389–396.

Samsung Electronics Co. (2015). *5G vision*. white paper.

Sanjay, B. (2013). Agricultural Plant Leaf Disease Detection Using Image Processing. *International Journal of Advance Research in Electrical, Electronics and Instrumentation Engineering*, 2(1), 599–602.

Sarkar, S. (2017). *Convergence of Big Data, IoT and Cloud Computing for Better Future, Big Data Cloud Computing Internet of Things*. https://www.analyticsinsight.net/convergence-of-big-data-iot-and-cloud-computing-for-better-future/

Sarma, H. K. D., Kar, A., & Mall, R. (2010). Energy efficient and reliable routing for mobile wireless sensor networks. *2010 International Conference on Distributed Computing in Sensor Systems Workshops (DCOSSW 2010)*, 1-6. 10.1109/DCOSSW.2010.5593277

Shakkottai, S., Srikant, R., & Shroff, N. (2003). Unreliable Sensor Grids: Coverage, Connectivity and Diameter. *Proc. of Twenty-Second Annual Joint Conference of the IEEE Computer and Communications Societies*, 2, 1073-1083. 10.1109/INFCOM.2003.1208944

Sharma, L. (2018). *Object detection with background subtraction. LAP LAMBERT Academic Publishing, SIA OmniScriptum Publishing Brivibas gatve 197*. European Union.

Sharma, L., Lohan, N., & Yadav, D. K. (2017). A study of challenging issues on video surveillance system for object detection. *International Conference on Electrical, Electronic Communication, Industrial Engineering and Technology Management Collaboration: Breaking the Barriers.*

Shen, X., Chen, J., Zhi, W., & Sun, Y. (2006). Grid Scan: A Simple and Effective Approach for Coverage Issue in Wireless Sensor Networks. *Proc. Of IEEE International Communications Conference*, 8, 3480-3484. 10.1109/ICC.2006.255611

Shi, E., & Perrig, A. (2004). Designing secure sensor networks. *IEEE Wireless Commun Mag*, *11*(6), 38–43. doi:10.1109/MWC.2004.1368895

Sidhu, P., Woungang, I., Carvalho, G. H. S., Anpalagan, A., & Dhurandher, S. K. (2015). An Analysis of Machine-Type-Communication on Human-Type-Communication over Wireless Communication Networks. *IEEE 29th International Conference in Advanced Information Networking and Applications Workshops (WAINA)*, 332–337.

SIITAg. (2018). *Satellite-enabled Intelligent internet of things for agriculture.* https://business.esa.int/projects/siitag

Singhal, S., & Daniel, A. K. (2014). Cluster head selection protocol under node degree, competence level and goodness factor for mobile ad hoc network using AI technique. *2014 Fourth International Conference on Advanced Computing & Communication Technologies (ACCT)*, 415-420. 10.1109/ACCT.2014.82

Singh, D., Tripathi, G., & Jara, A. J. (2014). A survey of Internet-of-Things: Future vision architecture challenges and services. *Proc. IEEE World Forum Internet Things*, 287-292. 10.1109/WF-IoT.2014.6803174

Sonka, M., Hlavac, V., & Boyle, R. (1998). *Image Processing, Analysis and Machine Vision.* PWS Publishing.

Stergiou, C., Psannis, K. E., & Andreas, P. (2017). Architecture for security monitoring in IoT environments. *IEEE 26th International Symposium on Industrial Electronics (ISIE).*

Stokes, P. (2018). *IoT applications in agriculture: the potential of smart farming on the current stage.* https://medium.com/datadriveninvestor/iot-applications-in-agriculture-the-potential-of-smart-farming-on-the-current-stage-275066f946d8

Taghikhaki, Z., Meratnia, N., & Havinga, P. J. (2013). A trust-based probabilistic coverage algorithm for wireless sensor networks. *Procedia Computer Science*, *21*, 455–464. doi:10.1016/j.procs.2013.09.061

Tan, L., & Wang, N. (2010). Future internet: The internet of things. In *IEEE 2010 3rd International Conference on Advanced Computer Theory and Engineering*, (vol. 5, pp. 376-380). IEEE.

Tehranipoor, M., & Koushanfar, F. (2010). A survey of hardware Trojan taxonomy and detection. *IEEE Design & Test of Computers*, *27*(1), 10–25. doi:10.1109/MDT.2010.7

Thai, M. T., Wang, F., Du, D. H., & Jia, X. (2008). Coverage problems in wireless sensor networks: Designs and analysis. *International Journal of Sensor Networks, 3*(3), 191–200. doi:10.1504/IJSNET.2008.018482

Thakurdesai, P. A., Kole, P. L., & Pareek, R. P. (2004). Evaluation of the quality and contents of diabetes mellitus patient education on Internet. *Patient Education and Counseling, 53,* 309–313.

Tian, D., & Georganas, N. D. (2002). A coverage-preserving node scheduling scheme for large wireless sensor networks. In *Proceedings of the 1st ACM international workshop on Wireless sensor networks and applications (WSNA '02).* Association for Computing Machinery. 10.1145/570738.570744

Tomovic, S., Pejanovic-Djurisic, M., & Radusinovic, I. (2014). SDN based mobile networks: Concepts and benefits. *Wireless Personal Communications, 78*(3), 1629–1644. doi:10.100711277-014-1909-6

Tostes, A., Izabel, J., Fátima, de L. P., Assuncao, R., Salles, J., & Loureiroet, A. A. F. (2013). From data to knowledge: City-wide traffic flows analysis and prediction using bing maps. *Proceedings of the 2nd ACM SIGKDD International Workshop on Urban Computing,* 12.

Trivisonno, R., Guerzoni, R., Vaishnavi, I., & Soldani, D. (2015). SDN-based 5G mobile networks: Architecture, functions, procedures and backward compatibility, Transmission. *Emerging Telecommunication Technology, 26*(1), 82–92. doi:10.1002/ett.2915

Verma, A. (2018). *The Relationship between IoT, Big Data, and Cloud Computing.* https://www.whizlabs.com/blog/relationship-between-iot-big-data-cloud-computing/

Wang, H. (2012). Image Recognition of Plant Diseases. *5th International Congress on Image and Signal Processing,* 894-90.

Wang, G., Cao, G., & La Porta, T. F. (2006). Movement-assisted sensor deployment. *IEEE Transactions on Mobile Computing, 5*(6), 640–652. doi:10.1109/TMC.2006.80

Wang, G., Cao, G., & Porta, T. L. (2003). A Bidding Protocol for Deploying Mobile Sensors Network Protocols. *Proc. of 11th IEEE International Conference on Network Protocols,* 315 – 324. 10.1109/ICNP.2003.1249781

Wang, J., & Zhong, N. (2006). Efficient point coverage in wireless sensor networks. *Journal of Combinatorial Optimization, 11*(3), 291–304. doi:10.100710878-006-7909-z

Want, R. (2004). Enabling ubiquitous sensing with RFID. *Computer, 37*(4), 84–86.

Wunder, G., Jung, P., Kasparick, M., Wild, T., Schaich, F., Chen, Y., Brink, S., Gaspar, I., Michailow, N., Festag, A., Mendes, L., Cassiau, N., Ktenas, D., Dryjanski, M., Pietrzyk, S., Eged, B., Vago, P., & Wiedmann, F. (2014). 5GNOW: Non-orthogonal, asynchronous waveforms for future mobile applications. *IEEE Communications Magazine, 52*(2), 97–105. doi:10.1109/MCOM.2014.6736749

Xu, X., & Sahni, S. (2007). Approximation algorithms for sensor deployment. *IEEE Transactions on Computers*, *56*(12), 1681–1695. doi:10.1109/TC.2007.1063

Yap, K. K., Sherwood, R., Kobayashi, M., Huang, T.-Y., Chan, M., Handigol, N., McKeown, N., & Parulkar, G. (2010). Blueprint for introducing innovation into wireless mobile networks. *ACM Proceedings of the Second ACM SIGCOMM Workshop on Virtualized Infrastructure Systems and Architectures, VISA '10*, 25–32.

Ye, Zhong, Cheng, Lu, & Zhang. (2003). PEAS: A Robust Energy Conserving Protocol for Long-lived Sensor Networks. In *Proceedings of the 23rd International Conference on Distributed Computing Systems (ICDCS '03)*. IEEE Computer Society.

Yick, J., Mukherjee, B., & Ghoshal, D. (2008). Wireless sensor networks survey. *Computer Networks*, *52*(12), 2292–2330. doi:10.1016/j.comnet.2008.04.002

Yun, Z., Yuguang, F., & Yanchao, Z. (2008). Securing wireless sensor networks: A survey. *IEEE Communications Surveys and Tutorials*, *10*(3), 6–28. doi:10.1109/COMST.2008.4625802

Zhou, Z., Das, S., & Gupta, H. (2004, October). Connected k-coverage problem in sensor networks. In *Proceedings. 13th International Conference on Computer Communications and Networks* (pp. 373-378). IEEE.

Zou, Y., & Chakrabarty, K. (2004). Sensor deployment and target localization in distributed sensor networks. *ACM Transactions on Embedded Computing Systems*, *3*(1), 61–91. doi:10.1145/972627.972631

Related References

To continue our tradition of advancing information science and technology research, we have compiled a list of recommended IGI Global readings. These references will provide additional information and guidance to further enrich your knowledge and assist you with your own research and future publications.

Adesina, K., Ganiu, O., & R., O. S. (2018). Television as Vehicle for Community Development: A Study of Lotunlotun Programme on (B.C.O.S.) Television, Nigeria. In A. Salawu, & T. Owolabi (Eds.), *Exploring Journalism Practice and Perception in Developing Countries* (pp. 60-84). Hershey, PA: IGI Global. doi:10.4018/978-1-5225-3376-4.ch004

Adigun, G. O., Odunola, O. A., & Sobalaje, A. J. (2016). Role of Social Networking for Information Seeking in a Digital Library Environment. In A. Tella (Ed.), *Information Seeking Behavior and Challenges in Digital Libraries* (pp. 272–290). Hershey, PA: IGI Global. doi:10.4018/978-1-5225-0296-8.ch013

Ahmad, M. B., Pride, C., & Corsy, A. K. (2016). Free Speech, Press Freedom, and Democracy in Ghana: A Conceptual and Historical Overview. In L. Mukhongo & J. Macharia (Eds.), *Political Influence of the Media in Developing Countries* (pp. 59–73). Hershey, PA: IGI Global. doi:10.4018/978-1-4666-9613-6.ch005

Ahmad, R. H., & Pathan, A. K. (2017). A Study on M2M (Machine to Machine) System and Communication: Its Security, Threats, and Intrusion Detection System. In M. Ferrag & A. Ahmim (Eds.), *Security Solutions and Applied Cryptography in Smart Grid Communications* (pp. 179–214). Hershey, PA: IGI Global. doi:10.4018/978-1-5225-1829-7.ch010

Akanni, T. M. (2018). In Search of Women-Supportive Media for Sustainable Development in Nigeria. In A. Salawu & T. Owolabi (Eds.), *Exploring Journalism Practice and Perception in Developing Countries* (pp. 126–149). Hershey, PA: IGI Global. doi:10.4018/978-1-5225-3376-4.ch007

Akçay, D. (2017). The Role of Social Media in Shaping Marketing Strategies in the Airline Industry. In V. Benson, R. Tuninga, & G. Saridakis (Eds.), *Analyzing the Strategic Role of Social Networking in Firm Growth and Productivity* (pp. 214–233). Hershey, PA: IGI Global. doi:10.4018/978-1-5225-0559-4.ch012

Al-Rabayah, W. A. (2017). Social Media as Social Customer Relationship Management Tool: Case of Jordan Medical Directory. In W. Al-Rabayah, R. Khasawneh, R. Abu-shamaa, & I. Alsmadi (Eds.), *Strategic Uses of Social Media for Improved Customer Retention* (pp. 108–123). Hershey, PA: IGI Global. doi:10.4018/978-1-5225-1686-6.ch006

Almjeld, J. (2017). Getting "Girly" Online: The Case for Gendering Online Spaces. In E. Monske & K. Blair (Eds.), *Handbook of Research on Writing and Composing in the Age of MOOCs* (pp. 87–105). Hershey, PA: IGI Global. doi:10.4018/978-1-5225-1718-4.ch006

Altaş, A. (2017). Space as a Character in Narrative Advertising: A Qualitative Research on Country Promotion Works. In R. Yılmaz (Ed.), *Narrative Advertising Models and Conceptualization in the Digital Age* (pp. 303–319). Hershey, PA: IGI Global. doi:10.4018/978-1-5225-2373-4.ch017

Altıparmak, B. (2017). The Structural Transformation of Space in Turkish Television Commercials as a Narrative Component. In R. Yılmaz (Ed.), *Narrative Advertising Models and Conceptualization in the Digital Age* (pp. 153–166). Hershey, PA: IGI Global. doi:10.4018/978-1-5225-2373-4.ch009

An, Y., & Harvey, K. E. (2016). Public Relations and Mobile: Becoming Dialogic. In X. Xu (Ed.), *Handbook of Research on Human Social Interaction in the Age of Mobile Devices* (pp. 284–311). Hershey, PA: IGI Global. doi:10.4018/978-1-5225-0469-6.ch013

Assay, B. E. (2018). Regulatory Compliance, Ethical Behaviour, and Sustainable Growth in Nigeria's Telecommunications Industry. In I. Oncioiu (Ed.), *Ethics and Decision-Making for Sustainable Business Practices* (pp. 90–108). Hershey, PA: IGI Global. doi:10.4018/978-1-5225-3773-1.ch006

Averweg, U. R., & Leaning, M. (2018). The Qualities and Potential of Social Media. In M. Khosrow-Pour, D.B.A. (Ed.), Encyclopedia of Information Science and Technology, Fourth Edition (pp. 7106-7115). Hershey, PA: IGI Global. doi:10.4018/978-1-5225-2255-3.ch617

Azemi, Y., & Ozuem, W. (2016). Online Service Failure and Recovery Strategy: The Mediating Role of Social Media. In W. Ozuem & G. Bowen (Eds.), *Competitive Social Media Marketing Strategies* (pp. 112–135). Hershey, PA: IGI Global. doi:10.4018/978-1-4666-9776-8.ch006

Baarda, R. (2017). Digital Democracy in Authoritarian Russia: Opportunity for Participation, or Site of Kremlin Control? In R. Luppicini & R. Baarda (Eds.), *Digital Media Integration for Participatory Democracy* (pp. 87–100). Hershey, PA: IGI Global. doi:10.4018/978-1-5225-2463-2.ch005

Bacallao-Pino, L. M. (2016). Radical Political Communication and Social Media: The Case of the Mexican #YoSoy132. In T. Deželan & I. Vobič (Eds.), *R)evolutionizing Political Communication through Social Media* (pp. 56–74). Hershey, PA: IGI Global. doi:10.4018/978-1-4666-9879-6.ch004

Baggio, B. G. (2016). Why We Would Rather Text than Talk: Personality, Identity, and Anonymity in Modern Virtual Environments. In B. Baggio (Ed.), *Analyzing Digital Discourse and Human Behavior in Modern Virtual Environments* (pp. 110–125). Hershey, PA: IGI Global. doi:10.4018/978-1-4666-9899-4.ch006

Başal, B. (2017). Actor Effect: A Study on Historical Figures Who Have Shaped the Advertising Narration. In R. Yılmaz (Ed.), *Narrative Advertising Models and Conceptualization in the Digital Age* (pp. 34–60). Hershey, PA: IGI Global. doi:10.4018/978-1-5225-2373-4.ch003

Behjati, M., & Cosmas, J. (2017). Self-Organizing Network Solutions: A Principal Step Towards Real 4G and Beyond. In D. Singh (Ed.), *Routing Protocols and Architectural Solutions for Optimal Wireless Networks and Security* (pp. 241–253). Hershey, PA: IGI Global. doi:10.4018/978-1-5225-2342-0.ch011

Bekafigo, M., & Pingley, A. C. (2017). Do Campaigns "Go Negative" on Twitter? In Y. Ibrahim (Ed.), *Politics, Protest, and Empowerment in Digital Spaces* (pp. 178–191). Hershey, PA: IGI Global. doi:10.4018/978-1-5225-1862-4.ch011

Bender, S., & Dickenson, P. (2016). Utilizing Social Media to Engage Students in Online Learning: Building Relationships Outside of the Learning Management System. In P. Dickenson & J. Jaurez (Eds.), *Increasing Productivity and Efficiency in Online Teaching* (pp. 84–105). Hershey, PA: IGI Global. doi:10.4018/978-1-5225-0347-7.ch005

Bermingham, N., & Prendergast, M. (2016). Bespoke Mobile Application Development: Facilitating Transition of Foundation Students to Higher Education. In L. Briz-Ponce, J. Juanes-Méndez, & F. García-Peñalvo (Eds.), *Handbook of Research on Mobile Devices and Applications in Higher Education Settings* (pp. 222–249). Hershey, PA: IGI Global. doi:10.4018/978-1-5225-0256-2.ch010

Bishop, J. (2017). Developing and Validating the "This Is Why We Can't Have Nice Things Scale": Optimising Political Online Communities for Internet Trolling. In Y. Ibrahim (Ed.), *Politics, Protest, and Empowerment in Digital Spaces* (pp. 153–177). Hershey, PA: IGI Global. doi:10.4018/978-1-5225-1862-4.ch010

Bolat, N. (2017). The Functions of the Narrator in Digital Advertising. In R. Yılmaz (Ed.), *Narrative Advertising Models and Conceptualization in the Digital Age* (pp. 184–201). Hershey, PA: IGI Global. doi:10.4018/978-1-5225-2373-4.ch011

Bowen, G., & Bowen, D. (2016). Social Media: Strategic Decision Making Tool. In W. Ozuem & G. Bowen (Eds.), *Competitive Social Media Marketing Strategies* (pp. 94–111). Hershey, PA: IGI Global. doi:10.4018/978-1-4666-9776-8.ch005

Brown, M. A. Sr. (2017). SNIP: High Touch Approach to Communication. In *Solutions for High-Touch Communications in a High-Tech World* (pp. 71–88). Hershey, PA: IGI Global. doi:10.4018/978-1-5225-1897-6.ch004

Brown, M. A. Sr. (2017). Comparing FTF and Online Communication Knowledge. In *Solutions for High-Touch Communications in a High-Tech World* (pp. 103–113). Hershey, PA: IGI Global. doi:10.4018/978-1-5225-1897-6.ch006

Brown, M. A. Sr. (2017). Where Do We Go from Here? In *Solutions for High-Touch Communications in a High-Tech World* (pp. 137–159). Hershey, PA: IGI Global. doi:10.4018/978-1-5225-1897-6.ch008

Brown, M. A. Sr. (2017). Bridging the Communication Gap. In *Solutions for High-Touch Communications in a High-Tech World* (pp. 1–22). Hershey, PA: IGI Global. doi:10.4018/978-1-5225-1897-6.ch001

Brown, M. A. Sr. (2017). Key Strategies for Communication. In *Solutions for High-Touch Communications in a High-Tech World* (pp. 179–202). Hershey, PA: IGI Global. doi:10.4018/978-1-5225-1897-6.ch010

Bryant, K. N. (2017). WordUp!: Student Responses to Social Media in the Technical Writing Classroom. In K. Bryant (Ed.), *Engaging 21st Century Writers with Social Media* (pp. 231–245). Hershey, PA: IGI Global. doi:10.4018/978-1-5225-0562-4.ch014

Buck, E. H. (2017). Slacktivism, Supervision, and #Selfies: Illuminating Social Media Composition through Reception Theory. In K. Bryant (Ed.), *Engaging 21st Century Writers with Social Media* (pp. 163–178). Hershey, PA: IGI Global. doi:10.4018/978-1-5225-0562-4.ch010

Bucur, B. (2016). Sociological School of Bucharest's Publications and the Romanian Political Propaganda in the Interwar Period. In A. Fox (Ed.), *Global Perspectives on Media Events in Contemporary Society* (pp. 106–120). Hershey, PA: IGI Global. doi:10.4018/978-1-4666-9967-0.ch008

Bull, R., & Pianosi, M. (2017). Social Media, Participation, and Citizenship: New Strategic Directions. In V. Benson, R. Tuninga, & G. Saridakis (Eds.), *Analyzing the Strategic Role of Social Networking in Firm Growth and Productivity* (pp. 76–94). Hershey, PA: IGI Global. doi:10.4018/978-1-5225-0559-4.ch005

Camillo, A. A., & Camillo, I. C. (2016). The Ethics of Strategic Managerial Communication in the Global Context. In A. Normore, L. Long, & M. Javidi (Eds.), *Handbook of Research on Effective Communication, Leadership, and Conflict Resolution* (pp. 566–590). Hershey, PA: IGI Global. doi:10.4018/978-1-4666-9970-0.ch030

Cassard, A., & Sloboda, B. W. (2016). Faculty Perception of Virtual 3-D Learning Environment to Assess Student Learning. In D. Choi, A. Dailey-Hebert, & J. Simmons Estes (Eds.), *Emerging Tools and Applications of Virtual Reality in Education* (pp. 48–74). Hershey, PA: IGI Global. doi:10.4018/978-1-4666-9837-6.ch003

Castellano, S., & Khelladi, I. (2017). Play It Like Beckham!: The Influence of Social Networks on E-Reputation – The Case of Sportspeople and Their Online Fan Base. In A. Mesquita (Ed.), *Research Paradigms and Contemporary Perspectives on Human-Technology Interaction* (pp. 43–61). Hershey, PA: IGI Global. doi:10.4018/978-1-5225-1868-6.ch003

Castellet, A. (2016). What If Devices Take Command: Content Innovation Perspectives for Smart Wearables in the Mobile Ecosystem. *International Journal of Handheld Computing Research*, 7(2), 16–33. doi:10.4018/IJHCR.2016040102

Chugh, R., & Joshi, M. (2017). Challenges of Knowledge Management amidst Rapidly Evolving Tools of Social Media. In R. Chugh (Ed.), *Harnessing Social Media as a Knowledge Management Tool* (pp. 299–314). Hershey, PA: IGI Global. doi:10.4018/978-1-5225-0495-5.ch014

Cockburn, T., & Smith, P. A. (2016). Leadership in the Digital Age: Rhythms and the Beat of Change. In A. Normore, L. Long, & M. Javidi (Eds.), *Handbook of Research on Effective Communication, Leadership, and Conflict Resolution* (pp. 1–20). Hershey, PA: IGI Global. doi:10.4018/978-1-4666-9970-0.ch001

Cole, A. W., & Salek, T. A. (2017). Adopting a Parasocial Connection to Overcome Professional Kakoethos in Online Health Information. In M. Folk & S. Apostel (Eds.), *Establishing and Evaluating Digital Ethos and Online Credibility* (pp. 104–120). Hershey, PA: IGI Global. doi:10.4018/978-1-5225-1072-7.ch006

Cossiavelou, V. (2017). ACTA as Media Gatekeeping Factor: The EU Role as Global Negotiator. *International Journal of Interdisciplinary Telecommunications and Networking*, 9(1), 26–37. doi:10.4018/IJITN.2017010103

Costanza, F. (2017). Social Media Marketing and Value Co-Creation: A System Dynamics Approach. In S. Rozenes & Y. Cohen (Eds.), *Handbook of Research on Strategic Alliances and Value Co-Creation in the Service Industry* (pp. 205–230). Hershey, PA: IGI Global. doi:10.4018/978-1-5225-2084-9.ch011

Cross, D. E. (2016). Globalization and Media's Impact on Cross Cultural Communication: Managing Organizational Change. In A. Normore, L. Long, & M. Javidi (Eds.), *Handbook of Research on Effective Communication, Leadership, and Conflict Resolution* (pp. 21–41). Hershey, PA: IGI Global. doi:10.4018/978-1-4666-9970-0.ch002

Damásio, M. J., Henriques, S., Teixeira-Botelho, I., & Dias, P. (2016). Mobile Media and Social Interaction: Mobile Services and Content as Drivers of Social Interaction. In J. Aguado, C. Feijóo, & I. Martínez (Eds.), *Emerging Perspectives on the Mobile Content Evolution* (pp. 357–379). Hershey, PA: IGI Global. doi:10.4018/978-1-4666-8838-4.ch018

Davis, A., & Foley, L. (2016). Digital Storytelling. In B. Guzzetti & M. Lesley (Eds.), *Handbook of Research on the Societal Impact of Digital Media* (pp. 317–342). Hershey, PA: IGI Global. doi:10.4018/978-1-4666-8310-5.ch013

Davis, S., Palmer, L., & Etienne, J. (2016). The Geography of Digital Literacy: Mapping Communications Technology Training Programs in Austin, Texas. In B. Passarelli, J. Straubhaar, & A. Cuevas-Cerveró (Eds.), *Handbook of Research on Comparative Approaches to the Digital Age Revolution in Europe and the Americas* (pp. 371–384). Hershey, PA: IGI Global. doi:10.4018/978-1-4666-8740-0.ch022

Delello, J. A., & McWhorter, R. R. (2016). New Visual Literacies and Competencies for Education and the Workplace. In B. Guzzetti & M. Lesley (Eds.), *Handbook of Research on the Societal Impact of Digital Media* (pp. 127–162). Hershey, PA: IGI Global. doi:10.4018/978-1-4666-8310-5.ch006

Di Virgilio, F., & Antonelli, G. (2018). Consumer Behavior, Trust, and Electronic Word-of-Mouth Communication: Developing an Online Purchase Intention Model. In F. Di Virgilio (Ed.), *Social Media for Knowledge Management Applications in Modern Organizations* (pp. 58–80). Hershey, PA: IGI Global. doi:10.4018/978-1-5225-2897-5.ch003

Dixit, S. K. (2016). eWOM Marketing in Hospitality Industry. In A. Singh, & P. Duhan (Eds.), Managing Public Relations and Brand Image through Social Media (pp. 266-280). Hershey, PA: IGI Global. doi:10.4018/978-1-5225-0332-3.ch014

Duhan, P., & Singh, A. (2016). Facebook Experience Is Different: An Empirical Study in Indian Context. In S. Rathore & A. Panwar (Eds.), *Capturing, Analyzing, and Managing Word-of-Mouth in the Digital Marketplace* (pp. 188–212). Hershey, PA: IGI Global. doi:10.4018/978-1-4666-9449-1.ch011

Dunne, D. J. (2016). The Scholar's Ludo-Narrative Game and Multimodal Graphic Novel: A Comparison of Fringe Scholarship. In A. Connor & S. Marks (Eds.), *Creative Technologies for Multidisciplinary Applications* (pp. 182–207). Hershey, PA: IGI Global. doi:10.4018/978-1-5225-0016-2.ch008

DuQuette, J. L. (2017). Lessons from Cypris Chat: Revisiting Virtual Communities as Communities. In G. Panconesi & M. Guida (Eds.), *Handbook of Research on Collaborative Teaching Practice in Virtual Learning Environments* (pp. 299–316). Hershey, PA: IGI Global. doi:10.4018/978-1-5225-2426-7.ch016

Ekhlassi, A., Niknejhad Moghadam, M., & Adibi, A. (2018). The Concept of Social Media: The Functional Building Blocks. In *Building Brand Identity in the Age of Social Media: Emerging Research and Opportunities* (pp. 29–60). Hershey, PA: IGI Global. doi:10.4018/978-1-5225-5143-0.ch002

Ekhlassi, A., Niknejhad Moghadam, M., & Adibi, A. (2018). Social Media Branding Strategy: Social Media Marketing Approach. In *Building Brand Identity in the Age of Social Media: Emerging Research and Opportunities* (pp. 94–117). Hershey, PA: IGI Global. doi:10.4018/978-1-5225-5143-0.ch004

Ekhlassi, A., Niknejhad Moghadam, M., & Adibi, A. (2018). The Impact of Social Media on Brand Loyalty: Achieving "E-Trust" Through Engagement. In *Building Brand Identity in the Age of Social Media: Emerging Research and Opportunities* (pp. 155–168). Hershey, PA: IGI Global. doi:10.4018/978-1-5225-5143-0.ch007

Elegbe, O. (2017). An Assessment of Media Contribution to Behaviour Change and HIV Prevention in Nigeria. In O. Nelson, B. Ojebuyi, & A. Salawu (Eds.), *Impacts of the Media on African Socio-Economic Development* (pp. 261–280). Hershey, PA: IGI Global. doi:10.4018/978-1-5225-1859-4.ch017

Endong, F. P. (2018). Hashtag Activism and the Transnationalization of Nigerian-Born Movements Against Terrorism: A Critical Appraisal of the #BringBackOurGirls Campaign. In F. Endong (Ed.), *Exploring the Role of Social Media in Transnational Advocacy* (pp. 36–54). Hershey, PA: IGI Global. doi:10.4018/978-1-5225-2854-8.ch003

Erragcha, N. (2017). Using Social Media Tools in Marketing: Opportunities and Challenges. In M. Brown Sr., (Ed.), *Social Media Performance Evaluation and Success Measurements* (pp. 106–129). Hershey, PA: IGI Global. doi:10.4018/978-1-5225-1963-8.ch006

Ezeh, N. C. (2018). Media Campaign on Exclusive Breastfeeding: Awareness, Perception, and Acceptability Among Mothers in Anambra State, Nigeria. In A. Salawu & T. Owolabi (Eds.), *Exploring Journalism Practice and Perception in Developing Countries* (pp. 172–193). Hershey, PA: IGI Global. doi:10.4018/978-1-5225-3376-4.ch009

Fawole, O. A., & Osho, O. A. (2017). Influence of Social Media on Dating Relationships of Emerging Adults in Nigerian Universities: Social Media and Dating in Nigeria. In M. Wright (Ed.), *Identity, Sexuality, and Relationships among Emerging Adults in the Digital Age* (pp. 168–177). Hershey, PA: IGI Global. doi:10.4018/978-1-5225-1856-3.ch011

Fayoyin, A. (2017). Electoral Polling and Reporting in Africa: Professional and Policy Implications for Media Practice and Political Communication in a Digital Age. In N. Mhiripiri & T. Chari (Eds.), *Media Law, Ethics, and Policy in the Digital Age* (pp. 164–181). Hershey, PA: IGI Global. doi:10.4018/978-1-5225-2095-5.ch009

Fayoyin, A. (2018). Rethinking Media Engagement Strategies for Social Change in Africa: Context, Approaches, and Implications for Development Communication. In A. Salawu & T. Owolabi (Eds.), *Exploring Journalism Practice and Perception in Developing Countries* (pp. 257–280). Hershey, PA: IGI Global. doi:10.4018/978-1-5225-3376-4.ch013

Fechine, Y., & Rêgo, S. C. (2018). Transmedia Television Journalism in Brazil: Jornal da Record News as Reference. In R. Gambarato & G. Alzamora (Eds.), *Exploring Transmedia Journalism in the Digital Age* (pp. 253–265). Hershey, PA: IGI Global. doi:10.4018/978-1-5225-3781-6.ch015

Feng, J., & Lo, K. (2016). Video Broadcasting Protocol for Streaming Applications with Cooperative Clients. In D. Kanellopoulos (Ed.), *Emerging Research on Networked Multimedia Communication Systems* (pp. 205–229). Hershey, PA: IGI Global. doi:10.4018/978-1-4666-8850-6.ch006

Fiore, C. (2017). The Blogging Method: Improving Traditional Student Writing Practices. In K. Bryant (Ed.), *Engaging 21st Century Writers with Social Media* (pp. 179–198). Hershey, PA: IGI Global. doi:10.4018/978-1-5225-0562-4.ch011

Fleming, J., & Kajimoto, M. (2016). The Freedom of Critical Thinking: Examining Efforts to Teach American News Literacy Principles in Hong Kong, Vietnam, and Malaysia. In M. Yildiz & J. Keengwe (Eds.), *Handbook of Research on Media Literacy in the Digital Age* (pp. 208–235). Hershey, PA: IGI Global. doi:10.4018/978-1-4666-9667-9.ch010

Gambarato, R. R., Alzamora, G. C., & Tárcia, L. P. (2018). 2016 Rio Summer Olympics and the Transmedia Journalism of Planned Events. In R. Gambarato & G. Alzamora (Eds.), *Exploring Transmedia Journalism in the Digital Age* (pp. 126–146). Hershey, PA: IGI Global. doi:10.4018/978-1-5225-3781-6.ch008

Ganguin, S., Gemkow, J., & Haubold, R. (2017). Information Overload as a Challenge and Changing Point for Educational Media Literacies. In R. Marques & J. Batista (Eds.), *Information and Communication Overload in the Digital Age* (pp. 302–328). Hershey, PA: IGI Global. doi:10.4018/978-1-5225-2061-0.ch013

Gao, Y. (2016). Reviewing Gratification Effects in Mobile Gaming. In X. Xu (Ed.), *Handbook of Research on Human Social Interaction in the Age of Mobile Devices* (pp. 406–428). Hershey, PA: IGI Global. doi:10.4018/978-1-5225-0469-6.ch017

Gardner, G. C. (2017). The Lived Experience of Smartphone Use in a Unit of the United States Army. In F. Topor (Ed.), *Handbook of Research on Individualism and Identity in the Globalized Digital Age* (pp. 88–117). Hershey, PA: IGI Global. doi:10.4018/978-1-5225-0522-8.ch005

Giessen, H. W. (2016). The Medium, the Content, and the Performance: An Overview on Media-Based Learning. In B. Khan (Ed.), *Revolutionizing Modern Education through Meaningful E-Learning Implementation* (pp. 42–55). Hershey, PA: IGI Global. doi:10.4018/978-1-5225-0466-5.ch003

Giltenane, J. (2016). Investigating the Intention to Use Social Media Tools Within Virtual Project Teams. In G. Silvius (Ed.), *Strategic Integration of Social Media into Project Management Practice* (pp. 83–105). Hershey, PA: IGI Global. doi:10.4018/978-1-4666-9867-3.ch006

Golightly, D., & Houghton, R. J. (2018). Social Media as a Tool to Understand Behaviour on the Railways. In S. Kohli, A. Kumar, J. Easton, & C. Roberts (Eds.), *Innovative Applications of Big Data in the Railway Industry* (pp. 224–239). Hershey, PA: IGI Global. doi:10.4018/978-1-5225-3176-0.ch010

Goovaerts, M., Nieuwenhuysen, P., & Dhamdhere, S. N. (2016). VLIR-UOS Workshop 'E-Info Discovery and Management for Institutes in the South': Presentations and Conclusions, Antwerp, 8-19 December, 2014. In E. de Smet, & S. Dhamdhere (Eds.), E-Discovery Tools and Applications in Modern Libraries (pp. 1-40). Hershey, PA: IGI Global. doi:10.4018/978-1-5225-0474-0.ch001

Grützmann, A., Carvalho de Castro, C., Meireles, A. A., & Rodrigues, R. C. (2016). Organizational Architecture and Online Social Networks: Insights from Innovative Brazilian Companies. In G. Jamil, J. Poças Rascão, F. Ribeiro, & A. Malheiro da Silva (Eds.), *Handbook of Research on Information Architecture and Management in Modern Organizations* (pp. 508–524). Hershey, PA: IGI Global. doi:10.4018/978-1-4666-8637-3.ch023

Gundogan, M. B. (2017). In Search for a "Good Fit" Between Augmented Reality and Mobile Learning Ecosystem. In G. Kurubacak & H. Altinpulluk (Eds.), *Mobile Technologies and Augmented Reality in Open Education* (pp. 135–153). Hershey, PA: IGI Global. doi:10.4018/978-1-5225-2110-5.ch007

Gupta, H. (2018). Impact of Digital Communication on Consumer Behaviour Processes in Luxury Branding Segment: A Study of Apparel Industry. In S. Dasgupta, S. Biswal, & M. Ramesh (Eds.), *Holistic Approaches to Brand Culture and Communication Across Industries* (pp. 132–157). Hershey, PA: IGI Global. doi:10.4018/978-1-5225-3150-0.ch008

Hai-Jew, S. (2017). Creating "(Social) Network Art" with NodeXL. In S. Hai-Jew (Ed.), *Social Media Data Extraction and Content Analysis* (pp. 342–393). Hershey, PA: IGI Global. doi:10.4018/978-1-5225-0648-5.ch011

Hai-Jew, S. (2017). Employing the Sentiment Analysis Tool in NVivo 11 Plus on Social Media Data: Eight Initial Case Types. In N. Rao (Ed.), *Social Media Listening and Monitoring for Business Applications* (pp. 175–244). Hershey, PA: IGI Global. doi:10.4018/978-1-5225-0846-5.ch010

Hai-Jew, S. (2017). Conducting Sentiment Analysis and Post-Sentiment Data Exploration through Automated Means. In S. Hai-Jew (Ed.), *Social Media Data Extraction and Content Analysis* (pp. 202–240). Hershey, PA: IGI Global. doi:10.4018/978-1-5225-0648-5.ch008

Hai-Jew, S. (2017). Applied Analytical "Distant Reading" using NVivo 11 Plus. In S. Hai-Jew (Ed.), *Social Media Data Extraction and Content Analysis* (pp. 159–201). Hershey, PA: IGI Global. doi:10.4018/978-1-5225-0648-5.ch007

Hai-Jew, S. (2017). Flickering Emotions: Feeling-Based Associations from Related Tags Networks on Flickr. In S. Hai-Jew (Ed.), *Social Media Data Extraction and Content Analysis* (pp. 296–341). Hershey, PA: IGI Global. doi:10.4018/978-1-5225-0648-5.ch010

Hai-Jew, S. (2017). Manually Profiling Egos and Entities across Social Media Platforms: Evaluating Shared Messaging and Contents, User Networks, and Metadata. In V. Benson, R. Tuninga, & G. Saridakis (Eds.), *Analyzing the Strategic Role of Social Networking in Firm Growth and Productivity* (pp. 352–405). Hershey, PA: IGI Global. doi:10.4018/978-1-5225-0559-4.ch019

Hai-Jew, S. (2017). Exploring "User," "Video," and (Pseudo) Multi-Mode Networks on YouTube with NodeXL. In S. Hai-Jew (Ed.), *Social Media Data Extraction and Content Analysis* (pp. 242–295). Hershey, PA: IGI Global. doi:10.4018/978-1-5225-0648-5.ch009

Hai-Jew, S. (2018). Exploring "Mass Surveillance" Through Computational Linguistic Analysis of Five Text Corpora: Academic, Mainstream Journalism, Microblogging Hashtag Conversation, Wikipedia Articles, and Leaked Government Data. In *Techniques for Coding Imagery and Multimedia: Emerging Research and Opportunities* (pp. 212–286). Hershey, PA: IGI Global. doi:10.4018/978-1-5225-2679-7.ch004

Hai-Jew, S. (2018). Exploring Identity-Based Humor in a #Selfies #Humor Image Set From Instagram. In *Techniques for Coding Imagery and Multimedia: Emerging Research and Opportunities* (pp. 1–90). Hershey, PA: IGI Global. doi:10.4018/978-1-5225-2679-7.ch001

Hai-Jew, S. (2018). See Ya!: Exploring American Renunciation of Citizenship Through Targeted and Sparse Social Media Data Sets and a Custom Spatial-Based Linguistic Analysis Dictionary. In *Techniques for Coding Imagery and Multimedia: Emerging Research and Opportunities* (pp. 287–393). Hershey, PA: IGI Global. doi:10.4018/978-1-5225-2679-7.ch005

Han, H. S., Zhang, J., Peikazadi, N., Shi, G., Hung, A., Doan, C. P., & Filippelli, S. (2016). An Entertaining Game-Like Learning Environment in a Virtual World for Education. In S. D'Agustino (Ed.), *Creating Teacher Immediacy in Online Learning Environments* (pp. 290–306). Hershey, PA: IGI Global. doi:10.4018/978-1-4666-9995-3.ch015

Harrin, E. (2016). Barriers to Social Media Adoption on Projects. In G. Silvius (Ed.), *Strategic Integration of Social Media into Project Management Practice* (pp. 106–124). Hershey, PA: IGI Global. doi:10.4018/978-1-4666-9867-3.ch007

Harvey, K. E. (2016). Local News and Mobile: Major Tipping Points. In X. Xu (Ed.), *Handbook of Research on Human Social Interaction in the Age of Mobile Devices* (pp. 171–199). Hershey, PA: IGI Global. doi:10.4018/978-1-5225-0469-6.ch009

Harvey, K. E., & An, Y. (2016). Marketing and Mobile: Increasing Integration. In X. Xu (Ed.), *Handbook of Research on Human Social Interaction in the Age of Mobile Devices* (pp. 220–247). Hershey, PA: IGI Global. doi:10.4018/978-1-5225-0469-6.ch011

Harvey, K. E., Auter, P. J., & Stevens, S. (2016). Educators and Mobile: Challenges and Trends. In X. Xu (Ed.), *Handbook of Research on Human Social Interaction in the Age of Mobile Devices* (pp. 61–95). Hershey, PA: IGI Global. doi:10.4018/978-1-5225-0469-6.ch004

Hasan, H., & Linger, H. (2017). Connected Living for Positive Ageing. In S. Gordon (Ed.), *Online Communities as Agents of Change and Social Movements* (pp. 203–223). Hershey, PA: IGI Global. doi:10.4018/978-1-5225-2495-3.ch008

Hashim, K., Al-Sharqi, L., & Kutbi, I. (2016). Perceptions of Social Media Impact on Social Behavior of Students: A Comparison between Students and Faculty. *International Journal of Virtual Communities and Social Networking*, 8(2), 1–11. doi:10.4018/IJVCSN.2016040101

Henriques, S., & Damasio, M. J. (2016). The Value of Mobile Communication for Social Belonging: Mobile Apps and the Impact on Social Interaction. *International Journal of Handheld Computing Research*, 7(2), 44–58. doi:10.4018/IJHCR.2016040104

Hersey, L. N. (2017). CHOICES: Measuring Return on Investment in a Nonprofit Organization. In M. Brown Sr., (Ed.), *Social Media Performance Evaluation and Success Measurements* (pp. 157–179). Hershey, PA: IGI Global. doi:10.4018/978-1-5225-1963-8.ch008

Heuva, W. E. (2017). Deferring Citizens' "Right to Know" in an Information Age: The Information Deficit in Namibia. In N. Mhiripiri & T. Chari (Eds.), *Media Law, Ethics, and Policy in the Digital Age* (pp. 245–267). Hershey, PA: IGI Global. doi:10.4018/978-1-5225-2095-5.ch014

Hopwood, M., & McLean, H. (2017). Social Media in Crisis Communication: The Lance Armstrong Saga. In V. Benson, R. Tuninga, & G. Saridakis (Eds.), *Analyzing the Strategic Role of Social Networking in Firm Growth and Productivity* (pp. 45–58). Hershey, PA: IGI Global. doi:10.4018/978-1-5225-0559-4.ch003

Hotur, S. K. (2018). Indian Approaches to E-Diplomacy: An Overview. In S. Bute (Ed.), *Media Diplomacy and Its Evolving Role in the Current Geopolitical Climate* (pp. 27–35). Hershey, PA: IGI Global. doi:10.4018/978-1-5225-3859-2.ch002

Ibadildin, N., & Harvey, K. E. (2016). Business and Mobile: Rapid Restructure Required. In X. Xu (Ed.), *Handbook of Research on Human Social Interaction in the Age of Mobile Devices* (pp. 312–350). Hershey, PA: IGI Global. doi:10.4018/978-1-5225-0469-6.ch014

Iwasaki, Y. (2017). Youth Engagement in the Era of New Media. In M. Adria & Y. Mao (Eds.), *Handbook of Research on Citizen Engagement and Public Participation in the Era of New Media* (pp. 90–105). Hershey, PA: IGI Global. doi:10.4018/978-1-5225-1081-9.ch006

Jamieson, H. V. (2017). We have a Situation!: Cyberformance and Civic Engagement in Post-Democracy. In R. Shin (Ed.), *Convergence of Contemporary Art, Visual Culture, and Global Civic Engagement* (pp. 297–317). Hershey, PA: IGI Global. doi:10.4018/978-1-5225-1665-1.ch017

Jimoh, J., & Kayode, J. (2018). Imperative of Peace and Conflict-Sensitive Journalism in Development. In A. Salawu & T. Owolabi (Eds.), *Exploring Journalism Practice and Perception in Developing Countries* (pp. 150–171). Hershey, PA: IGI Global. doi:10.4018/978-1-5225-3376-4.ch008

Johns, R. (2016). Increasing Value of a Tangible Product through Intangible Attributes: Value Co-Creation and Brand Building within Online Communities – Virtual Communities and Value. In R. English & R. Johns (Eds.), *Gender Considerations in Online Consumption Behavior and Internet Use* (pp. 112–124). Hershey, PA: IGI Global. doi:10.4018/978-1-5225-0010-0.ch008

Kanellopoulos, D. N. (2018). Group Synchronization for Multimedia Systems. In M. Khosrow-Pour, D.B.A. (Ed.), Encyclopedia of Information Science and Technology, Fourth Edition (pp. 6435-6446). Hershey, PA: IGI Global. doi:10.4018/978-1-5225-2255-3.ch559

Kapepo, M. I., & Mayisela, T. (2017). Integrating Digital Literacies Into an Undergraduate Course: Inclusiveness Through Use of ICTs. In C. Ayo & V. Mbarika (Eds.), *Sustainable ICT Adoption and Integration for Socio-Economic Development* (pp. 152–173). Hershey, PA: IGI Global. doi:10.4018/978-1-5225-2565-3.ch007

Karahoca, A., & Yengin, İ. (2018). Understanding the Potentials of Social Media in Collaborative Learning. In M. Khosrow-Pour, D.B.A. (Ed.), Encyclopedia of Information Science and Technology, Fourth Edition (pp. 7168-7180). Hershey, PA: IGI Global. doi:10.4018/978-1-5225-2255-3.ch623

Karataş, S., Ceran, O., Ülker, Ü., Gün, E. T., Köse, N. Ö., Kılıç, M., ... Tok, Z. A. (2016). A Trend Analysis of Mobile Learning. In D. Parsons (Ed.), *Mobile and Blended Learning Innovations for Improved Learning Outcomes* (pp. 248–276). Hershey, PA: IGI Global. doi:10.4018/978-1-5225-0359-0.ch013

Kasemsap, K. (2016). Role of Social Media in Brand Promotion: An International Marketing Perspective. In A. Singh & P. Duhan (Eds.), *Managing Public Relations and Brand Image through Social Media* (pp. 62–88). Hershey, PA: IGI Global. doi:10.4018/978-1-5225-0332-3.ch005

Kasemsap, K. (2016). The Roles of Social Media Marketing and Brand Management in Global Marketing. In W. Ozuem & G. Bowen (Eds.), *Competitive Social Media Marketing Strategies* (pp. 173–200). Hershey, PA: IGI Global. doi:10.4018/978-1-4666-9776-8.ch009

Kasemsap, K. (2017). Professional and Business Applications of Social Media Platforms. In V. Benson, R. Tuninga, & G. Saridakis (Eds.), *Analyzing the Strategic Role of Social Networking in Firm Growth and Productivity* (pp. 427–450). Hershey, PA: IGI Global. doi:10.4018/978-1-5225-0559-4.ch021

Kasemsap, K. (2017). Mastering Social Media in the Modern Business World. In N. Rao (Ed.), *Social Media Listening and Monitoring for Business Applications* (pp. 18–44). Hershey, PA: IGI Global. doi:10.4018/978-1-5225-0846-5.ch002

Kato, Y., & Kato, S. (2016). Mobile Phone Use during Class at a Japanese Women's College. In M. Yildiz & J. Keengwe (Eds.), *Handbook of Research on Media Literacy in the Digital Age* (pp. 436–455). Hershey, PA: IGI Global. doi:10.4018/978-1-4666-9667-9.ch021

Kaufmann, H. R., & Manarioti, A. (2017). Consumer Engagement in Social Media Platforms. In *Encouraging Participative Consumerism Through Evolutionary Digital Marketing: Emerging Research and Opportunities* (pp. 95–123). Hershey, PA: IGI Global. doi:10.4018/978-1-68318-012-8.ch004

Kavoura, A., & Kefallonitis, E. (2018). The Effect of Social Media Networking in the Travel Industry. In M. Khosrow-Pour, D.B.A. (Ed.), Encyclopedia of Information Science and Technology, Fourth Edition (pp. 4052-4063). Hershey, PA: IGI Global. doi:10.4018/978-1-5225-2255-3.ch351

Kawamura, Y. (2018). Practice and Modeling of Advertising Communication Strategy: Sender-Driven and Receiver-Driven. In T. Ogata & S. Asakawa (Eds.), *Content Generation Through Narrative Communication and Simulation* (pp. 358–379). Hershey, PA: IGI Global. doi:10.4018/978-1-5225-4775-4.ch013

Kell, C., & Czerniewicz, L. (2017). Visibility of Scholarly Research and Changing Research Communication Practices: A Case Study from Namibia. In A. Esposito (Ed.), *Research 2.0 and the Impact of Digital Technologies on Scholarly Inquiry* (pp. 97–116). Hershey, PA: IGI Global. doi:10.4018/978-1-5225-0830-4.ch006

Khalil, G. E. (2016). Change through Experience: How Experiential Play and Emotional Engagement Drive Health Game Success. In D. Novák, B. Tulu, & H. Brendryen (Eds.), *Handbook of Research on Holistic Perspectives in Gamification for Clinical Practice* (pp. 10–34). Hershey, PA: IGI Global. doi:10.4018/978-1-4666-9522-1.ch002

Kılınç, U. (2017). Create It! Extend It!: Evolution of Comics Through Narrative Advertising. In R. Yılmaz (Ed.), *Narrative Advertising Models and Conceptualization in the Digital Age* (pp. 117–132). Hershey, PA: IGI Global. doi:10.4018/978-1-5225-2373-4.ch007

Kim, J. H. (2016). Pedagogical Approaches to Media Literacy Education in the United States. In M. Yildiz & J. Keengwe (Eds.), *Handbook of Research on Media Literacy in the Digital Age* (pp. 53–74). Hershey, PA: IGI Global. doi:10.4018/978-1-4666-9667-9.ch003

Kirigha, J. M., Mukhongo, L. L., & Masinde, R. (2016). Beyond Web 2.0. Social Media and Urban Educated Youths Participation in Kenyan Politics. In L. Mukhongo & J. Macharia (Eds.), *Political Influence of the Media in Developing Countries* (pp. 156–174). Hershey, PA: IGI Global. doi:10.4018/978-1-4666-9613-6.ch010

Krochmal, M. M. (2016). Training for Mobile Journalism. In D. Mentor (Ed.), *Handbook of Research on Mobile Learning in Contemporary Classrooms* (pp. 336–362). Hershey, PA: IGI Global. doi:10.4018/978-1-5225-0251-7.ch017

Kumar, P., & Sinha, A. (2018). Business-Oriented Analytics With Social Network of Things. In H. Bansal, G. Shrivastava, G. Nguyen, & L. Stanciu (Eds.), *Social Network Analytics for Contemporary Business Organizations* (pp. 166–187). Hershey, PA: IGI Global. doi:10.4018/978-1-5225-5097-6.ch009

Kunock, A. I. (2017). Boko Haram Insurgency in Cameroon: Role of Mass Media in Conflict Management. In N. Mhiripiri & T. Chari (Eds.), *Media Law, Ethics, and Policy in the Digital Age* (pp. 226–244). Hershey, PA: IGI Global. doi:10.4018/978-1-5225-2095-5.ch013

Labadie, J. A. (2018). Digitally Mediated Art Inspired by Technology Integration: A Personal Journey. In A. Ursyn (Ed.), *Visual Approaches to Cognitive Education With Technology Integration* (pp. 121–162). Hershey, PA: IGI Global. doi:10.4018/978-1-5225-5332-8.ch008

Lefkowith, S. (2017). Credibility and Crisis in Pseudonymous Communities. In M. Folk & S. Apostel (Eds.), *Establishing and Evaluating Digital Ethos and Online Credibility* (pp. 190–236). Hershey, PA: IGI Global. doi:10.4018/978-1-5225-1072-7.ch010

Lemoine, P. A., Hackett, P. T., & Richardson, M. D. (2016). The Impact of Social Media on Instruction in Higher Education. In L. Briz-Ponce, J. Juanes-Méndez, & F. García-Peñalvo (Eds.), *Handbook of Research on Mobile Devices and Applications in Higher Education Settings* (pp. 373–401). Hershey, PA: IGI Global. doi:10.4018/978-1-5225-0256-2.ch016

Liampotis, N., Papadopoulou, E., Kalatzis, N., Roussaki, I. G., Kosmides, P., Sykas, E. D., ... Taylor, N. K. (2016). Tailoring Privacy-Aware Trustworthy Cooperating Smart Spaces for University Environments. In A. Panagopoulos (Ed.), *Handbook of Research on Next Generation Mobile Communication Systems* (pp. 410–439). Hershey, PA: IGI Global. doi:10.4018/978-1-4666-8732-5.ch016

Luppicini, R. (2017). Technoethics and Digital Democracy for Future Citizens. In R. Luppicini & R. Baarda (Eds.), *Digital Media Integration for Participatory Democracy* (pp. 1–21). Hershey, PA: IGI Global. doi:10.4018/978-1-5225-2463-2.ch001

Mahajan, I. M., Rather, M., Shafiq, H., & Qadri, U. (2016). Media Literacy Organizations. In M. Yildiz & J. Keengwe (Eds.), *Handbook of Research on Media Literacy in the Digital Age* (pp. 236–248). Hershey, PA: IGI Global. doi:10.4018/978-1-4666-9667-9.ch011

Maher, D. (2018). Supporting Pre-Service Teachers' Understanding and Use of Mobile Devices. In J. Keengwe (Ed.), *Handbook of Research on Mobile Technology, Constructivism, and Meaningful Learning* (pp. 160–177). Hershey, PA: IGI Global. doi:10.4018/978-1-5225-3949-0.ch009

Makhwanya, A. (2018). Barriers to Social Media Advocacy: Lessons Learnt From the Project "Tell Them We Are From Here". In F. Endong (Ed.), *Exploring the Role of Social Media in Transnational Advocacy* (pp. 55–72). Hershey, PA: IGI Global. doi:10.4018/978-1-5225-2854-8.ch004

Manli, G., & Rezaei, S. (2017). Value and Risk: Dual Pillars of Apps Usefulness. In S. Rezaei (Ed.), *Apps Management and E-Commerce Transactions in Real-Time* (pp. 274–292). Hershey, PA: IGI Global. doi:10.4018/978-1-5225-2449-6.ch013

Manrique, C. G., & Manrique, G. G. (2017). Social Media's Role in Alleviating Political Corruption and Scandals: The Philippines during and after the Marcos Regime. In K. Demirhan & D. Çakır-Demirhan (Eds.), *Political Scandal, Corruption, and Legitimacy in the Age of Social Media* (pp. 205–222). Hershey, PA: IGI Global. doi:10.4018/978-1-5225-2019-1.ch009

Manzoor, A. (2016). Cultural Barriers to Organizational Social Media Adoption. In A. Goel & P. Singhal (Eds.), *Product Innovation through Knowledge Management and Social Media Strategies* (pp. 31–45). Hershey, PA: IGI Global. doi:10.4018/978-1-4666-9607-5.ch002

Manzoor, A. (2016). Social Media for Project Management. In G. Silvius (Ed.), *Strategic Integration of Social Media into Project Management Practice* (pp. 51–65). Hershey, PA: IGI Global. doi:10.4018/978-1-4666-9867-3.ch004

Marovitz, M. (2017). Social Networking Engagement and Crisis Communication Considerations. In M. Brown Sr., (Ed.), *Social Media Performance Evaluation and Success Measurements* (pp. 130–155). Hershey, PA: IGI Global. doi:10.4018/978-1-5225-1963-8.ch007

Mathur, D., & Mathur, D. (2016). Word of Mouth on Social Media: A Potent Tool for Brand Building. In S. Rathore & A. Panwar (Eds.), *Capturing, Analyzing, and Managing Word-of-Mouth in the Digital Marketplace* (pp. 45–60). Hershey, PA: IGI Global. doi:10.4018/978-1-4666-9449-1.ch003

Maulana, I. (2018). Spontaneous Taking and Posting Selfie: Reclaiming the Lost Trust. In S. Hai-Jew (Ed.), *Selfies as a Mode of Social Media and Work Space Research* (pp. 28–50). Hershey, PA: IGI Global. doi:10.4018/978-1-5225-3373-3.ch002

Mayo, S. (2018). A Collective Consciousness Model in a Post-Media Society. In M. Khosrow-Pour (Ed.), *Enhancing Art, Culture, and Design With Technological Integration* (pp. 25–49). Hershey, PA: IGI Global. doi:10.4018/978-1-5225-5023-5.ch002

Mazur, E., Signorella, M. L., & Hough, M. (2018). The Internet Behavior of Older Adults. In M. Khosrow-Pour, D.B.A. (Ed.), Encyclopedia of Information Science and Technology, Fourth Edition (pp. 7026-7035). Hershey, PA: IGI Global. doi:10.4018/978-1-5225-2255-3.ch609

McGuire, M. (2017). Reblogging as Writing: The Role of Tumblr in the Writing Classroom. In K. Bryant (Ed.), *Engaging 21st Century Writers with Social Media* (pp. 116–131). Hershey, PA: IGI Global. doi:10.4018/978-1-5225-0562-4.ch007

McKee, J. (2018). Architecture as a Tool to Solve Business Planning Problems. In M. Khosrow-Pour, D.B.A. (Ed.), Encyclopedia of Information Science and Technology, Fourth Edition (pp. 573-586). Hershey, PA: IGI Global. doi:10.4018/978-1-5225-2255-3.ch050

McMahon, D. (2017). With a Little Help from My Friends: The Irish Radio Industry's Strategic Appropriation of Facebook for Commercial Growth. In V. Benson, R. Tuninga, & G. Saridakis (Eds.), *Analyzing the Strategic Role of Social Networking in Firm Growth and Productivity* (pp. 157–171). Hershey, PA: IGI Global. doi:10.4018/978-1-5225-0559-4.ch009

McPherson, M. J., & Lemon, N. (2017). The Hook, Woo, and Spin: Academics Creating Relations on Social Media. In A. Esposito (Ed.), *Research 2.0 and the Impact of Digital Technologies on Scholarly Inquiry* (pp. 167–187). Hershey, PA: IGI Global. doi:10.4018/978-1-5225-0830-4.ch009

Melro, A., & Oliveira, L. (2018). Screen Culture. In M. Khosrow-Pour, D.B.A. (Ed.), Encyclopedia of Information Science and Technology, Fourth Edition (pp. 4255-4266). Hershey, PA: IGI Global. doi:10.4018/978-1-5225-2255-3.ch369

Merwin, G. A. Jr, McDonald, J. S., Bennett, J. R. Jr, & Merwin, K. A. (2016). Social Media Applications Promote Constituent Involvement in Government Management. In G. Silvius (Ed.), *Strategic Integration of Social Media into Project Management Practice* (pp. 272–291). Hershey, PA: IGI Global. doi:10.4018/978-1-4666-9867-3.ch016

Mhiripiri, N. A., & Chikakano, J. (2017). Criminal Defamation, the Criminalisation of Expression, Media and Information Dissemination in the Digital Age: A Legal and Ethical Perspective. In N. Mhiripiri & T. Chari (Eds.), *Media Law, Ethics, and Policy in the Digital Age* (pp. 1–24). Hershey, PA: IGI Global. doi:10.4018/978-1-5225-2095-5.ch001

Miliopoulou, G., & Cossiavelou, V. (2016). Brands and Media Gatekeeping in the Social Media: Current Trends and Practices – An Exploratory Research. *International Journal of Interdisciplinary Telecommunications and Networking*, 8(4), 51–64. doi:10.4018/IJITN.2016100105

Miron, E., Palmor, A., Ravid, G., Sharon, A., Tikotsky, A., & Zirkel, Y. (2017). Principles and Good Practices for Using Wikis within Organizations. In R. Chugh (Ed.), *Harnessing Social Media as a Knowledge Management Tool* (pp. 143–176). Hershey, PA: IGI Global. doi:10.4018/978-1-5225-0495-5.ch008

Mishra, K. E., Mishra, A. K., & Walker, K. (2016). Leadership Communication, Internal Marketing, and Employee Engagement: A Recipe to Create Brand Ambassadors. In A. Normore, L. Long, & M. Javidi (Eds.), *Handbook of Research on Effective Communication, Leadership, and Conflict Resolution* (pp. 311–329). Hershey, PA: IGI Global. doi:10.4018/978-1-4666-9970-0.ch017

Moeller, C. L. (2018). Sharing Your Personal Medical Experience Online: Is It an Irresponsible Act or Patient Empowerment? In S. Sekalala & B. Niezgoda (Eds.), *Global Perspectives on Health Communication in the Age of Social Media* (pp. 185–209). Hershey, PA: IGI Global. doi:10.4018/978-1-5225-3716-8.ch007

Mosanako, S. (2017). Broadcasting Policy in Botswana: The Case of Botswana Television. In O. Nelson, B. Ojebuyi, & A. Salawu (Eds.), *Impacts of the Media on African Socio-Economic Development* (pp. 217–230). Hershey, PA: IGI Global. doi:10.4018/978-1-5225-1859-4.ch014

Nazari, A. (2016). Developing a Social Media Communication Plan. In G. Silvius (Ed.), *Strategic Integration of Social Media into Project Management Practice* (pp. 194–217). Hershey, PA: IGI Global. doi:10.4018/978-1-4666-9867-3.ch012

Neto, B. M. (2016). From Information Society to Community Service: The Birth of E-Citizenship. In B. Passarelli, J. Straubhaar, & A. Cuevas-Cerveró (Eds.), *Handbook of Research on Comparative Approaches to the Digital Age Revolution in Europe and the Americas* (pp. 101–123). Hershey, PA: IGI Global. doi:10.4018/978-1-4666-8740-0.ch007

Noguti, V., Singh, S., & Waller, D. S. (2016). Gender Differences in Motivations to Use Social Networking Sites. In R. English & R. Johns (Eds.), *Gender Considerations in Online Consumption Behavior and Internet Use* (pp. 32–49). Hershey, PA: IGI Global. doi:10.4018/978-1-5225-0010-0.ch003

Noor, R. (2017). Citizen Journalism: News Gathering by Amateurs. In M. Adria & Y. Mao (Eds.), *Handbook of Research on Citizen Engagement and Public Participation in the Era of New Media* (pp. 194–229). Hershey, PA: IGI Global. doi:10.4018/978-1-5225-1081-9.ch012

Nwagbara, U., Oruh, E. S., & Brown, C. (2016). State Fragility and Stakeholder Engagement: New Media and Stakeholders' Voice Amplification in the Nigerian Petroleum Industry. In W. Ozuem & G. Bowen (Eds.), *Competitive Social Media Marketing Strategies* (pp. 136–154). Hershey, PA: IGI Global. doi:10.4018/978-1-4666-9776-8.ch007

Obermayer, N., Csepregi, A., & Kővári, E. (2017). Knowledge Sharing Relation to Competence, Emotional Intelligence, and Social Media Regarding Generations. In A. Bencsik (Ed.), *Knowledge Management Initiatives and Strategies in Small and Medium Enterprises* (pp. 269–290). Hershey, PA: IGI Global. doi:10.4018/978-1-5225-1642-2.ch013

Obermayer, N., Gaál, Z., Szabó, L., & Csepregi, A. (2017). Leveraging Knowledge Sharing over Social Media Tools. In R. Chugh (Ed.), *Harnessing Social Media as a Knowledge Management Tool* (pp. 1–24). Hershey, PA: IGI Global. doi:10.4018/978-1-5225-0495-5.ch001

Ogwezzy-Ndisika, A. O., & Faustino, B. A. (2016). Gender Responsive Election Coverage in Nigeria: A Score Card of 2011 General Elections. In L. Mukhongo & J. Macharia (Eds.), *Political Influence of the Media in Developing Countries* (pp. 234–249). Hershey, PA: IGI Global. doi:10.4018/978-1-4666-9613-6.ch015

Okoroafor, O. E. (2018). New Media Technology and Development Journalism in Nigeria. In A. Salawu & T. Owolabi (Eds.), *Exploring Journalism Practice and Perception in Developing Countries* (pp. 105–125). Hershey, PA: IGI Global. doi:10.4018/978-1-5225-3376-4.ch006

Olaleye, S. A., Sanusi, I. T., & Ukpabi, D. C. (2018). Assessment of Mobile Money Enablers in Nigeria. In F. Mtenzi, G. Oreku, D. Lupiana, & J. Yonazi (Eds.), *Mobile Technologies and Socio-Economic Development in Emerging Nations* (pp. 129–155). Hershey, PA: IGI Global. doi:10.4018/978-1-5225-4029-8.ch007

Ozuem, W., Pinho, C. A., & Azemi, Y. (2016). User-Generated Content and Perceived Customer Value. In W. Ozuem & G. Bowen (Eds.), *Competitive Social Media Marketing Strategies* (pp. 50–63). Hershey, PA: IGI Global. doi:10.4018/978-1-4666-9776-8.ch003

Pacchiega, C. (2017). An Informal Methodology for Teaching Through Virtual Worlds: Using Internet Tools and Virtual Worlds in a Coordinated Pattern to Teach Various Subjects. In G. Panconesi & M. Guida (Eds.), *Handbook of Research on Collaborative Teaching Practice in Virtual Learning Environments* (pp. 163–180). Hershey, PA: IGI Global. doi:10.4018/978-1-5225-2426-7.ch009

Pase, A. F., Goss, B. M., & Tietzmann, R. (2018). A Matter of Time: Transmedia Journalism Challenges. In R. Gambarato & G. Alzamora (Eds.), *Exploring Transmedia Journalism in the Digital Age* (pp. 49–66). Hershey, PA: IGI Global. doi:10.4018/978-1-5225-3781-6.ch004

Passarelli, B., & Paletta, F. C. (2016). Living inside the NET: The Primacy of Interactions and Processes. In B. Passarelli, J. Straubhaar, & A. Cuevas-Cerveró (Eds.), *Handbook of Research on Comparative Approaches to the Digital Age Revolution in Europe and the Americas* (pp. 1–15). Hershey, PA: IGI Global. doi:10.4018/978-1-4666-8740-0.ch001

Patkin, T. T. (2017). Social Media and Knowledge Management in a Crisis Context: Barriers and Opportunities. In R. Chugh (Ed.), *Harnessing Social Media as a Knowledge Management Tool* (pp. 125–142). Hershey, PA: IGI Global. doi:10.4018/978-1-5225-0495-5.ch007

Pavlíček, A. (2017). Social Media and Creativity: How to Engage Users and Tourists. In A. Kiráľová (Ed.), *Driving Tourism through Creative Destinations and Activities* (pp. 181–202). Hershey, PA: IGI Global. doi:10.4018/978-1-5225-2016-0.ch009

Pillay, K., & Maharaj, M. (2017). The Business of Advocacy: A Case Study of Greenpeace. In V. Benson, R. Tuninga, & G. Saridakis (Eds.), *Analyzing the Strategic Role of Social Networking in Firm Growth and Productivity* (pp. 59–75). Hershey, PA: IGI Global. doi:10.4018/978-1-5225-0559-4.ch004

Piven, I. P., & Breazeale, M. (2017). Desperately Seeking Customer Engagement: The Five-Sources Model of Brand Value on Social Media. In V. Benson, R. Tuninga, & G. Saridakis (Eds.), *Analyzing the Strategic Role of Social Networking in Firm Growth and Productivity* (pp. 283–313). Hershey, PA: IGI Global. doi:10.4018/978-1-5225-0559-4.ch016

Pokharel, R. (2017). New Media and Technology: How Do They Change the Notions of the Rhetorical Situations? In B. Gurung & M. Limbu (Eds.), *Integration of Cloud Technologies in Digitally Networked Classrooms and Learning Communities* (pp. 120–148). Hershey, PA: IGI Global. doi:10.4018/978-1-5225-1650-7.ch008

Popoola, I. S. (2016). The Press and the Emergent Political Class in Nigeria: Media, Elections, and Democracy. In L. Mukhongo & J. Macharia (Eds.), *Political Influence of the Media in Developing Countries* (pp. 45–58). Hershey, PA: IGI Global. doi:10.4018/978-1-4666-9613-6.ch004

Porlezza, C., Benecchi, E., & Colapinto, C. (2018). The Transmedia Revitalization of Investigative Journalism: Opportunities and Challenges of the Serial Podcast. In R. Gambarato & G. Alzamora (Eds.), *Exploring Transmedia Journalism in the Digital Age* (pp. 183–201). Hershey, PA: IGI Global. doi:10.4018/978-1-5225-3781-6.ch011

Ramluckan, T., Ally, S. E., & van Niekerk, B. (2017). Twitter Use in Student Protests: The Case of South Africa's #FeesMustFall Campaign. In M. Korstanje (Ed.), *Threat Mitigation and Detection of Cyber Warfare and Terrorism Activities* (pp. 220–253). Hershey, PA: IGI Global. doi:10.4018/978-1-5225-1938-6.ch010

Rao, N. R. (2017). Social Media: An Enabler for Governance. In N. Rao (Ed.), *Social Media Listening and Monitoring for Business Applications* (pp. 151–164). Hershey, PA: IGI Global. doi:10.4018/978-1-5225-0846-5.ch008

Rathore, A. K., Tuli, N., & Ilavarasan, P. V. (2016). Pro-Business or Common Citizen?: An Analysis of an Indian Woman CEO's Tweets. *International Journal of Virtual Communities and Social Networking, 8*(1), 19–29. doi:10.4018/IJVCSN.2016010102

Redi, F. (2017). Enhancing Coopetition Among Small Tourism Destinations by Creativity. In A. Kiráľová (Ed.), *Driving Tourism through Creative Destinations and Activities* (pp. 223–244). Hershey, PA: IGI Global. doi:10.4018/978-1-5225-2016-0.ch011

Reeves, M. (2016). Social Media: It Can Play a Positive Role in Education. In R. English & R. Johns (Eds.), *Gender Considerations in Online Consumption Behavior and Internet Use* (pp. 82–95). Hershey, PA: IGI Global. doi:10.4018/978-1-5225-0010-0.ch006

Reis, Z. A. (2016). Bring the Media Literacy of Turkish Pre-Service Teachers to the Table. In M. Yildiz & J. Keengwe (Eds.), *Handbook of Research on Media Literacy in the Digital Age* (pp. 405–422). Hershey, PA: IGI Global. doi:10.4018/978-1-4666-9667-9.ch019

Resuloğlu, F., & Yılmaz, R. (2017). A Model for Interactive Advertising Narration. In R. Yılmaz (Ed.), *Narrative Advertising Models and Conceptualization in the Digital Age* (pp. 1–20). Hershey, PA: IGI Global. doi:10.4018/978-1-5225-2373-4.ch001

Ritzhaupt, A. D., Poling, N., Frey, C., Kang, Y., & Johnson, M. (2016). A Phenomenological Study of Games, Simulations, and Virtual Environments Courses: What Are We Teaching and How? *International Journal of Gaming and Computer-Mediated Simulations, 8*(3), 59–73. doi:10.4018/IJGCMS.2016070104

Ross, D. B., Eleno-Orama, M., & Salah, E. V. (2018). The Aging and Technological Society: Learning Our Way Through the Decades. In V. Bryan, A. Musgrove, & J. Powers (Eds.), *Handbook of Research on Human Development in the Digital Age* (pp. 205–234). Hershey, PA: IGI Global. doi:10.4018/978-1-5225-2838-8.ch010

Rusko, R., & Merenheimo, P. (2017). Co-Creating the Christmas Story: Digitalizing as a Shared Resource for a Shared Brand. In I. Oncioiu (Ed.), *Driving Innovation and Business Success in the Digital Economy* (pp. 137–157). Hershey, PA: IGI Global. doi:10.4018/978-1-5225-1779-5.ch010

Sabao, C., & Chikara, T. O. (2018). Social Media as Alternative Public Sphere for Citizen Participation and Protest in National Politics in Zimbabwe: The Case of #thisflag. In F. Endong (Ed.), *Exploring the Role of Social Media in Transnational Advocacy* (pp. 17–35). Hershey, PA: IGI Global. doi:10.4018/978-1-5225-2854-8. ch002

Samarthya-Howard, A., & Rogers, D. (2018). Scaling Mobile Technologies to Maximize Reach and Impact: Partnering With Mobile Network Operators and Governments. In S. Takavarasha Jr & C. Adams (Eds.), *Affordability Issues Surrounding the Use of ICT for Development and Poverty Reduction* (pp. 193–211). Hershey, PA: IGI Global. doi:10.4018/978-1-5225-3179-1.ch009

Sandoval-Almazan, R. (2017). Political Messaging in Digital Spaces: The Case of Twitter in Mexico's Presidential Campaign. In Y. Ibrahim (Ed.), *Politics, Protest, and Empowerment in Digital Spaces* (pp. 72–90). Hershey, PA: IGI Global. doi:10.4018/978-1-5225-1862-4.ch005

Schultz, C. D., & Dellnitz, A. (2018). Attribution Modeling in Online Advertising. In K. Yang (Ed.), *Multi-Platform Advertising Strategies in the Global Marketplace* (pp. 226–249). Hershey, PA: IGI Global. doi:10.4018/978-1-5225-3114-2.ch009

Schultz, C. D., & Holsing, C. (2018). Differences Across Device Usage in Search Engine Advertising. In K. Yang (Ed.), *Multi-Platform Advertising Strategies in the Global Marketplace* (pp. 250–279). Hershey, PA: IGI Global. doi:10.4018/978-1-5225-3114-2.ch010

Senadheera, V., Warren, M., Leitch, S., & Pye, G. (2017). Facebook Content Analysis: A Study into Australian Banks' Social Media Community Engagement. In S. Hai-Jew (Ed.), *Social Media Data Extraction and Content Analysis* (pp. 412–432). Hershey, PA: IGI Global. doi:10.4018/978-1-5225-0648-5.ch013

Sharma, A. R. (2018). Promoting Global Competencies in India: Media and Information Literacy as Stepping Stone. In M. Yildiz, S. Funk, & B. De Abreu (Eds.), *Promoting Global Competencies Through Media Literacy* (pp. 160–174). Hershey, PA: IGI Global. doi:10.4018/978-1-5225-3082-4.ch010

Sillah, A. (2017). Nonprofit Organizations and Social Media Use: An Analysis of Nonprofit Organizations' Effective Use of Social Media Tools. In M. Brown Sr., (Ed.), *Social Media Performance Evaluation and Success Measurements* (pp. 180–195). Hershey, PA: IGI Global. doi:10.4018/978-1-5225-1963-8.ch009

Škorić, M. (2017). Adaptation of Winlink 2000 Emergency Amateur Radio Email Network to a VHF Packet Radio Infrastructure. In A. El Oualkadi & J. Zbitou (Eds.), *Handbook of Research on Advanced Trends in Microwave and Communication Engineering* (pp. 498–528). Hershey, PA: IGI Global. doi:10.4018/978-1-5225-0773-4.ch016

Skubida, D. (2016). Can Some Computer Games Be a Sport?: Issues with Legitimization of eSport as a Sporting Activity. *International Journal of Gaming and Computer-Mediated Simulations*, 8(4), 38–52. doi:10.4018/IJGCMS.2016100103

Sonnenberg, C. (2016). Mobile Content Adaptation: An Analysis of Techniques and Frameworks. In J. Aguado, C. Feijóo, & I. Martínez (Eds.), *Emerging Perspectives on the Mobile Content Evolution* (pp. 177–199). Hershey, PA: IGI Global. doi:10.4018/978-1-4666-8838-4.ch010

Sonnevend, J. (2016). More Hope!: Ceremonial Media Events Are Still Powerful in the Twenty-First Century. In A. Fox (Ed.), *Global Perspectives on Media Events in Contemporary Society* (pp. 132–140). Hershey, PA: IGI Global. doi:10.4018/978-1-4666-9967-0.ch010

Sood, T. (2017). Services Marketing: A Sector of the Current Millennium. In T. Sood (Ed.), *Strategic Marketing Management and Tactics in the Service Industry* (pp. 15–42). Hershey, PA: IGI Global. doi:10.4018/978-1-5225-2475-5.ch002

Stairs, G. A. (2016). The Amplification of the Sunni-Shia Divide through Contemporary Communications Technology: Fear and Loathing in the Modern Middle East. In S. Gibson & A. Lando (Eds.), *Impact of Communication and the Media on Ethnic Conflict* (pp. 214–231). Hershey, PA: IGI Global. doi:10.4018/978-1-4666-9728-7.ch013

Stokinger, E., & Ozuem, W. (2016). The Intersection of Social Media and Customer Retention in the Luxury Beauty Industry. In W. Ozuem & G. Bowen (Eds.), *Competitive Social Media Marketing Strategies* (pp. 235–258). Hershey, PA: IGI Global. doi:10.4018/978-1-4666-9776-8.ch012

Sudarsanam, S. K. (2017). Social Media Metrics. In N. Rao (Ed.), *Social Media Listening and Monitoring for Business Applications* (pp. 131–149). Hershey, PA: IGI Global. doi:10.4018/978-1-5225-0846-5.ch007

Swiatek, L. (2017). Accessing the Finest Minds: Insights into Creativity from Esteemed Media Professionals. In N. Silton (Ed.), *Exploring the Benefits of Creativity in Education, Media, and the Arts* (pp. 240–263). Hershey, PA: IGI Global. doi:10.4018/978-1-5225-0504-4.ch012

Switzer, J. S., & Switzer, R. V. (2016). Virtual Teams: Profiles of Successful Leaders. In B. Baggio (Ed.), *Analyzing Digital Discourse and Human Behavior in Modern Virtual Environments* (pp. 1–24). Hershey, PA: IGI Global. doi:10.4018/978-1-4666-9899-4.ch001

Tabbane, R. S., & Debabi, M. (2016). Electronic Word of Mouth: Definitions and Concepts. In S. Rathore & A. Panwar (Eds.), *Capturing, Analyzing, and Managing Word-of-Mouth in the Digital Marketplace* (pp. 1–27). Hershey, PA: IGI Global. doi:10.4018/978-1-4666-9449-1.ch001

Tellería, A. S. (2016). The Role of the Profile and the Digital Identity on the Mobile Content. In J. Aguado, C. Feijóo, & I. Martínez (Eds.), *Emerging Perspectives on the Mobile Content Evolution* (pp. 263–282). Hershey, PA: IGI Global. doi:10.4018/978-1-4666-8838-4.ch014

Teurlings, J. (2017). What Critical Media Studies Should Not Take from Actor-Network Theory. In M. Spöhrer & B. Ochsner (Eds.), *Applying the Actor-Network Theory in Media Studies* (pp. 66–78). Hershey, PA: IGI Global. doi:10.4018/978-1-5225-0616-4.ch005

Tomé, V. (2018). Assessing Media Literacy in Teacher Education. In M. Yildiz, S. Funk, & B. De Abreu (Eds.), *Promoting Global Competencies Through Media Literacy* (pp. 1–19). Hershey, PA: IGI Global. doi:10.4018/978-1-5225-3082-4.ch001

Toscano, J. P. (2017). Social Media and Public Participation: Opportunities, Barriers, and a New Framework. In M. Adria & Y. Mao (Eds.), *Handbook of Research on Citizen Engagement and Public Participation in the Era of New Media* (pp. 73–89). Hershey, PA: IGI Global. doi:10.4018/978-1-5225-1081-9.ch005

Trauth, E. (2017). Creating Meaning for Millennials: Bakhtin, Rosenblatt, and the Use of Social Media in the Composition Classroom. In K. Bryant (Ed.), *Engaging 21st Century Writers with Social Media* (pp. 151–162). Hershey, PA: IGI Global. doi:10.4018/978-1-5225-0562-4.ch009

Ugangu, W. (2016). Kenya's Difficult Political Transitions Ethnicity and the Role of Media. In L. Mukhongo & J. Macharia (Eds.), *Political Influence of the Media in Developing Countries* (pp. 12–24). Hershey, PA: IGI Global. doi:10.4018/978-1-4666-9613-6.ch002

Uprety, S. (2018). Print Media's Role in Securitization: National Security and Diplomacy Discourses in Nepal. In S. Bute (Ed.), *Media Diplomacy and Its Evolving Role in the Current Geopolitical Climate* (pp. 56–82). Hershey, PA: IGI Global. doi:10.4018/978-1-5225-3859-2.ch004

Van der Merwe, L. (2016). Social Media Use within Project Teams: Practical Application of Social Media on Projects. In G. Silvius (Ed.), *Strategic Integration of Social Media into Project Management Practice* (pp. 139–159). Hershey, PA: IGI Global. doi:10.4018/978-1-4666-9867-3.ch009

van der Vyver, A. G. (2018). A Model for Economic Development With Telecentres and the Social Media: Overcoming Affordability Constraints. In S. Takavarasha Jr & C. Adams (Eds.), *Affordability Issues Surrounding the Use of ICT for Development and Poverty Reduction* (pp. 112–140). Hershey, PA: IGI Global. doi:10.4018/978-1-5225-3179-1.ch006

van Dokkum, E., & Ravesteijn, P. (2016). Managing Project Communication: Using Social Media for Communication in Projects. In G. Silvius (Ed.), *Strategic Integration of Social Media into Project Management Practice* (pp. 35–50). Hershey, PA: IGI Global. doi:10.4018/978-1-4666-9867-3.ch003

van Niekerk, B. (2018). Social Media Activism From an Information Warfare and Security Perspective. In F. Endong (Ed.), *Exploring the Role of Social Media in Transnational Advocacy* (pp. 1–16). Hershey, PA: IGI Global. doi:10.4018/978-1-5225-2854-8.ch001

Varnali, K., & Gorgulu, V. (2017). Determinants of Brand Recall in Social Networking Sites. In W. Al-Rabayah, R. Khasawneh, R. Abu-shamaa, & I. Alsmadi (Eds.), *Strategic Uses of Social Media for Improved Customer Retention* (pp. 124–153). Hershey, PA: IGI Global. doi:10.4018/978-1-5225-1686-6.ch007

Varty, C. T., O'Neill, T. A., & Hambley, L. A. (2017). Leading Anywhere Workers: A Scientific and Practical Framework. In Y. Blount & M. Gloet (Eds.), *Anywhere Working and the New Era of Telecommuting* (pp. 47–88). Hershey, PA: IGI Global. doi:10.4018/978-1-5225-2328-4.ch003

Vatikiotis, P. (2016). Social Media Activism: A Contested Field. In T. Deželan & I. Vobič (Eds.), *R)evolutionizing Political Communication through Social Media* (pp. 40–54). Hershey, PA: IGI Global. doi:10.4018/978-1-4666-9879-6.ch003

Velikovsky, J. T. (2018). The Holon/Parton Structure of the Meme, or The Unit of Culture. In M. Khosrow-Pour, D.B.A. (Ed.), Encyclopedia of Information Science and Technology, Fourth Edition (pp. 4666-4678). Hershey, PA: IGI Global. doi:10.4018/978-1-5225-2255-3.ch405

Venkatesh, R., & Jayasingh, S. (2017). Transformation of Business through Social Media. In N. Rao (Ed.), *Social Media Listening and Monitoring for Business Applications* (pp. 1–17). Hershey, PA: IGI Global. doi:10.4018/978-1-5225-0846-5.ch001

Vesnic-Alujevic, L. (2016). European Elections and Facebook: Political Advertising and Deliberation? In T. Deželan & I. Vobič (Eds.), *R)evolutionizing Political Communication through Social Media* (pp. 191–209). Hershey, PA: IGI Global. doi:10.4018/978-1-4666-9879-6.ch010

Virkar, S. (2017). Trolls Just Want to Have Fun: Electronic Aggression within the Context of E-Participation and Other Online Political Behaviour in the United Kingdom. In M. Korstanje (Ed.), *Threat Mitigation and Detection of Cyber Warfare and Terrorism Activities* (pp. 111–162). Hershey, PA: IGI Global. doi:10.4018/978-1-5225-1938-6.ch006

Wakabi, W. (2017). When Citizens in Authoritarian States Use Facebook for Social Ties but Not Political Participation. In Y. Ibrahim (Ed.), *Politics, Protest, and Empowerment in Digital Spaces* (pp. 192–214). Hershey, PA: IGI Global. doi:10.4018/978-1-5225-1862-4.ch012

Weisberg, D. J. (2016). Methods and Strategies in Using Digital Literacy in Media and the Arts. In M. Yildiz & J. Keengwe (Eds.), *Handbook of Research on Media Literacy in the Digital Age* (pp. 456–471). Hershey, PA: IGI Global. doi:10.4018/978-1-4666-9667-9.ch022

Weisgerber, C., & Butler, S. H. (2016). Debranding Digital Identity: Personal Branding and Identity Work in a Networked Age. *International Journal of Interactive Communication Systems and Technologies*, 6(1), 17–34. doi:10.4018/IJICST.2016010102

Wijngaard, P., Wensveen, I., Basten, A., & de Vries, T. (2016). Projects without Email, Is that Possible? In G. Silvius (Ed.), *Strategic Integration of Social Media into Project Management Practice* (pp. 218–235). Hershey, PA: IGI Global. doi:10.4018/978-1-4666-9867-3.ch013

Wright, K. (2018). "Show Me What You Are Saying": Visual Literacy in the Composition Classroom. In A. August (Ed.), *Visual Imagery, Metadata, and Multimodal Literacies Across the Curriculum* (pp. 24–49). Hershey, PA: IGI Global. doi:10.4018/978-1-5225-2808-1.ch002

Yang, K. C. (2018). Understanding How Mexican and U.S. Consumers Decide to Use Mobile Social Media: A Cross-National Qualitative Study. In K. Yang (Ed.), *Multi-Platform Advertising Strategies in the Global Marketplace* (pp. 168–198). Hershey, PA: IGI Global. doi:10.4018/978-1-5225-3114-2.ch007

Yang, K. C., & Kang, Y. (2016). Exploring Female Hispanic Consumers' Adoption of Mobile Social Media in the U.S. In R. English & R. Johns (Eds.), *Gender Considerations in Online Consumption Behavior and Internet Use* (pp. 185–207). Hershey, PA: IGI Global. doi:10.4018/978-1-5225-0010-0.ch012

Yao, Q., & Wu, M. (2016). Examining the Role of WeChat in Advertising. In X. Xu (Ed.), *Handbook of Research on Human Social Interaction in the Age of Mobile Devices* (pp. 386–405). Hershey, PA: IGI Global. doi:10.4018/978-1-5225-0469-6. ch016

Yarchi, M., Wolfsfeld, G., Samuel-Azran, T., & Segev, E. (2017). Invest, Engage, and Win: Online Campaigns and Their Outcomes in an Israeli Election. In M. Brown Sr., (Ed.), *Social Media Performance Evaluation and Success Measurements* (pp. 225–248). Hershey, PA: IGI Global. doi:10.4018/978-1-5225-1963-8.ch011

Yeboah-Banin, A. A., & Amoakohene, M. I. (2018). The Dark Side of Multi-Platform Advertising in an Emerging Economy Context. In K. Yang (Ed.), *Multi-Platform Advertising Strategies in the Global Marketplace* (pp. 30–53). Hershey, PA: IGI Global. doi:10.4018/978-1-5225-3114-2.ch002

Yılmaz, R., Çakır, A., & Resuloğlu, F. (2017). Historical Transformation of the Advertising Narration in Turkey: From Stereotype to Digital Media. In R. Yılmaz (Ed.), *Narrative Advertising Models and Conceptualization in the Digital Age* (pp. 133–152). Hershey, PA: IGI Global. doi:10.4018/978-1-5225-2373-4.ch008

Yusuf, S., Hassan, M. S., & Ibrahim, A. M. (2018). Cyberbullying Among Malaysian Children Based on Research Evidence. In M. Khosrow-Pour, D.B.A. (Ed.), Encyclopedia of Information Science and Technology, Fourth Edition (pp. 1704-1722). Hershey, PA: IGI Global. doi:10.4018/978-1-5225-2255-3.ch149

Zervas, P., & Alexandraki, C. (2016). Facilitating Open Source Software and Standards to Assembly a Platform for Networked Music Performance. In D. Kanellopoulos (Ed.), *Emerging Research on Networked Multimedia Communication Systems* (pp. 334–365). Hershey, PA: IGI Global. doi:10.4018/978-1-4666-8850-6.ch011

About the Contributors

Sunil Kumar is currently working as an Associate Professor in the Computer Science and Engineering Department of Amity School of Engineering & Technology, Amity University, Noida, India. He has rich experience in teaching & training the undergraduate and postgraduate classes. He has published 3 textbooks and 20 research papers publications in different International Journals and in Proceedings of International Conferences of repute. Dr. Sunil completed his Ph.D. in Computer Science & Engineering from Amity University, Noida, India. He Completed his M.Tech (Computer Engineering) in 2011 and B.Tech (Information Technology) in 2007 from Uttar Pradesh Technical University, Lucknow. He has 11 years of teaching, training and research experience with leading institutions. His area of interest includes computer networks, distributed systems, wireless sensor networks, and network security. He filed 2 international patents in the field of networks. He is Cisco & Tech Mahindra certified instructor for CCNA routing & switching course and CCNA & CCNP certified. http://auup.amity.edu/faculty-detail.aspx?facultyID=22561

Munesh Chandra Trivedi is currently works as a Professor in Computer Science and Engineering Department, ABES Engineering College, Ghaziabad, India. He has published 20 text books and 81 research papers publications in different International Journals and in Proceedings of International Conferences of repute. He has received Young Scientist Visiting Fellowship and numerous awards from different national as well international forum. He has organized several international conferences technically sponsored by IEEE, ACM and Springers. He has delivered numerous invited and plenary conference presentations and seminars throughout Country and chaired the technical sessions in International and national conferences in India. He has also delivered many invited talks in India. He has been appointed member of board of studies as well as in Syllabus committee of different private Indian universities and member of organizing committee for various national and international seminars/workshops. He is Executive Committee Member of IEEE UP Section, IEEE computer Socity Chapter India Council and also IEEE Asia Pacific Region-10.

Priya Ranjan, Ph.D. (ECE-University of Maryland, USA), MS (EE-University of Maryland, USA), B. Tech. (EE-IIT Kharagpur), Professor-EEE, Amity School of Engineering and Technology (ASET) (India).

* * *

Pooja Chaturvedi is currently working as Assistant Professor in School of Management Sciences, Varanasi. She has completed her Ph. D. from Department of Computer Science and Engineering, M.M.M. University of Technology, Gorakhpur in the year 2018 and has 5 years of teaching experience. She has received her Master's degree from the Amity University, Uttar Pradesh, Lucknow in 2012. She has received her B. Tech. from the Ideal Institute of Technology, Ghaziabad in 2010. She has published and presented more than 30 papers in national and international conferences. Her research interest includes wireless sensor network protocols using AI techniques.

A. K. Daniel is currently working as a Professor in the Department of Computer Science and Engineering, M.M.M. University of Technology, Gorakhpur and has an experience of over 30 years in teaching and research. He had served as a member in the technical committee of various national and international conferences. He is a senior member of IEEE, ACM, CSI and various others. He had published over 100 papers in the national as well as international conferences and journals. He has guided a number of research scholars of post graduate level. His research interest includes wireless communication, artificial intelligence and mobile adhoc network protocols.

Pradeep Garg is currently serving as Professor in Geomatics Engineering Group, Civil Engineering Department at Indian Institute of Technology (IIT) Roorkee, Uttarakhand, India. He completed B.Tech (Civil Engg.) in 1980 and M.Tech (Civil Engg) in 1982 both from the University of Roorkee (now IIT Roorkee). He is a recipient of Gold Medal at IIT Roorkee to stand first during M.Tech programme, Commonwealth Scholarship Award for doing Ph.D. from University of Bristol (UK), and Commonwealth Fellowship Award to carry out post-doctoral research work at University of Reading (UK). He joined the Department of Civil Engg at IIT Roorkee in 1982, and gradually advancing his career rose to the position of Head of the Civil Engg Department at IIT Roorkee in 2015, and then Vice Chancellor, Uttarakhand Technical University, Dehradun from 2015-2018. Prof. Garg has published more than 310 technical papers in national and international conferences and journals. He has undertaken 26 research projects and provided technical services to 94 consultancy projects on various aspects of Civil Engineering, generating funds for the Institute.

He has authored a text book on Remote Sensing and another on Geoinformatics, Edited two books and produced two technical films on Story of Mapping. He has developed several new courses and practical exercises in Geomatics Engineering. Besides, supervising a large number of undergraduate projects, he has guided about 71 M.Tech and 27 Ph.D. Thesis. He is instrumental in prestigious MHRD funded projects on e-learning; Development of Virtual Labs, Pedagogy and courses under NPTEL. He has served as experts on various national committees, including Ministry of Environment & Forest, EAEC Committee, NBA (AICTE) and Project Evaluation Committee, DST, New Delhi. Prof. Garg has reviewed a large number of papers for national and international journals. Considering the need to train the human resource in the country, he has successfully organized 40 programmes in advanced areas of Surveying, Photogrammetry, Remote Sensing, GIS and GPS. He has successfully organized more than 10 conferences and workshops. He is a life member of 24 professional societies, out of which he is a Fellow member of 8 societies. For academic work, Prof. Garg has travelled widely, nationally and internationally.

Ashish Sharma is currently working with Lebanese French University, Erbil, Kurdistan, Iraq as an Assistant Professor, Department of Computer Networking, College of Engineering & Computer Science. I have a total of Twelve Years (12 Years) of Experience in the field of Industry, Academics, Research, and Training. My areas of interest in research work: Education Improvement Research, Computer Networks, Cloud Computing, Blockchain, Hyperledger. I have presented and attended various Training, Workshops, and Seminars to enhance or share my knowledge/ideas. I have completed Master of Computer Applications (MCA) from UP Technical University, Lucknow, UP, India, and also completed M. Tech. (CSE) from Jamia Hamdard University, New Delhi, Delhi, India. So far I have published Four (04) Research Articles in various reputed International Journals.

Rajesh Kumar Yadav received his B.E(CSE) from G.B.Pant Engineering College Pauri (H.N.B Garahwal University), M.Tech(CS) from UPTU, Lucknow and PhD(Computer Engineering) from Delhi Technological University (Formerly Delhi College of Engineering), New Delhi, India. Presently he is working as an Assistant Professor in the department of Computer Science & Engineering at Delhi Technological University. His areas of research interest are Mobile ad-hoc Networks, Wireless Sensor Networks and Internet of Things (IoT).

Index

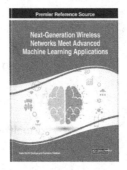
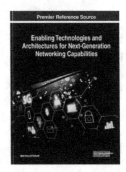

Ensure Quality Research is Introduced to the Academic Community

Become an IGI Global Reviewer for Authored Book Projects

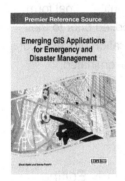

Premier Reference Source

Emerging GIS Applications for Emergency and Disaster Management

Premier Reference Source

Managerial Strategies and Green Solutions for Project Sustainability

Premier Reference Source

Comparative Approaches to Using R and Python for Statistical Data Analysis

Premier Reference Source

Solutions for High-Touch Communications in a High-Tech World

The overall success of an authored book project is dependent on quality and timely reviews.

In this competitive age of scholarly publishing, constructive and timely feedback significantly expedites the turnaround time of manuscripts from submission to acceptance, allowing the publication and discovery of forward-thinking research at a much more expeditious rate. Several IGI Global authored book projects are currently seeking highly-qualified experts in the field to fill vacancies on their respective editorial review boards:

Applications and Inquiries may be sent to:
development@igi-global.com

Applicants must have a doctorate (or an equivalent degree) as well as publishing and reviewing experience. Reviewers are asked to complete the open-ended evaluation questions with as much detail as possible in a timely, collegial, and constructive manner. All reviewers' tenures run for one-year terms on the editorial review boards and are expected to complete at least three reviews per term. Upon successful completion of this term, reviewers can be considered for an additional term.

If you have a colleague that may be interested in this opportunity, we encourage you to share this information with them.

IGI Global's Transformative Open Access (OA) Model:

How to Turn Your University Library's Database Acquisitions Into a Source of OA Funding

In response to the OA movement and well in advance of Plan S, IGI Global, early last year, unveiled their OA Fee Waiver (Read & Publish) Initiative.

Under this initiative, librarians who invest in IGI Global's InfoSci-Books (5,300+ reference books) and/or InfoSci-Journals (185+ scholarly journals) databases will be able to subsidize their patron's OA article processing charges (APC) when their work is submitted and accepted (after the peer review process) into an IGI Global journal. *See website for details.

How Does it Work?

1. When a library subscribes or perpetually purchases IGI Global's InfoSci-Databases and/or their discipline/subject-focused subsets, IGI Global will match the library's investment with a fund of equal value to go toward subsidizing the OA article processing charges (APCs) for their patrons.

   Researchers: **Be sure to recommend the InfoSci-Books and InfoSci-Journals to take advantage of this initiative.**

2. When a student, faculty, or staff member submits a paper and it is accepted (following the peer review) into one of IGI Global's 185+ scholarly journals, the author will have the option to have their paper published under a traditional publishing model or as OA.

3. When the author chooses to have their paper published under OA, IGI Global will notify them of the OA Fee Waiver (Read & Publish) Initiative. If the author decides they would like to take advantage of this initiative, IGI Global will deduct the US$ 2,000 APC from the created fund.

4. This fund will be offered on an annual basis and will renew as the subscription is renewed for each year thereafter. IGI Global will manage the fund and award the APC waivers unless the librarian has a preference as to how the funds should be managed.

Hear From the Experts on This Initiative:

"I'm very happy to have been able to make one of my recent research contributions, "Visualizing the Social Media Conversations of a National Information Technology Professional Association" featured in the *International Journal of Human Capital and Information Technology Professionals*, freely available along with having access to the valuable resources found within IGI Global's InfoSci-Journals database."

– **Prof. Stuart Palmer,**
Deakin University, Australia